Old Boy, dir. Park Chan-Wook (2003)

Monsters Inc, dir. Pete Docter, David Silverman, and Lee Unkrich (2001)

Roman Polanski

Terminator 3, dir. Jonathan Mostow (2003)

My Name is Khan, dir. Karan Johar (2010)

Antichrist, dir. Lars von Trier (2008)

Miami Vice, dir. Michael Mann (2006)

SERIES EDITED BY ÉLISABETH COUTURIER

JEAN-BAPTISTE THORET

talk about cinema

Flammarion

CONTENTS

PREFACE

I remember how, in *A Personal Journey Through American Movies*, or perhaps somewhere else, Martin Scorsese traced the origin of his passion for the cinema back, not to *Citizen Kane* (a traditional catalyst), but to Howard Hawks's—on the face of it unremarkable—sword and sandals epic of 1955, *Land of the Pharaohs*.

Whether one likes it or not, to see a film, to talk or to write about one, means—first and foremost—eavesdropping on an intimate conversation between movies as they really are and the first, often hypothetical, sometimes fantasized cinematographic experience. Its subject is a generational thing, since a love of cinema cannot always be spawned by the same movies. My own *Land of the Pharaohs* was a many-headed hydra: *The Wild Bunch*, *Suspiria*, *Big Deal on Madonna Street*, *The Red Circle*, *Assault on Precinct 13*, and more broadly the "genre" movies of the 1970s. The history of cinema is a living, moving, tumultuous discipline, perpetually on the go, a regular march-past of last rites and exhumations.

At root, undertaking this history has meant putting the movies we deal with through a kind of critical health check to see if their heart is still beating. Some of them (the movies of Hitchcock, Lang, Ford, and Renoir) remain in fine fettle, as fit as the day they hit the screens. Others (those of Melville, Peckinpah, or Sirk) seem to have positively improved. Unjustly neglected by the critics of yesteryear, they have become classics of today—keystones sometimes in what has become known as "contemporary" cinema. And then there are others that are beginning to show their age, sacred cows we politely nod to as we hurry past: Peter Greenaway, Jean Cocteau, even Wim Wenders.

Today, so overwhelming is the sheer number of films, filmmakers, movements, genres, sub-genres, periods, filmographies, and technical innovations, no one in their right mind (the author of the present volume included) would seriously embark on a history of cinema in its "totality." Hollywood cinema alone, however well charted its pre-1960s waters are today, constitutes such a vast and eclectic expanse that to deal with it in a single sweep has become impossible. And what can one say about the cinemas of Asia and all those countries where movie production has recently mushroomed (South Korea, Taiwan, Thailand, and Hong Kong in the 1980s and 1990s)? Who remembers today that, before 1951 and the screening of *Rashomon* at the Venice Film Festival, Japanese movies were almost never shown in the West? This gives rise to the following paradox: the more the history of cinema progresses, the more time is required to catch up with it—even if access to film has massively improved with the creation of the DVD and the Internet.

Every year, vast swathes of this history resurface before the eyes of amazed audiences and, as in a piece of architecture, each new stone alters the whole building—from the still largely unexplored genre film of the 1960s and 1970s to Mexican melodramas whose very existence was hardly suspected; not to mention Bollywood, and now Nollywood, the film industry of Nigeria, the second biggest in the world just behind that of the United States.

We have then to choose the required focal distance, the right viewpoint or trajectory so as to zero in on just one of many possible histories of cinema, one that is perfectly complementary and compatible with a thousand other ways of presenting the lineage of film.

So what are our guidelines? First, we want the images themselves, freed from their hierarchies, to be left to move around. Then we would like to offer the *soliti ignoti* of cinema history their rightful place. Finally, it is our firm conviction that cinema is less an affair of new beginnings than of consciously acknowledged affiliations. Here, in a democratic approach worthy of John Ford, each, from wherever he hails, will be allowed a place at the table. A film's background will not be held against it: and how could it be otherwise, now that in 2011 the Centre Pompidou opened its eminent portals to Hammer's monsters and the French Cinémathèque showcases Jess Franco and the godfather of Japanese "Roman Porno," Koji Wakamastu?

JEAN-BAPTISTE THORET

WHAT IS
CONTEMPORARY CINEMA?

"Being contemporary means receiving smack in the face

the beam of darkness coming from the era in which one lives."

Giorgio Agamben, "What's contemporary?" 2008

MIX AND MATCH

Imagine a moviegoer from a distant planet, or a kind of Rip Van VVinkle vvho, after a sleep lasting thirty years, vvanted some idea of so-called "contemporary" cinema. VVhat vvould they find?

They would see a star of the 1980s, Mickey Rourke, who, after a short-lived career as a boxer and fifteen years in acting purgatory, mounting a successful comeback in the ring as *The Wrestler*. Strange, super-low-budget movies made with portable phones alongside saccharine melodramas made in Bombay. Whole phalanxes of remakes (*King Kong*, *The Planet of the Apes*, *True Grit*, *The Texas Chainsaw Massacre*) and teenagers too cool for school (*Elephant*, *Ken Park*). A director, Gus Van Sant, who decides to reshoot the script of Hitchcock's *Psycho* frame by frame, and a superhero (Batman in *The Dark Knight*) consumed by doubts. They would see blockbusters striving to imitate indie films (*Rec*, *Cloverfield*, *Diary of the Dead*), a cohort of new media (HD, 35 mm, video), and, with Bruno Dumont, non-professional actors (*Humanité*, *Twenty-Nine Palms*) vying for top of the bill with deathless legends. They would witness some unexpected meetings: Cecil B. De Mille and Nietzsche having a fireside chat in *A Christmas Tale* as retold by Arnaud Desplechin, a Korean monster film (*The Host*) that switches from social chronicle to set-piece mayhem, a trilogy (*The Matrix*) that elevated the blockbuster to the status of a theoretical-cum-mythical product, and overlays technological wizardry with a philosophical veneer that intercuts Plato with Jean Baudrillard. **A quick glance at Hollywood movies of the last ten years would also tell them that a traumatic event had overtaken America and left deep scars on US cinema: September 11, 2001**, of course, and the extraordinary spectacle of the decapitation of a city, visible not only in Steven Spielberg's *War of the Worlds* but also in Spike Lee's *25th Hour*. They would then, of course, come across some new directors: Gaspar Noé, David Fincher, Park Chan-VVook, Xavier Giannoli, Rob Zombie, Paul Thomas Anderson, and Jia Zhang-Ke. Then, in that reconfiguration of *The VVizard of Oz* that is James Cameron's *Avatar*, they would be amazed by a blue-tinged planet emerging into a sparkling Eden; they would be pleased to see there's still life in ole 007 (*Casino Royal*), and perhaps even in Italian cinema (*Il Divo*, *The Solitude of Prime Numbers*), and would scratch his head over the proliferation of 3D glasses on moviegoers' noses. They could hardly help noticing an explosion in documentary (from Michael Moore's polemics to Jonathan Nossiter's ecological fables) and the emergence of new forms—"docufiction," "mockumentary"—mixing genres once thought impermeable. Thus, on the edge of their seat watching *Armadillo* by the Dane Janus Metz, they follows a unit of young soldiers sent to Afghanistan to fight the Taliban in 2001, with all the tricks and treats of the feature-film trade: fearful expectation, ambush, panic, paranoia, and even photographs in a mirror redolent of Ridley Scott's *Black Hawk Down*.

In spite of the occasional flash in the pan (*OSS 117*, *The Secret of the Grain*, *Irreversible*, *The Life of Jesus*, *Mesrine*), they would be surprised to see French cinema is still waiting for its second wind, while South Korean film is on the up. On closer inspection, they would discover new media, new ways to make film, and the emergence of uncharted worlds: the burlesque melancholy of VVes Anderson (*The Royal Tenenbaums*), the New York clan films of James Gray (*VVe Own the Night*), as well as those funny little digital creatures labeled "Pixar" which, since *Toy Story* in 1995, have invaded movie screens (*Cars*, *Up*, *Wall-E*).

Then, next to all the up-and-coming young Turks, he would recognize a few veterans who are far from finished yet: Clint Eastwood, Alain Resnais, Marco Bellocchio, Terrence Malick, William Friedkin, and Roman Polanski, all still in the director's chair.

The Dark Knight, dir. Christopher Nolan (2008)

OSS 117: Cairo, Nest of Spies, dir. Michel Hazanavicius (2005)

The Solitude of Prime Numbers, dir. Saverio Costanzo (2010)

FACING PAGE
TOP:
The Host,
dir. Bong Joon-Ho
(2006)
BOTTOM:
Bowling for Columbine,
dir. Michael Moore
(2002)

A CONTEMPORARY APPROACH

Although bandied about in the cultural arena, the expressions "contemporary cinema" and "contemporary film" are hardly self-explanatory. VVhat is vvorse, they refer neither to a vvell-defined critical category (unlike "contemporary art," for example, vvhich—roughly speaking—designates artvvorks produced since the 1960s), nor to a functioning aesthetic category, since the cinema, vvhenever it is contemporary, is naturally contemporary vvith the era in vvhich it vvas shot, and vvith a present in particular. At base, some films have alvvays been contemporary, vvhile others vvere never so—even on the day they came out. So is a contemporary film one vvhich, although anchored in the concerns of its epoch, passes the test of time?

The Deer Hunter, for example, today, as in 1979, speaks as much to those who lived through the Vietnam VVar in "real time" as to those who, decades later, have little inkling of the events it retells. And if Tod Browning's *Freaks* and Jean Vigo's *L'Atalante*, two major films of the 1930s, were made today, people would scarcely turn a hair. *VVe VVon't Grow Old Together* by Maurice Pialat and the films of John Cassavetes have not aged. Conversely, *Amélie* (Jean-Pierre Jeunet, 2001), *Pearl Harbor* (Michael Bay, 2001), and *The Round-Up* (Roselyne Bosch, 2010), like a substantial proportion of the cinema of their time, with their sometimes academic forms, already seem outmoded, passé: full of well-worn recipes and stale processes, they are films made today that look out of date. VVriting on *The Good, the Bad, and the Ugly* (1966), Serge Daney said of Sergio Leone's film that he was a "lap ahead of his time." In other words that he was "on time." **This could be an ideal definition of "the contemporary" in film: movies which, by their themes, their obsessions, by the way they look at the world and their characters, are "on time."**

One has, then, to distinguish two *presents*: on one side, are all those trappings that attach a film to the age in which it was made (and which can be as banal as a cumbersome mobile telephone or bell-bottoms as indicators of a specific decade); on the other side lurks something less obvious, the "beam of darkness" that Agamben mentions above, which reveals the less palpable, hidden atmosphere of a period—those ghosts of politics (or those ghosts of form) that stalk it.

A movie is contemporary whenever it manages to resolve the paradox of being at once datable and timeless; a film that is patently anchored in its epoch, but which is also able to address some of the seminal ideas that underpin the age. It focuses at one and the same time on the individual and on his world, on the story and on History with a capital "H," on both the here and now and the universal.

Take Michael Mann 's *Miami Vice* (2006), for instance: sure, it is a (first-rate) action film that satisfies all the rules of the genre (shoot-ups, manhunts, white knuckles, etc.), but also, in a very subtle yet powerful manner, captures the melancholic and disillusioned mood of the first decade of the century, that grinding down of human relationships in an age of globalized capitalism, the loneliness of those powerless to stop it.

She Wore a Yellow Ribbon, dir. John Ford (1949)

Sunchaser, dir. Michael Cimino (1995)

The Last of the Mohicans, dir. Michael Mann (1992)

SHARED OBSESSIONS

If one looks at movies from just the last thirty years—with the 1970s being undoubtedly the decade that laid the foundations for today's cinema—in every genre, and wherever the films hail from (Taiwan or Hollywood, Hong Kong or Brazil, Paris or Berlin), they are infused with a common state of mind that is evidenced in recurrent themes, character types, acting styles, ways of filming people and society.

All the same? If cinema has constituted the ideal mechanism for recording the world as it has developed over the last thirty years, it has been characterized first and foremost by an increasingly standardized imagination, as visible as much in the films of Hou Hsiao Hsien (*Millennium Mambo, Café Light, Flowers of Shanghai*) as in those of Alejandro Gonzáles Iñárritu (*Amores Perros, Biutiful*). The figurehead of the new Taiwanese cinema shows consummate rigor in delineating themes such as the collapse of family structure, the description of a rootless youth fed up with consumerism and prey to the obsession of memory. Starting with *Babel,* the Mexican Iñárritu's "world films" reveal a significant taste for the butterfly effect (a wing-beat here has unaccountable repercussions on the other side of the planet), while the narrative ignores frontiers, and shifts back and forth over the US-Mexican border or leaps from Japan to Morocco. All different, perhaps, but at root all similar, since, from the geographical desert in which a Berber family ekes out a living. to the inner desert of a young woman in Japan, the loneliness, the aspirations, and the dreams are now basically one and the same.

The cinema as backdrop. Cast our minds back. At the beginning of the 1970s, there appeared a new generation of film-buff filmmakers (Martin Scorsese, Joe Dante, Brian de Palma, John Carpenter, Steven Spielberg), for whom death is also, and perhaps primarily, the image and the sound of dead bodies tumbling down a movie screen. Today, cinema has become more than ever a screen for film itself—a permanent dialogue underwritten by tributes, references, quotations, borrowings, and remakes. If the unspoken model for Gus Van Sant's *Gerry* is *The Shooting* by Monte Hellman, Peter Weir's *Picnic at Hanging Rock* runs like an underground river through Sofia Coppola's *Virgin Suicides*; Tsui Hark, meanwhile, reactivates all the figures of the *wu-xapian* (the Chinese swordplay film). As for Hitchcock's films, the shower sequence in *Psycho* in particular has been amply revisited by all those, from Brian De Palma to Quentin Tarantino, who make quotation and recognizing past films one of the driving forces behind today's cinema. *Jackie Brown* harks back to blaxploitation, offering one of its iconic figures, Pam Grier, the role of her career, while *Death Proof* doffs its hat to the B movies of the 1970s (*Duel, Race with the Devil, The Car, Vanishing Point*) in perfect pastiche (noncontinuity editing and original angles, old film stock, jump shots and gaps, sudden slow-downs and speed-ups).

The Virgin Suicides,
dir. Sofia Coppola
(1999)

Millennium Mambo,
dir. Hou Hsiao-Hsien
(2001)

Picnic at Hanging Rock,
dir. Peter Weir
(1975)

Memory loss.

Then there's the Jason Bourne syndrome, from the name of a successful four-parter that kicked off in 2007, tracking an ex-CIA agent who, following a botched operation, tries to recover his memory and crisscrosses the world in the search of what he once was. Amnesia, the difficulty in precisely recalling the past or in coming to terms with some painful event (Algeria in French cinema, the regime of Franco in Spanish film, the *anni di piombo* for the Italians), has become a seminal theme in contemporary cinema, from *eXistenz* to *Memento*, via *Mulholland Drive*, *Shutter Island*, Neil Jordan's *Ondine*, and Aki Kaurismäki's *The Man Without a Past*. **Be it on an individual (who am I?) or collective level (who are we?), the theme of memory loss speaks volumes in a world that has also lost its bearings and which, in an age of globalization and the Internet, wants to get back to its origins, or, less ambitiously, forge itself an identity.**

FACING PAGE

TOP:

The Bourne Supremacy,
dir. Paul Greengrass
(2004)

BOTTOM:

Kinatay,
dir. Brillante Mendoza
(2009)

Cinema in all its forms.

The cinema, as André Malraux already wrote in 1946, is also an industry. Today, nothing has really changed. The cinema is more than ever an industry, although since the mid-2000s it has been only the second most bankable in the so-called "cultural" sector—just behind video gaming.

But what has one actually *said* about cinema, about its forms, about the ambitions of all those who make films, once we repeat that it is, and always has been, an art of the masses, or perhaps (to use a less loaded phrase) of "popular consumption," designed to maximize ticket sales and turn a profit? Industrial and mainstream cinema, indie and auteur film, B movies and genre: all these categories of which institutional criticism used to be so fond have been exploded by a new generation of filmmakers who emerged in the 1990s (David Fincher, Rob Zombie, James Gray, Quentin Tarantino) and who take what they want where they find it. The old categories present the added disadvantage of assuming synergy between aesthetic value and the unquestionable economic realities (the budget of *Kinatay*, by the Filipino filmmaker Brillante Mendoza, was 1/200th of that for *Avatar*). The history of cinema proves that a film can possess aesthetic qualities, or amount to an academic exercise whatever its genre, while the downshift from the mass to the niche market does not invariably reap artistic benefits. The auteur director approach does not necessarily equate to a blueprint for fine filmmaking. One just has to take a look at the films of Dario Argento (*Inferno*) or Alain Resnais (*Same Old Song*) to see how today "high" and "low" culture have become inextricably mixed. Or take the case of Steven Soderbergh, who follows super-productions like *Ocean's Twelve* with independent films like *Bubble*, and Bernardo Bertolucci who, in a career spanning some thirty-seven years, has constructed an atypical oeuvre ranging from European *films d'auteur* (*The Strategy of the Spider*, *Before the Revolution*) to political lampoons (on Fascist Italy of the 1930s in *The Conformist*), from steamy potboilers (*Last Tango in Paris*, starring Brando) to Hollywood spectaculars (*The Last Emperor*, *Little Buddha*).

HISTORY AND RUPTURE

But vvhen did contemporary film begin? At the birth of cinema, one is tempted to reply. From the first films by the Lumière brothers, or the famous *Arrival of a Train at La Ciotat*, filmed in 1895, that already heralded an as-yet-unarticulated sense that these moving and sometimes frightening pictures vvould constitute the very essence of tvventieth-century art. But the story of cinema, like that of art itself, unfolds in tvvo parallel histories: constantly intersecting, they some-times run over vvidely differing paths, at other times they are one and the same; one day advancing hand in hand, the next violently at odds.

Because history itself is twofold: on the one side, there is what one could term chronological history, and on the other—more interestingly—there is the history of forms. One is made up of topical, present-day concerns (that can be as cross as a type of computer attesting to the date of creation of a film), the other is informed by what is really contemporary, by those forms and themes that, because they capture the essential spirit of a time, are destined to outlast it.

Rome, Open City, dir.
Roberto Rossellini
(1945)

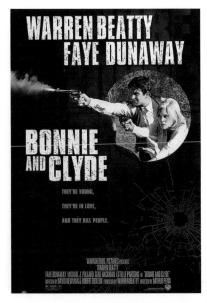

In 1969, Dennis Hopper and Peter Fonda embarked on the adventure that was shooting *Easy Rider*. That same year, Ray Kellog and John Wayne rolled out *The Green Berets*. From the point of view of chronological history, these two movies are obviously contemporary, but from the point of view of the history of form, they are light-years apart. Whatever *Easy Rider* may be, its rather slapdash innovations (its jump cuts, rock soundtrack, loose idiom, and determination to learn from the lessons of the European New Wave) make it a far cry from the sclerosis and anachronism of the second, as obvious as in its agenda (a binary ethical vision coupled to a paean to an all-conquering and triumphant United States) as in its formal ideas.

For all that, the evolution of cinema *is* marked by rupture and step-change (economic, technological, and sociohistorical). "A film is not revolutionary because it is about a revolution, but because it revolutionizes something in the world," as Nicole Brenez, a historian of avant-garde cinema, so neatly put it.

ABOVE, LEFT:
Poster for Arthur Penn's *Bonnie and Clyde* (1967)

ABOVE:
Poster for Dennis Hopper's *Easy Rider* (1969)

LEFT:
Poster for Arthur Penn's *Alice's Restaurant* (1969)

And evolutionary leaps? Admittedly they have been numerous, ongoing, but one seems positively seismic: the 1960s, a countercultural wind of change that seemed to blow all over the world. It is this that seems to us to inform a large slice of "contemporary" production—even more than the great shifts that traditional film history places at the turn of the 1950s, between, in short, the onset of Italian neorealism (1945) and the emergence of the French New Wave (1959).

Repulsion,
dir. Roman Polanski
(1965)

Starting from the mid-1960s, and for a raft of economic and historical reasons (the takeover of the majors by financial consortia, the development of television and the multiplex, diverse assassinations and political scandals, the emergence of a counterculture), a world riven by protest movements began to aspire to greater freedom. In the United States, the demise of the studios, coupled with the emergence of a younger generation of filmmakers who were both film and TV buffs (the "movie brats"), spawned New Hollywood—that period during which American cinema, pushed and shoved by the likes of Scorsese, Coppola, Ashby, Altman, and Rafelson, embarked on a wholesale critical analysis of its history, myths, and classics.

In Brazil, there was the emergence of cinema novo led by Glauber Rocha (*Black God, White Devil, Antonio das Mortes,* aka *The Dragon of Evil Against the Warrior Saint*); in England, the "free cinema" of Tony Richardson and Lindsay Anderson was a million miles away from the pleasures of Ealing Studios; in Czechoslovakia as it was still, the short-lived Prague Spring allowed filmmakers like Milos Forman (*Loves of a Blonde,* 1965) and Jiri Menzel (*Closely Watched Trains,* 1965) to come to prominence. And then there was Roman Polanski in Poland (*Repulsion,* 1965), Miklos Jancso in Hungary (*The Round-Up,* 1966; *Silence and Cry,* 1998) and, in Italy, Michelangelo Antonioni, Bernardo Bertolucci, and Marco Bellocchio (*Fists in the Pocket,* 1966).

Loves of a Blonde,
dir. Milos Forman
(1965)

The Bird with the Crystal Plumage, dir. Dario Argento (1970)

MODELS AND INNOVATION

Breaking with the past does not (inevitably) mean a tabula rasa, and many filmmakers of today, like those of yesterday, claim descent from former directors or their movies. The interrelationships are many and various, and the model has often become an object of worship or guiding light, a source of inspiration or aesthetic compass. Every filmmaker has their models, of course: Robert Bresson, Douglas Sirk, Sergio Leone, David Lean, John Cassavetes, and many others, and among the classics, Fritz Lang, F.W. Murnau, and Jean Renoir. Then there are the bonds that the work of Brian De Palma weaves with Alfred Hitchcock; the considerable influence of the films of Jean-Pierre Melville and Sergio Leone on contemporary output; the constant references to Stanley Kubrick's *2001: A Space Odyssey* by Gaspar Noé; and the tribute paid by Tarantino to Godard when, as the expert in deconstructing stories that he is, the director of *Inglourious Basterds* baptized his production company "A Band Apart," in reference to the eponymous film that arranged a detective thriller's scenes in nonlinear order and blew the genre apart. There is also Peter Sellers's reincarnation—in Blake Edwards's *The Party* and *Pink Panther*—of the unflappability and chaotic power of Jacques Tati's Hulot. And finally there is the contemporary cinema of fear which, from Spain (Jaume Balagueró, Alex de la Iglesia) to Hollywood is constantly acknowledging its debts to John Carpenter, George A. Romero, Larry Cohen, and Wes Craven.

2001: A Space Odyssey, dir. Stanley Kubrick (1968)

John Ford

THREE CLASSICS

Gangs of New York, dir. Martin Scorsese (2002)

The children of John Ford

John Ford or the Holy Writ of American cinema: sacred cow and totem. With 137 feature films made between 1929 and 1966 to his name, the oeuvre of John Ford straddles the history of contemporary America like a colossus and provides a glorious reflection of its development. Every film by the Irishman Ford is imprinted by an undying humanism and shot through by the burning questions often asked by members of a diaspora: What is a community? And how can it hold together, remain open to the Other, and yet survive? Most of all, every one of them, from *The Searchers* to his last film, *7 Women*, proclaims the idea blurted out by Tom Joad (Henry Fonda) in the final reel of *The Grapes of Wrath*: "A fellow ain't got a soul of his own, just little piece of a big soul, the one big soul that belongs to everybody" That is to say, *the* great subject of the American movie: What is a people? A mystery that percolates through the films of Michael Cimino (*Heaven's Gate*, 1980; *Year of the Dragon*, 1984), Martin Scorsese (*Gangs of New York*, 2002), Hal Ashby (*Bound for Glory*, 1976), and Robert Altman (*Nashville*, 1975).

The children of Jean-Pierre Melville

The aesthetic influence exerted by Melville's films (from *Samurai* to *The Red Circle*) on contemporary cinema is such that his name has become an epithet: "Melvillian," referring to a dark, pared-down style, complete with a mysterious, reclusive, raincoat-wearing hero, a fantastical, Japanized America—a ghost world where, like depressed children, people play at cops and robbers. Melville's impact can be seen in films from around the globe, from Japan (the thrillers of Hideo Gosha and Seijun Susuzi) to Italy (Fernando di Leo), from the United States (Michael Winner, Jim Jarmusch or Michael Mann) to France (the detective films of Alain Corneau). (See pages 172–173.)

Dirty Money, dir. Jean-Pierre Melville (1972)

Mulholland Drive,
dir. David Lynch
(2001)

That Obscure
Object of Desire,
dir. Luis Buñuel
(1977)

The children of Luis Buñuel

What strange and unexpected link is there between Marco Ferreri's *Max, My Love* (1985) and Tobe Hooper's *Texas Chain Saw Massacre* (1973)? One of the thirty-two films made by Luis Buñuel between 1929 and 1977. And has there ever been a more clamorous entrance into cinema than that of Buñuel? In 1929: standing at a window, a man (Buñuel in person), slices through the eye of a woman with a razor. Close-up of a cloud flitting across the moon (that's metaphor for you), then on the organ discharging its fluid (that's actualization). This is an image early in *Un chien andalou*, Buñuel's lurching dream, soon taken up by Dali (a hand from which emerges a steady stream of ants). For Buñuel, metaphor is literal: if two men cackle like hens (*The Phantom of Liberty*), there's a shot of some poultry. When a terrifying "beast" roams the woods ready to rape and kill a little girl (*Diary of a Chambermaid*), there's shots of a wild boar. The complexity of female desire implies that each woman in fact harbors several. Then, in *This Obscure Object of Desire*, two different actresses, Carole Bouquet and Angela Molina, will play one and the same character. Buñuel has no truck with simile. Reality is sufficiently undecipherable: there's no need to make it more complicated. Originally, *Un chien andalou* was

not entitled "An Andalusian Dog," but "It is forbidden to lean inside" (as against "outside")—a plausible definition of filmmaking for Buñuel. Once upon a time, there was the eye, just any old eye—puritan, blinkered, blind—and it was put to death by a sharp blade. Then a new eye was born and, with it, a new way of looking at the world—that of surrealism (*Un chien andalou* began existence as one of its party pieces), that of a filmmaker determined to remove our chronic cataracts. What do men look like when we really look at them? Like a film by Buñuel. Like *The Discreet Charm of the Bourgeoisie*, where the borders between reality and fiction merge to the point that they no longer pose a problem. Like *The Milky Way*, too, a theological road movie containing much tub-thumping about religious doctrine, after which one is left wondering whether the body of Christ is not to the Host what the jugged hare is to the pie. In other words, his movies possess the singular ability to simultaneously keep two contradictory but not incompatible realities in the air at the same time. Because nothing is more alien to Buñuel's universe than judgment,

*That Obscure
Object of Desire,*
dir. Luis Buñuel
(1977)

which presupposes a closed vision of reality and its conflicts, the phantasm of a total comprehension of events, which his films are intelligent enough to avoid like the plague. His oeuvre, however, has often wrongly been interpreted as a dyed-in-the-wool critique of middle-class values; values against which, as everyone knows, it requires no effort to take the moral high ground. It is enough, however, to take another look at *Diary of a Chambermaid* to experience all the subtle power of Buñuel. There, the quagmire in which the servants wallow (opportunism, spinelessness, racism, extreme right-wing beliefs) is no better and no worse than that of their employers—pampered bourgeois ne'er-do-wells who hide the muddy boots of their suppressed desires at the back of the bedroom closet. Any criticism, then, is two-edged: of the middle classes and the proletariat. The same can be said of the believers and non-believers in *The Milky Way*. That is Buñuel's true subversive act. He is an "and," not an "or" filmmaker: the willful enemy of "good sense," wherever it hails from.

I Am a Cyborg,
dir. Park Chan-Wook
(2006)

2

WHAT'S REALLY CHANGED?

"The more things change, the more they stay the same."

Kurt Russell in *Los Angeles 2013*, dir. John Carpenter, 1996.

IS EVERYONE A FILMMAKER NOW?

In *Cloverfield* by Matt Reeves—a cross between an action film and *Godzilla*—the point of view of the amateur filmmakers trapped within some incomprehensible catastrophe appears falsely disorganized, chaotic, subjected to ever-changing circumstances. Matt Reeves supercharges the subjective dimension of the narrative (though only optically: "I see solely what the videomaker-cum-witness shoots"), but eliminates the author. It's certainly one particular individual who is filming, but this individual could be anyone.

A film "is being made." Basically, like many others (*Rec, Redacted, Paranormal Activity, The Last Exorcism*), this studio film simply confirms a tendency that surfaced in the early 1970s: the illusion of the disappearance of the movie author-director, in opposition to the traditional conception of the all-seeing, all-powerful filmmaker, whose word is law in the little world he creates. A camera that jumps about in time with the cameraman's movements, as if he too was part of the fiction, translates the anguish of the person holding a camera as he shoots what's there. Remember *The Blair Witch Project* or *Man Bites Dog*, the first to systematize the use of this documentary effect within the framework of a fiction film; that feeling of being immersed in the action like a war reporter, which can also be seen in the opening sequence of *The Wild Bunch*, as well in the documentary shorts embedded in *Cannibal Holocaust*? **Thirty years later, the launch of the DV camera, and still more its increased availability to the general public, introduced a novel form of scriptwriting: faster, more democratic, less cumbersome to shoot.**

In 2000, Lars von Trier receives the Palme d'Or at Cannes for his *Dancer in the Dark*, shot in HD, like Melvin Van Peebles's *Bellyful* and *Baise-moi* by Virginia Despentes and Coralie Trinh Thi, as well as Agnès Varda's *The Gleaners and I*, Alexander Sokurov's *Russian Ark*, and Claude Miller's *Of Women and Magic*.

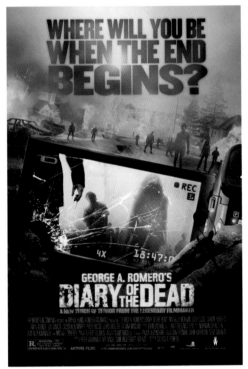

Poster for George Romero's *Diary of the Dead* (2007)

*The Blair Witch
Project*, dir. Daniel
Myrick and Eduardo
Sanchez (1999)

A WORLD IN SEARCH OF MEANING

This is one of the predominant features of modern cinema: the world, once complete and coherent, has mislaid its center of gravity. Today, more than ever, it appears divided, incomprehensible, up for grabs. So it has to be decoded—in the manner of David Hemmings in *Blow Up* or *Deep Red*. Yet, as we know, the mind, like nature, abhors a vacuum, and will use anything—including fiction—to fill in the gaps.

CONSPIRACY THEORIES

The imagination begins to see plotting everywhere, in a tendency whose heyday came in the 1970s with *The Parallax View*, *The Conversation*, *Three Days of the Condor*. Today, in everything from run-of-the-mill thriller series to porn, the conspiracy has become a widespread narrative ploy. By "them," conspiracy lovers mean those who, behind the scenes, really control the world, manipulating events and the march of history, who yesterday decided to assassinate President Kennedy and who tomorrow will engineer a run on food prices.

You can't see them, you don't know who they are, but "they" are everywhere—like the invisible invaders who terrorized David Vincent, and the fantasy insects of William Friedkin's more recent *Bug*. At the very summit of the state, in the senate or in cabinet, in your company, behind your mirror, they peer into your home and probably even into your bed. The horizon of conspiracy pathology lies in an irrational belief in the global interdependence of all events, from the world shattering to the trifling. It derives from the phantasm of a totality made up of infinite ramifications and directed by an invisible, omnipotent mastermind. "They" fill in the gaps in what is an ungovernable and thus mysterious world.

Conspiracy theories. Like totalitarian propaganda, such as Hannah Arendt analyzed it, the theory of the plot, the unacknowledged cousin of many a noxious ideology, "sets up a world that competes with the real world, whose great disadvantage is not to be logical, coherent and organized." It exploits an enduring failing of the human psyche: faced with an incomplete picture, a sometimes incomprehensible reality, it invents a coherent narrative, however bizarre it may be.

For discontinuous and uncertain reality, the conspiracy theorist substitutes rounded, credible fiction. What, though, is the "credible," if not reality as desire wants it to be? Even where the facts are verifiable, the way they hang together stems from speculative fiction. This is the key manipulative practice of the genre: just like the paranoiac, conspiracy theorists extract from reality only that material that supports their chosen fiction, and reject from consideration anything that might go against it. For them, truth is just one facet of falsehood, manipulation just one aspect of the interpretation, and reality is a lie not yet unmasked.

Zodiac,
dir. David Fincher
(2007)

Rather than seeking to impose any specific truth ("them" is sufficient), conspiracy theorists, exploiting our innate mistrust of predominant systems and offering to simplify the world, posit the existence of one conspiring power. Hence, it is objectively impossible to disprove their theories: in the autistic bubble of the conspiracy theorist, truth is not the opposite of a lie—it simply magnifies it. Consequently no proof, not even the most indisputable, can slake a thirst for conspiracy since it is fed precisely by what contradicts it. The moral of the story: the more an event looks true (the Shoah, the Gulf Wars, the massacres in Rwanda, September 11, etc.), the more likely it is to be fake.

RADICAL CHIC AND MAINSTREAM

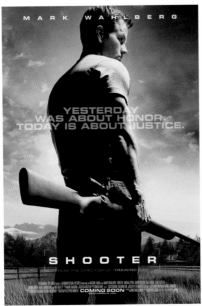

Poster for *Shooter*, dir. Antoine Fuqua (2007)

In *Shooter* (Antoine Fuqua, 2007), a retired sniper living in the woods, like a latter-day Jeremiah Johnson, is contacted by men from the FBI to help thwart a plot intended to assassinate the US president. What, they ask, would Bob Lee Swagger (Mark Wahlberg) do in the assassin's place? The question will be answered when the man realizes, but all too late, that it's all a setup, and he will be framed for the assassination of an Ethiopian dignitary possessing compromising information. It bears repeating more than once that Hollywood movies, and especially the most mainstream, often articulate ideas that in France, for instance, tend to appear on the margins of the film industry, in low-budget "political" or "*engagé*" independent films.

Shooter then works on two fronts: on the one side, it ticks all the right boxes for an action movie; on the other, it is yet another example of that quiet, challenging voice that has long pilloried the US government, poking fun at the "presence" of WMDs in Iraq that it knows is a secret no one ever believed, or casually denouncing the implication of the administration in various massacres (here, it's an African village up in arms against US oil interests), as if it were common knowledge.

Everything can be seen in this light: from Kennedy's assassination—that inaugural event that courses through the veins of anti-Bush America—to Abu Ghraib (everyone, from the Pentagon down to commanders in the field, "knew what was going on"), and nothing surprises anyone anymore. Ned Beatty, the cheery senator who masterminds the whole affair in the movie, parrots the cynical mantra about the power of private interests that already appeared in *Network* in 1976, condensing the basic tenet of contemporary cinema into a formula: "There are no Democrats or Republicans: there are just 'haves' and 'have-nots.'" The point here is less to reiterate the extreme porosity of genres and attitudes than to emphasize the astonishing, inexhaustible capacity of Hollywood to place center stage (in movies that are popular and fun, and hence made for the greatest number of popcorn-chomping militants), counter-arguments (*Wall-E* precisely on junk food, for example) which, in the United States, would make a radical activist look like a spineless social democrat. Bob Lee Swagger, rogue soldier and modern cowboy, is thus a kind of post-September 11 Rambo (the napalm attack on the FBI sniper's villa reactivates flashbacks of the Vietnam War); a man who has gained in cynicism what he has to jettison in patriotism.

Bug, dir. William Friedkin (2006)

THE END OF IDENTITY?

As a response to world cinema and to the standardization of the imagination and of lifestyles all over the globe, films have appeared that try to exacerbate national characteristics. Flirting with a mildly gamey nostalgia for a long-vanished world, French examples include the sanitized Montmartre of Jeunet's *Amélie* or the kind of flaky regionalism peddled by *Bienvenue chez les Ch'tis* by Dany Boon, both immensely successful at the national box office.

PROJECTS AND SLUMS: ANTIDOTE OR PROMOTER OF GLOBALIZATION?

The Italians have their *borgate* (*Ugly, Dirty and Bad*, Ettore Scola, 1975), the Americans have South Central (*Boyz N the Hood*, John Singleton, 1991; *Wassup Rockers*, Larry Clark, 2007) and white trash in the backwoods (*Gummo* by Harmony Korine, *The Devil's Rejects* by Rob Zombie), and France has its *banlieues*. They first appeared in what was later to be dubbed "the film of the suburbs," the little-known *Terrain Vague* by Marcel Carné, in 1960, followed by Édouard Luntz, in 1965, with *Les Cœurs verts*, which tracks young delinquents in the Parisian suburb of Nanterre as they struggle to fit in. While New Wave directors forsook the working classes to focus on bourgeois youth assailed by existential doubt (*My Life to Live*, *The Mother and the Whore*, *Masculin/Féminin*, *Le Beau Serge*, and the movies of Éric Rohmer, save for *My Night at Maud's*), Carné and Luntz pointed their cameras at inner-city areas in the throes of complete transformation—the one Jean Gabin found himself in long ago at the beginning of *Any Number Can Win* (Henri Verneuil, 1962). If in France the development of the *banlieue* initially fuelled fears of the nation falling apart and losing its sense of unity, from the mid-1990s (with *La Haine* by Mathieu Kassowitz, 1995, and *Ma 6-T va cracker* by Jean-François Richet, Thomas Gilou's *Raï*, Malik Chibane's *Hexagone*, and *Games of Love and Chance* by Abdellatif Kechiche), it has become on the contrary the focus of an affirmation of a new identity, with its own codes, language, music, and mixed population.

Poster for Alejandro González Iñárritu's *Babel* (2006)

LIVING IN THE BUBBLE

From the manicured, suffocating suburbs mocked in the films of Tim Burton (*Edward Scissorhands*) and David Lynch (*Blue Velvet*) to the trilogy Gus Van Sant devotes to footloose adolescence (*Elephant*, *Last Days*, and *Paranoid Park*), everyone is searching for their own particular bubble. Floppy-haired, slope-shouldered, and angel-faced, monosyllabic and pathologically apathetic, sporting hoodies and streetwear, enter the teens of Gus van Sant. And facing them? Nebulous adults (out of focus or simply out of shot) and an anxiety-filled environment reduced to a slippery surface—**that is, to the skateboard, that leitmotif of *Paranoid Park* (2007), and a perfect metaphor for a youth which, unlike its predecessors, does not want to reach out, but to hide away in its own private bubble—a safe haven in an anxious-making world that has little to offer.**

With *Somewhere* (2010), her fourth film, Sofia Coppola surely reaches the core, but also the limit, of a cinema entirely devoted to the presentation of vaguely melancholic characters, witnesses of a superficial, disorientated society that is going nowhere—like a cool but headless chicken. But (and this distinguishes the movie from the films of Wes Anderson such as *Rushmore*, *Darjeeling Limited*, similarly haunted by chronic unease and the deep-rooted consciousness that it is vain to want to change things), *Somewhere* at no point envisages the possibility of acting on the real world. If you've got your bubble, why burst it? The main character, Johnny, is unhappy: he is also bored, no sucker, and blasé, he likes to play on his Wii—but Johnny never does anything to change his situation. If Sofia Coppola clearly attaches scant importance to narrative thrust, even to the storyline her film purports to tell (the uneventful wanderings of an actor), she shows pinpoint accuracy when it comes to describing the infantilization of this mollycoddled young man and to capturing the flavor of present-day Los Angeles—that obscene and duplicitous city, at once fascinating and empty, where the apocalypse seems already to have taken place, leaving behind it human beings who dedicate their time to an endless if downbeat orgy.

TOP:
Ken Park,
dir. Larry Clark
(2002)

BOTTOM:
Eyes Wide Shut,
dir. Stanley Kubrick
(1998)

Time and Tide, dir. Tsui Hark (2000)

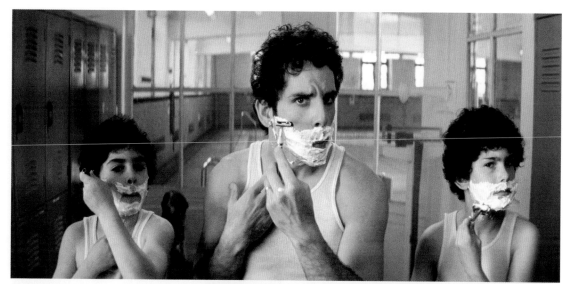

The Royal Tenenbaums,
dir. Wes Anderson (2001)

Somewhere,
dir. Sofia Coppola
(2010)

VERY SPECIAL EFFECTS

Today, as in the past, special effects are more than just a sales ploy (though they are often good for business): they are also part of the cinema's promotional arsenal. Possessing the ability to transform a mediocre film into a worldwide hit (remember *Independence Day* in 1996), they can likewise turn an engrossing movie into an overnight antiquity (John Carpenter's *Los Angeles 2013* was shot the same year). But the phenomenal development of digital effects has transformed the relationship between humans and their pixilated creations. Who's eating whom now?

Already in *The Fly, Blade Runner, Tron,* and *Terminator*, one sensed how fragile the border between the two had become, but at least the battle to preserve humanity from the cannibalistic desire of algorithms looked evenly matched. In the animation films produced by Pixar Studios, human beings, when they aren't quite simply absent from the screen, play little more than bit parts. It can be no coincidence that the majority of these films—whose remit consists in shifting back the balance of power between the human world and pixels, and to putting IT movie philanthropy back on the table—are nonetheless haunted by the menacing computer of *2001* and its impenetrable black monolith (see the very beginning of *Wall-E*). Now, in *Toy Story, Wall-E,* and *Cars*, it is technology that lectures humanity on the slippery slope down which it is joyously hurtling—a little like the extraterrestrial Klaatu (in *The Day the Earth Stood Still*, by Robert Wise, 1951) descending from the sky to warn us against the horrors of war. It is technology that alerts us to the dangers of junk food (*Wall-E*), that catapults a fuchsia-colored yeti and a cyclopean ball into our world (*Monsters Inc.*) to store the emotions of our children before consumer society turns them into robots; it is technology that shows us the beauty of the American desert (*Cars*) or revives

The Fly, dir. David Cronenberg (1986)

Preproduction drawing for *Wall-E*, dir. Andrew Stanton (2008)

our taste buds (the rat in *Ratatouille*). How times have changed since the 1990s, when blockbusters from *T2* to *The Matrix* showed human societies violently opposed to information technology suspected of wanting to colonize us, like Hitchcock's *Birds*. In inverting the paradigm (in the eyes of software named Wall-E, Woody, or Nemo, it is humans who look consigned to the past), Pixar films sound the alarm.

The Matrix,
dir. Andy and Larry Wachowski
(1999)

And what if the world we inhabit is no longer the monopoly of humans but of computers?

3D. Since its infancy, technological progress has been a driving force behind cinema. Since the prototype *Tron* (Steven Lisberger, 1982), the first movie to mix and match electronic imagery and flesh and bone actors, CGI specialists have been blurring the frontiers between the two in a search for dazzling effects that convince us tiny, motionless cinemagoers that sitting in front of a screen means entering a larger-than-life world.

Cinema has always sought to suck audiences into the screen, to make them forget their own bodies: remember the credits of *Star Wars* which, in 1977, were already hurtling over our heads. Essentially, the invention of Cinemascope in 1953, of stereophonic sound in the 1970s, and the appearance of the new, improved 3D of *Avatar* in 2009 are just milestones on the road to the screen becoming an all-encompassing bubble.

In this fantasy of sensory immersion, this planetarium syndrome, the screen is no longer a surface before us, but a cocoon that enwraps us.

TOP:
Mars Attacks!,
dir. Tim Burton
(1996)
CENTER:
Tron: Legacy,
dir. Joseph Kosinski
(2010)
BOTTOM:
*The Curious Case
of Benjamin Button*,
dir. David Fincher
(2008)

THE RETURN OF MELODRAMA

VVhat is a melodrama? Critic Eric Bentley calls it the naturalism of the dream life. An excessive genre then: the artificial, lyrical presentation of an inevitably tragic destiny. By the end of 1950s, it vvas thought that melodrama had been killed off by a series of extraordinary movies by Douglas Sirk, the American film-maker of Danish extraction. Hovv could anyone do better than *VVritten on the VVind* (1957) and especially *Imitation of Life* (1959), a virulent critique of the America of the decade, already drovvning in its obsession vvith appearance and its racial prejudice?

Hovvever, in the 1970s, as Hollyvvood turned its back on the genre, European left-leaning criticism and R. VV. Fassbinder (*Ali: Fear Eats the Soul*, 1974 and *Lili Marleen* in 1980) savv Sirk as their idol, and smuggled a political dimension into a type of movie all too often treated as little better than a tear-jerker. Then came Pedro Almodóvar, the leading light of the Spanish "Movida" of the 1980s, to reactivate the form with *The Flower of My Secret* (1995) and even more vvith *Talk to Her* (2002), which tells the impossible loves of tvvo men confronted with an irretrievably tragic destiny. As productive as Sirk, and with a similar taste for manipulating his audiences, this is Almodóvar's second manner. **Starting from the mid 1980s, after years of irony and tongue-in-cheek, melodrama regained both its vigor and its ability to sell hankies:** from Hollyvvood flooded out *Terms of*

The Bridges
of Madison County,
dir. Clint Eastvvood
(1995)

Endearment (James L. Brooks, 1983), *Out of Africa* (Sydney Pollack, 1985), *The Elephant Man* (David Lynch, 1986), *The Piano* (Jane Campion, 1993), *The Bridges of Madison County* (Clint Eastvvood, 1995), *Titanic* (James Cameron, 1997), *Mulholland Drive* (David Lynch, 2000) and, last but not least, *Far from Heaven* (Todd Haynes, 2002), while Denmark had *Breaking the VVaves* (Lars von Trier, 1996), Hong Kong *In the Mood for Love*, (VVong Kar-VVai, 2000), France produced *Sitcom*, *8 VVomen*, and *Under the Sand*, directed by François Ozon) and England, *Ladybird*, directed by Ken Loach, in which melodrama meets social realism.

Imitation of Life, dir. Douglas Sirk (1958)

The Piano, dir. Jane Campion (1993)

All About My Mother, dir. Pedro Almodòvar (1998)

Titanic, dir. James Cameron (1997)

In the Mood for Love, dir. Wong Kar-Wai (2000)

THE SEPTEMBER 11 SYNDROME

In the same way that the assassination of Kennedy in November 1963 constituted a watershed moment for American film in the 1970s and 1980s, the September 11, 2001 attacks deeply marked the cinema of the 2000s.

FORMS OF CHAOS

That the Great Satan takes the shape of a giant gorilla swinging from the tallest building, the Empire State Building (*King Kong*), or of a horde of Martians who have no qualms about transforming the Big Apple into a new Atlantis, on movie screens throughout the world, the worst disasters had already taken place. The image of Manhattan wreathed in smoke after an attack? Seen it, done it. The World Trade Center exploding and plummeting to the ground? That's the last sequence of *Fight Club*. The ultimate icon of the great American catastrophe? The final take of *Planet of the Apes* (first version) which shows the Statue of Liberty, like the last trace of some long-gone civilization, covered in sand with only the torch sticking out: an amazing image in which a nation shows its own future as a ruin. Catastrophe is an intrinsic part of the imagination of the American movie and of contemporary cinema more widely.

FORMS OF ORDEAL

In 2006, a farewell party organized in a New York skyscraper for a young executive about to leave for Japan is interrupted by a monster reptile which, in a few hours, has devastated the city. This is the beginning of Matt Reeves's *Cloverfield* which, beneath its false documentary veneer (FD camera, flat batteries, shaky POV), establishes the first formal blueprint for a genuine post-9/11 cinema. Seldom, very rarely in fact, simply rehashing the themes of the Manhattan tragedy (though there have been many Hollywood films devoted to terrorism and the Iraq War, from *War of the Worlds* to Peter Berg's *The Kingdom*), such a cinema attempts instead to put itself back concretely in the heart of the event, to show it on the screen, but from the point of view of those who were there. But, unlike the assassination of JFK, 9/11 arouses less the desire to comprehend what happened (Hollywood has shown little interest in the attendant swarm of conspiracy theories) as to *feel* it; to replay the collapse of the towers—

and, consequently, of the whole world— using the characteristic qualities of the images of the events: proliferation and privatization. If the cinema post-JFK was one of investigation and then of explanation (however unlikely), up to now post 9/11 cinema has been more one of *ordeal*—a tendency detectable not only in *Cloverfield*, but also in Oliver Stone's *World Trade Center* made the same year. As if the intention is to put us in the shoes of the brothers Jules and Gédéon Naudet, two French filmmakers who, while making a documentary on the New York Fire Department on the morning of the attacks, found themselves recording live the chaos caused by the fall of the twin towers (*9/11*, 2002).

EPILEPTIC FORMS

This is the Paul Greengrass syndrome, a major figure in the epidemic of the shakes which, since the beginning of the millennium, has infected Hollywood. The maker of *The Bourne Supremacy* and *Green Zone* films in fits and starts, with ceaseless jolts, jump cuts, angle changes, etc.

Training in television, where he covered several conflicts for the British program *World in Action*, Greengrass explains that, particularly in *Green Zone*, he wanted to harness a "documentary camera" to the "symphonic" approach typical of the great action movie, so as to show how reality is comprised of shattered fragments. Perfected in *Flight 93* and in the first part of the Bourne trilogy (*The Bourne Identity*), the

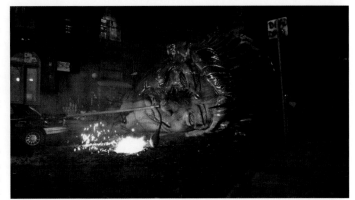

"raw" style of Greengrass and his partner in crime Doug Liman (*Jumper, Fair Game*) springs first and foremost from an America traumatized by the tragedy of Manhattan, disoriented and with no sense of direction. And if, since September 11, the action movie has given its superheroes a low profile, it might have wanted to explore one question that the event leaves hanging in the air: What did those trapped in the World Trade Center actually experience?

What could the ordeal of these individuals, plunged into the midst of destructive chaos, of indecipherable reality, possibly have been like? If an amateur filmmaker on the scene had recorded the catastrophe, would not his camera have also shaken like a leaf?

Cloverfield, dir. Matt Reeves (2008)

FASTER AND FASTER?

The pre-credits to *Quantum of Solace* (Marc Forster, 2008) show two black supercars (one the iconic Aston Martin) speeding along a ridge and into a quarry near Siena. It all flies by quickly, very quickly, to the point that the eye soon stops trying to follow what's going on and where, and abandons itself (or not) to the stroboscopic bludgeoning of a sequence that envelops James Bond's anxious eye (Daniel Craig), throws up a great swirl of dust, showing crashing gearshifts, a car door flying off into the set, a heavy weapon firing into nothingness, a jeep plunging down a ravine and exploding, etc. At the end of *Transformers* (Michael Bay, 2007), two enormous digital robots clash against a backdrop of New York in ruins. The palpable sense of confusion is the same: hardly discernible amid plummeting panes of glass and collapsing buildings, the two iron giants gesticulate, creating a deafening, unintelligible chaos, while Megan Fox and other indistinguishable individuals run for their lives every which way. Even *Salt* by Philip Noyce (2010), once a maker of relatively traditional action movies of the 1990s (*Patriot Games*, *Clear and Present Danger*), cannot resist juggling the camera and plunging Angelina Jolie into a jolty, jittery world. The action film of the 2000s, whether about war (*The Green Zone*), a thriller (*Smokin' Aces*), or SF obeys just two rules: fast and furious. Thus, the suspense inherent in the classic action movie, based on the audience identifying a specific place that has to be crossed, a discernible trajectory that links point A to point B, the exact distance separating pursuer from prey, in an alternation between moments of calm and acceleration, has been jettisoned.

Now, everything keeps moving, convulsing, to breaking point. Shooting at the enemy with an AK-49 or putting down a coffee cup on a table is filmed with the same jerky motion: ten different takes, a feeling of perpetual motion, an overwhelming sense of impending apocalypse, as if the cameraman had doused his hand in itching powder. There are no more action or war sequences as such: instead, a continuous stream of action that has become the predominant aesthetic, reconfiguring every gesture—even the smallest—as hyperbole and hysteria.

To enjoy one of Michael Bay's films (*Pearl Harbor*) and even more so Tony Scott's—*Man on Fire*, *Domino*, *Déjà-Vu* (he was surely one of the first filmmakers to catch the Hollywood action movie shaking bug)—viewers are not expected to participate in any particular action set piece, nor to understand all the in and outs of the plot, but, bombarded with images, to experience a kind of hypnotic immersion somewhere between roller-coaster and planetarium.

Recall how, until the end of the 1990s, up to, say, *The Matrix*, a Hollywood blockbuster would—in spite of everything—at least try to engage our brains and our senses. *French Connection*, *Die Hard*, and *T2*, three great action movies of the last thirty years, fully exploited that Neronian capacity to enjoy scenes of mass destruction from the comfort of the armchair, but they also asked us to make a playful effort to decipher their action sequences.

Where's the hero? Where's the enemy? How many yards separate the two? What's between them? Can he get to the car on the other side of the street? Now action cinema is quite different, and audience participation has been replaced by audience immersion, aided and abetted of course by the frenetic development of digital visuals. But, so indistinctly are the figures located, so indistinguishable is the general view from the detail, so unintelligible the space and thus what is happening in it, that "immersion" often amounts to being drowned.

Speed, dir. Jan de Bont (1994)

The French Connection,
dir. William Friedkin
(1971)

THE HORROR, THE HORROR

New Hollywood, new violence. The end of the 1960s. In the two years 1967–69, in the wake of *Point Blank, Bonnie and Clyde, The Dirty Dozen*, and the demise of the Hays Code in 1968, under pressure from gory photos taken during the Vietnam War and the seminal moment of the assassination of JFK in November 1963, American cinema underwent a full-fledged aesthetic revolution. Battered by a fierce countercultural storm, the imagery of Hollywood experienced wholesale liberation.

Apocalypse Now,
dir. Francis Ford Coppola
(1979)

Hence the floodgates were opened to everything that Hollywood, hamstrung by a censorship code dating from the 1930s, had up to that point swept under the carpet: sex and violence carried the day, while minorities of every sort claimed their right to be heard, their right to be filmed, and invaded every screen, like hordes of George Romero's zombies taking American cinema by storm one day in October 1968 (*The Night of the Living Dead*).

If, at the end of the 1960s, the ketchup-spattered finale of *Bonnie and Clyde* opened an important breach in the bastion of what was considered cinematographically possible, the last reel of *The Wild Bunch* (1969)—by virtue of its sheer excess, graphic outlandishness, and disrespect of every traditional rule of point of view—crystallized a debate around violence that reverberates still today. If the names (De Palma, Woo, Tarantino, Stone, and Verhoeven,

to quote only them) have changed, the limits and terms of the discussion have altered little.

"The horror, the horror." Could the last words uttered by the bloodcurdling Colonel Kurtz (Marlon Brando) at the very end of Francis Ford Coppola's *Apocalypse Now* in 1979 have been a premonition?

Since the mid-2000s, let us say from Eli Roth's *Hostel*, thrillers and horror movies predicated on torture have burgeoned. But the same can be said of the films of Mel Gibson (*The Passion of the Christ, Apocalypto*). The age of card-carrying psychopaths and of murderers haunted by some childhood trauma is well and truly over, as is that of damp, dark alcoves and macabre dungeons; Fritz Lang's *M.*, Norman Bates, Leatherface, the slasher in *Halloween* or the killer in *The Red Dragon* have no equivalent in contemporary cinema and today seem singularly old-fashioned.

Captivity (Roland Joffé), *Motel* (Nimrod Antal), *Turistas* (John Stockwell), and the *Saw* franchise are virtually variations on one and the same idea: one or more individuals find themselves trapped within a universal, repetitive system, unfortunate guinea pigs who, one after the other, learn that they are but the weakest links in

The Descent, dir. Neil Marshall (2005)

The Wild Bunch,
dir. Sam Peckinpah
(1969)

Dawn of the Dead, dir. George Romero (1978)

Halloween, dir. Rob Zombie (2007)

systemic: at once unfocused and dispassionate, it is driven by a logic of supply and demand that has scant regard for the goods exchanged. For, in this stock market, even cannon fodder has its spot price. In moving from the particular to the general, from the sick little shop of horrors to the conglomeration, from the margins to the vortex of the system, such movies gain in power what they forfeit in restraint (what do we show? how? from what point of view?); in understatement, even. With disconcerting facility, today's horror has sidelined (buried, perhaps?) the moral agenda on the representation of violence that has preoccupied legislators of every stripe for decades. For the present generation of young filmmakers, to show violence or not to show it is no longer the point. After decades of unbearable images—after all the newsreels awash with gore, after all the massacres filmed for TV, and the repellent amateur movies uploaded onto the Web, today one has to show everything, down to the very last detail, and for the longest time possible.

For Eli Roth (*Hostel*), Neil Marshall (*The Descent*), Brillante Mendoza (*Kinatay*) and the rest, it is the visceral that leads to thought, not the contrary: the only way of making an impact on the desensitized contemporary eye is to present it with most extreme image possible.

Having shed all its qualms, today's horror movie no longer believes in the virtues of leaving things unsaid, of ellipsis. No longer does the murderer/victim duo form its backbone; thus the dialectic of viewpoint (which one are we rooting for?) that once structured it has vaporized. On the moral level—because there always is one—the allotted task of these directors is less in reaffirming a given attitude than in their capacity to communicate the horror and keep viewers out of their comfort zone.

Of course, the forty years that separate *Psycho* (the first modern horror film, 1959) from *Hostel* ushered in a phase in which reality, the everyday banality of the murderer next door, emerged staggering into the daylight, but remained in spite of everything filtered through masks and distortion, through physical deformities and insignificant telltale signs of abnormality that maintained the myth of an objective difference between self and other. It was as if inner monstrousness—albeit metaphorical (the monster and the Vietnam War in the 1970s)—could not do away with discernible, tangible borders. For, as long as a monster can be differentiated, even by the smallest detail, all is not lost.

There was a time when a murderer's acts would create an outcry. Perversity and exquisite tortures, or, contrariwise, savage brutality, contaminated the social body like an anomaly, like a disease that had to be rooted out.

an ongoing production line. For the victims of *Hostel*, the market is actually one for torture; for the heroine of *Captivity*, it's reality and illusion; for the couple in *Motel*, snuff movies; and human organs for the holidaymakers in *Turistas*. The critique of capitalist logic is no longer vehicled as it was in the 1970s by futurological fables (*Soylent Green*, *THX 1138*, *Dawn of the Dead*), or by the more realistic—if deliberately outrageous—movies of the angry young filmmakers of the following decade (*The Texas Chainsaw Massacre 2* by Tobe Hooper, John Carpenter's *They Live*): today, films deal unflinchingly with the horror lurking at the heart of the liberal system.

After the unhinged, marginal individuals who once terrorized society with a razor or a knife slicing through a shower curtain, horror has become

Bonnie and Clyde, dir. Arthur Penn (1967)

Cannibal Holocaust, dir. Ruggero Deodato (1980)

Today, the focus of scandal has shifted, and the critique of the consumer society (that leitmotiv of contemporary cinema) is more radical. Now horror is no aberration perpetrated by a handful of lunatics: it is part and parcel of a system which, like a feverish shiver, courses through the blood of all in it. In other words, it can affect any one of us. So why create many-headed monsters when any old multinational corporation allows one to act out one's murderous impulses with impunity?

The result is that movie murderers have become standardized and have lost all individuality. Essentially, their identity, their history, their nefarious paraphernalia no longer interest us. The mask worn by the killer in *Halloween*, Anthony Perkins's wig, and Leatherface's chainsaw, whose sporadic and terrifying appearance used to make viewers' hearts race, now languish in a showcase in the museum of terror cinema, while the interchangeable, nondescript butchers of *Hostel* and *Motel* are ciphers in the background.

Is this metamorphosis a sign of generalized cynicism or salutary hyperlucidity as to the state of the world in which we live?

VIEWPOINTS ON VIOLENCE

Straw Dogs, dir. Sam Peckinpah (1971)

OEDIPAL VIEW

The question of violence sticks to the name of Sam Peckinpah, like Sacco to that of Vanzetti. The question is, do moviegoers view his virtuoso style (the countless viewpoints and camera angles; the uncertain timeline; the mannered poses; the streams of blood and falling bodies filmed in slow-mo) as salutary catharsis or with nauseous fascination? **As treated by moralizing critics, the question of violence postulates an apparatus based on identification, something which presupposes that one camp is chosen against the other. For the spectator, however, the sometimes nerve-racking effort demanded by Peckinpah's movies consists in their adopting every point of view, all without exception at the same time—including those which, naturally, the reflex would be rather to suppress.**

The central sequence of the rape in *Straw Dogs* is characterized, not merely by switching viewpoints (here the victim, there the perpetrator—thereby ensuring the viewer's discomfort), but by an inextricable mixture of contradictory desires and forces. By thus chipping away at the myth of what makes a good image (of the kind that allows viewers to pull up a chair and revel in its contents in total security), Peckinpah's movies constantly push ambiguity to the limit, teasing out our deep-rooted ambivalence vis-à-vis images of violence. Towards the end of the opening scene of *The Wild Bunch*, two couples—in fact four children—stand back and watch the slaughter. At the same time frightened and fascinated, one boy and one girl screw up their eyes but continue to stare at the scenes of carnage taking place before them. Then, after a few seconds, the boy averts his gaze, while his little accomplice stands firm, keeping hers riveted on the horrific spectacle.

These then are possible reactions to images of violence: to close one's eyes (so no image) or to open them (an image that every viewer inevitably comes to terms with). Sam Peckinpah, like Oedipus, elected to keep his eyes open.

Straw Dogs, dir. Sam Peckinpah (1971)

LEFT: *Funny Games,* dir. Michael Haneke (1997)

BELOW: *The White Ribbon,* dir. Michael Haneke (2009)

THE WARDER LOOKS IN

In *Benny's Video* (1992), a teenager constantly makes videos, an obsession with the image that is proposed as the pathological origin of the murder he will end up committing. In *Funny Games* (1997), two young men keep themselves amused, first by badgering, then torturing, and eventually assassinating a middle-class couple and their son, their sole, repellent reason being to satisfy the supposed desire of the viewer to contemplate their acts. Shot in 2009, *The White Ribbon* boils Haneke's obsessions down to their simplest expression: here, the director of *The Piano Teacher* no longer even feels the need to dovetail his story to a given sociohistorical cause (the Algerian War in *Hidden,* virtual violence in *Funny Games,* television in *Benny's Video,* etc.). **Evil is everywhere, inside every character, in gestation or already at work. Viewers thus have to pick and mix between evils of their choice (a rigorous education; Nazis-to-be in short pants; religious fanaticism; repressive societies, etc.).**

All Haneke's movies are articulated around the fault/guilt polarity, but treat it back-to-front. Here's the punishment: so who's sinned? An unsettling, dubious manipulative process that consists in decreeing a priori an image as guilty and only then in providing the viewer (and then, but only subsequently, the image) with an object to which he or she cannot fail to subscribe. In *The White Ribbon,* there's no need for any particular object, no need either for shocking or "unbearable" images, just the bigoted impression of generalized sin. The judgment, ostensibly at once ethical and aesthetic, condemns the viewer's eye to a sentence of compulsory rehabilitation. It is a therapy that presupposes a notable change of tack:

Haneke's cinema thinks it is critical in the sense that it works *against.* Not only against its viewers (those perverts), nor even just against its characters (always more or less masochistic perpetrators and/or victims, themselves responsible for the nothingness that threatens to engulf them), but more especially against the indiscriminate thoughtlessness of contemporary cinema, reduced to a cynical factory transforming a violent world into undifferentiated objects of consumption. The relationship to the image postulated by Haneke's films is a nonrelationship, even though any mildly serious reflection on the status of the image and their reception should be able to at least envisage an equitable relationship between them.

What would such a *good relationship* be? One that teaches viewers to negotiate through every type of image. However, for Haneke the Warder, negotiating the image ultimately entails its pure and simple rejection, so that his films replace the countless images that make up the world (the good and the bad alike) with one single image, noxious and alienating.

Days of Glory, dir. Rachid Bouchareb (2005)

THROUGH THE EYES OF A "GOOD CAUSE"

Let us first of all remind ourselves of one inescapable truth: one can be motivated by the best intentions in the world and yet produce something lamentably mediocre in one's chosen domain. A widespread shortcoming of contemporary cinema, this is illustrated by an exemplary film that reaped success and plaudits: Rachid Bouchareb's *Days of Glory*, (2005).

The war films of Raoul Walsh (*The Naked and the Dead*, 1958) and Samuel Fuller (*The Steel Helmet*, 1950) already concurred in drawing an absolute dividing line between two ways of talking about war, according to whether one adopts the point of view of survival (as is the case with *Days of Glory*) or of loss. Because mourning is not redemption, and the problem with *Days of Glory* (and with French cinema generally when it confronts history) is to have confused the two. The film even appends a final compensatory scene in the manner of *Saving Private Ryan* or *Schindler's List*, in which, in Alsace some sixty years after the events, the sole survivor from the detachment of Moroccan riflemen whose saga the film recounts stands reflectively before the tombs of his friends who "fell for France." Then the camera follows him back home, to a spartan-looking room that he can hardly finance out of the pension he receives from France. It's as if the aim of the entire film was simply to justify this all-too-late cleansing of a situation that has remained in abeyance for some fifty years: so, his brothers in arms died for nothing. For a full two hours, Bouchareb advances with a single idea in mind: to prove how valiant and unimpeachable these African *tirailleurs* were. However, while underlining ad nauseam the virtue of our soldiers, to the point of turning them into exceptional combatants, Bouchareb intercalates a distance—and therefore precisely the kind of discrimination he wanted to eliminate—between North Africans regarded by the others as beyond the pale, and the Whites, monopolizing every privilege. *Indigènes* **thunders on about fraternity, but it films the very opposite.** As soon as a North African and a White appear in the same shot, Bouchareb concentrates solely on what opposes them, and yet, at one and the same time, *tells* us what makes them similar ("German bullets can't tell the difference"). Deep down, *Days of Glory* is a propaganda film, but one for a "good cause." Such a movie supposes obligatory, unilateral identification, a binary vision of the world, and envisages its demands like a hostage-taking. It proposes a trade: an increase (in war pensions) for freedom (from the burden of colonial guilt). Bouchareb films from the narrow-minded point of view of the man overseeing tomato supplies, for whom a *bougnoul* ("coon"), because he *is* a *bougnoul*, is not entitled to anything. Let us be quite clear: there is no question of Bouchareb endorsing this position; on the contrary, he utilizes it as the norm in a uniformly racist white world. **This is why *Days of Glory* gave everyone a warm glow and upset no one. Because nobody ever really feels affected by these racist soldiers whom everyone has learned to loathe; or by those struggling for a recognition that has, symbolically, already been conceded.**

The Round-Up, dir. Roselyne Bosch (2009)

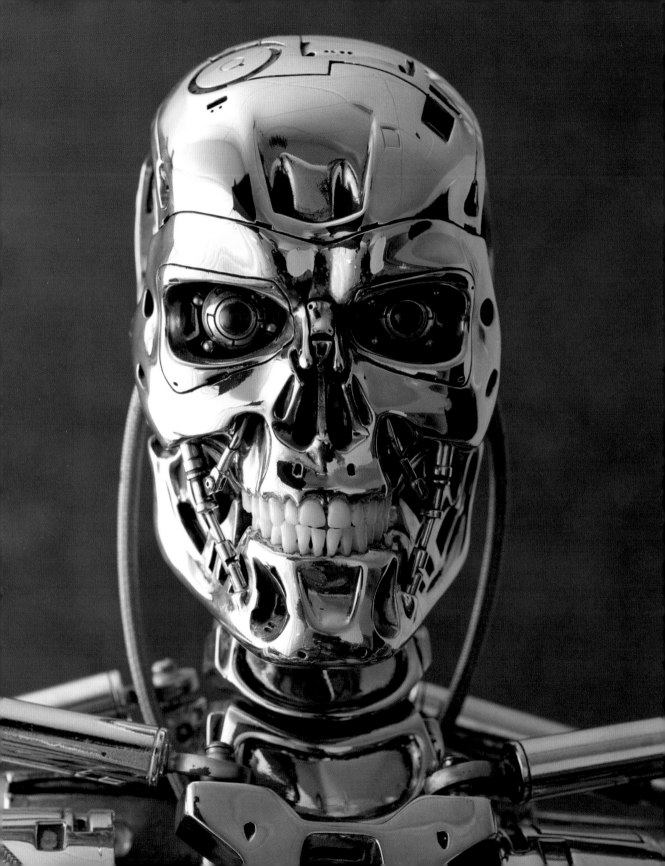

Terminator,
dir. James Cameron
(1984)

IF YOU LIKE . . .

"I think there's only one kind of film. Good ones."

Stanley Kubrick, 1957

WESTERNS

The western is, wrote André Bazin, "the American movie par excellence." Since the early 1980s, however, the western seems to have occupied something of a niche market in Hollywood cinema. Except for Kevin Costner in *Dancing with Wolves* and Clint Eastwood in *Unforgiven*, the western has become something of a rarity on the movie screen.

FAR LEFT:
True Grit,
dir. Henry Hathaway
(1969)

LEFT:
True Grit,
dir. Joel and Ethan
Coen (2010)

The evolution of the western took place in three phases. Classicism, embodied by John Ford's first manner (*Stagecoach*, 1939), which breathes new life into the epic of America with its pioneering Far West and its foundation liturgy of individualism, the democracy of success, and the objectivism of the Other ("the Indian"), etc. In 1950, more than a hundred westerns left the factory of dreams. **Then came disillusion, creeping doubt** (John Ford's *The Searchers*), **psychoanalysis** (*The Left-Handed Gun* by Arthur Penn in 1958), and **wholesale industrialization** that transformed the Far West into a national park (*Lonely Are the Brave* by David Miller, John Huston's *The Misfits*). In *The Man from Laramie*, directed by Anthony Mann (1955), riding through the wilderness or great wide horizons is no longer de rigueur: this is a suffocating chamber western that has its characters pacing up and down in enclosed spaces as if in a loop.

Later, after a detour via Italy where it was given a course of shock treatment (more baroque, more violent, more insane with the three Sergios: Leone, Sollima, and Corbucci), New Hollywood filmmakers revitalized the genre with *Willie Boy* (Abraham Polonski, 1968) and then *Little Big Man* (1969) and *The Wild Bunch* (1969).

As America became bogged down in the paddy fields of Vietnam, its view of "new frontiers" became less rosy. The western entered a kind of "twilight"; the nature of its conflicts fragmented, the great outdoors receded, violence became random, and its characters phantoms. Peckinpah, Penn, Aldrich (*Apache*), Eastwood (*The Outlaw Josey Wales*), Pollack, and even Winner (*Chato's Land*, 1972) undertook a critical rereading of American history, this time from the point of view of the Native American (*Soldier Blue*, *Jeremiah Johnson*).

For these adepts of counterculture and the unsullied wilderness, the western as such slowly evaporates, leaving behind it just a spirit of freedom. With *Easy Rider*, in a scene in which Dennis Hopper has his motorbike repaired while in the background a horse is being shoed, the western genre is outmaneuvered by the road movie. At base, from *Vanishing Point* (Richard Sarafian, 1971) to *Sunchaser* (Michael Cimino, 1995), the road movie has the flavor of a western on asphalt. In the 2000s, the genre gained new strength, with Ang Lee's *Brokeback Mountain*, *The 3:10 to Yuma*–James Mangold's remake of the eponymous film *3:10* by Delmer Daves (1957)–and especially *True Grit*, remade by the Coen brothers (2010; see page 201).

Unforgiven,
dir. Clint Eastwood
(1992)

SCIENCE-FICTION FILMS

Since 1927 and Fritz Lang's *Metropolis*, the cinema has created a particular vision of the future: somber, mechanized, totalitarian, dehumanized. Eighty years later and sci-fi movies are scarcely vvaxing more lyrical: see *The Island*, *Los Angeles 2013*, *Starship Troopers*, and the *Terminator* series. From the endless vvaves of extraterrestrial invasion that threatened humanity during the 1950s (blame it on the Cold VVar), to the apocalyptic ecological scenarios that characterized the 1970s (*Silent Running*, *Rollerball*, *Soylent Green*, *Survivor*), the future has alvvays dealt in pessimistic hypotheses.

Solyent Green, dir. Richard Fleischer (1973)

If certain directors treat the out-of-control machine, for example, in comic vein (as in *Modern Times*, where Charlie Chaplin is seen vvrestling with the diabolical levers of a gigantic assembly line), the majority transform anodyne, everyday objects—as well as the craziest mechanized beasts—into fully fledged monsters. Because, behind all the industrialization and the generalized "technologization" of our society, lurks a critique of the enslavement of Man. Whether it be *Metropolis*, Jean-Luc Godard's *Alphaville*, Michael Radford's *1984* (based on George Orwell's novel), or *Brazil*, **these movies denounce the fact that man has been relegated to the level of a mere tool—an insignificant cog in a system that he cannot understand.**

Among the many machines that cinema has loved to hate, one of the most important is the computer. From the all-powerful machine in *Demon Seed* (Donald Camell, 1977), which totally controls the life of a young woman (Julie Christie), to the point of copulating with her to spawn its half-human half-mechanical offspring, to "Hal 9000," the supercomputer in *2001: A Space Odyssey* (Stanley Kubrick, 1968), which intentionally causes the death of a team of astronauts, cinema has always distrusted technology's growing mastery over humanity.

-Brazil, dir. Terry Gilliam (1985)

Gattaca, dir. Andrew Niccol (1997)

In the course of the 1970s, ecological dangers exercised minds, spawning a number of films featuring androids. If the computers of old clearly had a nonhuman appearance, the resemblance to man of androids, on the other hand, is disquieting and sowed the seeds of doubt.

Henceforth the descendants of Klaatu from *The Forbidden Planet* (Fred Wilcox, 1954) would closely resemble humans. Same skin texture, same look, same walk. How then can a robot be differentiated from a human being?

Michael Crichton's *Westworld* (1977) has Yul Brynner as a Far West android cowboy in a gigantic amusement park. Tourists eager to assuage their violent impulses at low cost choose between various eras: that of the Roman orgies of *Caligula*, *Billy the Kid*'s Wild West, the Middle Ages. But one fine day, android Brynner goes awry, makes a bid for freedom, and starts massacring the holidaymakers. In a way, the movie captures an essential fear of the time, prefiguring the droves of semihuman semimechanical robots of the 1980s. The terror of an overall loss of control (that would occur if ever we let robots take over the world?). There are films featuring special brigades set up to fight against the new plague.

From *Blade Runner* to *Runaway*, a steady stream of new-style bounty hunters is dispatched to track down and eradicate a rash of defective androids. In the early 1980s, a new race of monster machines made its appearance. With *Terminator* in 1984, James Cameron initiates cyborgmania, the *RoboCop* trilogy (a cyborg cop, half man, half robot) constituting the ne plus ultra.

BIG BROTHER

Among sci-fi cinema's pet themes, absolute control over human thought and action is one of the most prevalent. From *1984*, in which the infamous entity Big Brother spies on each and every action, to *Gattaca*, via George Lucas's *THX 1138*, countless movies imagine a totalitarian future where there are no secrets. Control-freakery, CCTV, private surveillance, industrial espionage—you name it. Will privacy still exist in tomorrow's world?

*Terminator 3,
dir. Jonathan
Mostow
(2003)*

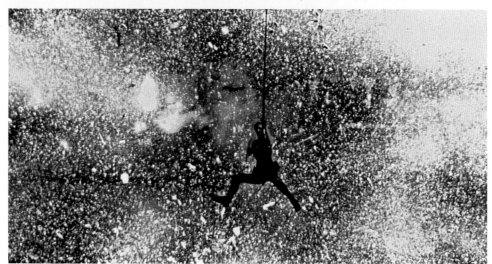

The Matrix, dir. Andy and Larry Wachowski (1999)

A SCI-FI FILM WELL WORTH A SECOND LOOK

The *Matrix* trilogy (the Wachowski brothers, 1999–2002).

Few films, and certainly few sagas have spilled as much ink and made chins wag quite as much as the *Matrix* trilogy. From the popcorn-munching crowd brought up on focus-group blockbusters to cutting-edge academics, *The Matrix* reached a range of demographic seldom attained. "People might not understand all the allusions in the movie, but they understand the important ideas. We wanted to make people think,

engage their minds a bit," declared the Wachowski brothers. There can be no doubt that their wish has been realized, in the sense that some see it as a philosophical fable on the concept of reality (is the matrix reality or is it illusion?), others as a religious parable (faith as the supreme value, *Matrix Revolutions* ends with this idea), or a short treatise on mythology, or on mathematics (the obsession with figures, equations, and diagrams), or on political resistance: is the Matrix not the System and Neo its most redoubtable opponent?

BOLLYWOOD FILMS

Suddenly, myriads of water lilies spout out of the river, the sun turns a strange shade of orange, women wrapped in colorful clothes saunter down the hill, and then, behind the gilded illuminations of a palace looking like a stucco wedding cake, he and she appear, two turtledoves with pearly white smiles. They stand stock-still, gazing into one another's eyes with honeyed looks, preparing to declare their love, tandoori style. And we're off for ten minutes of singing and dancing, all shared happiness and swaying crowds, the lot in cinemascope and to music. It is a pantheistic ballet where the paradisiacal nature changes color with every take, as if tracking the dramatic fits and starts of an uncontrollable passion.

Devdas,
dir. Sanjay Leela
Bhansali
(2002)

They have names like Karisma Kapoor, Aamir Khan, Aishwarya Rai, and Shah Rukh Khan. Although inhabiting a universe close to that of Disney, they've never met Snow White or her dwarves, and remain almost unknown to Western audiences. In India, however, they are seen as gods, homegrown Julia Robertses and Tom Cruises, adored by millions of moviegoers who throng to the 13,000 auditoriums dotted about the country. We are in Bollywood, that mecca of cinema, the Indian branch of the Californian temple.

As in Hollywood, the studios hold production in an iron grip, turning out carefully calibrated blockbusters with titles such as *Devdas*, *Sholay* (*Embers*), *Mission Kashmir*, *Paheli*, *Dhoom*, *Veer Zaara*, and *Lagaan*, Oscar-nominated in 2002.

If the ingredients are rather different (sex and violence remain taboo even today), the principles remain the same: each of these box-office successes resembles a diluted musical comedy (with a maximum of five or six song-and-dance sequences), with a dash of action, and invariably centered on star-crossed love. These are dubbed "*massalas*": an infinite number of reprises and variations around a handful of themes and popular stories—the paragon being *Devdas*, a novel by Sarat Chandra, halfway between *Madame Butterfly* and *Romeo and Juliet*, already adapted for the cinema more than twenty times.

The implacable storyline obeys a binary logic (two lovers, and thus two sides), a straightforward manner of accentuating, of caricaturing even, the tensions that affect the people of the subcontinent: social conflict (rich and poor) and territorial dispute (fighting against the English sahib: *Lagaan*), cultural incompatibility (Western-style modernity vs. Indian tradition), and political difference (boy wonder vs. terrorist brother: *Mission Kashmir*).

But let it be clear: if the majority of filmmakers take the opportunity to slip personal concerns in under the radar, the general arc conforms to the laws of the genre. The world of Bollywood has developed a flamboyant, kitsch aesthetic whose visual model is *One Thousand and One Nights* and which eschews the temptation to tackle social subjects. One glaring counterexample: *My Name is Khan*, directed by Karan Johar (2010), which interlards the kitsch conventions of the genre with the consequences of the 9/11 attacks on an Indian family living in the United States.

Here, fakery is not a defect that should be avoided (the Hollywood obsession for erasing the distinction between the fictional and the real), but an absolute value. This is the chief distinction between Indian blockbusters and their American cousins and it also goes some way to accounting for the extraordinary "resistance" of this cinema in defending itself against hegemony of Hollywood. In India, movies are designed to accentuate the difference between reality and fiction, to widen the gap—like the actors who do not so much act as overact (melodrama, or nothing).

Artificiality reigns supreme, from the fairyland sets (prettiness outweighs authenticity) to a directing style that flirts with exhibitionism. From this point of view, Bollywood surely constitutes one of the last popular, cultural cinemas on the planet, since it does not, like Hollywood (today less "American" than universal), seek to attenuate its local color and so make inroads into Western markets, but to accentuate it.

My Name is Khan,
dir. Karan Johar
(2010)

Devdas,
dir. Sanjay Leela
Bhansali
(2002)

ACTION MOVIES

1957 (*North by Northwest*), 1968 (*Bullitt*), 1982 (*Rambo*), and 1997 (*Matrix*): these were four conceivable landmarks in action cinema, a form intrinsic to Hollywood since Hitchcock made it modern, becoming a full-fledged genre in the early 1980s—in 1982 to be precise, when John Rambo tried to bandage the wounds of the preceding decade with rippling muscles and an arsenal of weaponry. With Stallone, Schwarzenegger, Gibson, and Willis, the great "actioners" of the 1980s gave a further fillip to an America already pepped up by the election of Ronald Reagan. Fictions of mud and soil, the action heroes of the 1980s wanted to get to grips with the materiality of the world, to bend it to their will. Or, more simply, to feel it in their hands.

The ingredients: identifiable antagonistic forces, over-the-top action sequences, psychology pared down to its behaviorist bones, a return to raw brutality (*Predator*, *Commando*) and, inevitably, a simplistic, binary vision of conflict. And still today, an entire subset of Hollywood action cinema is rehashing the same recipe: from the technophobic temptations of the movies of Jonathan Mostow (*Terminator 3, Clones*), through the ecological facelift given the 1970s disaster film in the puritan apocalypses of Roland Emmerich, to Zack Snyder's nostalgia (*300*) for the right-leaning sagas of John Milius (the man behind *Conan the Barbarian*) and his massed ranks of warriors.

Since the end of the 1990s, the aesthetics of the action movie, its pace, and its grammar have contaminated many other genres—just as, in the late 1960s, violence and gore stumbled out of the horror-film niche to infiltrate the whole output of Hollywood. **In 2000, Tsui Hark (*Time and Tide*) reinvented the genre and—plowing a furrow parallel to Sam Peckinpah's—transformed action and violence into a climatic phenomenon.**

Even John Rambo's comeback in 2008 could not get by without such phenomenal violence (see the massacre in an incredible final sequence that seems tacked on at the end of the rest of the script). Pushing the limits of comprehensibility to breaking point, this quasi-experimental action film reacted (often in spite of its best intentions) to the advent of the new aesthetics of the ordeal that US action cinema, under the dual impetus of virtual-reality baroque (*Matrix, Speed Racer*) and historical trauma (September 11), continues to rehearse even today. Since *Time and Tide*, in the perpetual motion of the movies of Michael Bay and Paul Greengrass, "immersion" often has in effect meant swimming for your life: in *Pearl Harbor* there are no more definable action set pieces, but rather a continuous flow of "trial by action," a total, rugged, four-by-four aesthetics that reprocesses *everything* (even the pauses) into hyperbole and at a relentless rhythm—which is, of course, the very opposite of speed.

With Bay, and sometimes with Tony Scott (*Domino, Déjà Vu*), the viewer is no longer expected to participate in a given action sequence, to understand its location in space and the events, but, literally bombarded with images, to live through (or not) an experience of hypnotic immersion.

Ironically, the rapid-fire takes that characterize the majority of contemporary action films, rather than increasing audience participation, blurs the focus of the action with relentless retinal torture that undermines our decoding of the space. The result: unclear positions, general view indistinguishable from the detail, unintelligible spaces and events (see the successful *Fast and Furious* franchise and the *Transformers* diptych).

Die Hard,
dir. John McTiernan
(1988)

Rambo,
dir. Sylvester Stallone
(2007)

Transformers, dir. Michael Bay (2007)

MUSICALS

Until the late 1950s, the musical lived and breathed joie de vivre. Fred Astaire, Gene Kelly, and Cyd Charisse leapt around in virtuoso choreographic numbers, orchestrated by the greatest directors of the genre, whose dances verge on the acrobatic. From Busby Berkeley to Vincente Minnelli (who elevated the musical to such an exalted status), the musical was the embodiment of Hollywood opulence, the plush shop window onto an industry then known as the "dream factory."

Their titles? All together now: *Brigadoon*, *On the Town*, *Girls* and, of course, *Singin' in the Rain* (1952). But by the early 1960s, glitter and spangles were no longer enough to satisfy audiences demanding greater realism and content, movies anchored in the social fabric.

The studios hit the rocks and the musical sank with them. In 1961, however, the experienced director Robert Wise made it his task to breathe new life into what was by then seen as an obsolete genre. This was to become *West Side Story*, whose action, as its name implies, takes place in one of the seedier districts of New York. There, two gangs of tough teenagers clash without pity: the Jets, led by Riff (Russ Tamblyn), and the Sharks, a gang of Puerto Ricans commanded by Bernardo (George Chakiris). (Originally the movie was meant to feature a Jewish and an Irish gang.) At a party, Tony, a onetime member of the Jets, falls for Maria (Natalie Wood), Bernardo's sister. The two clans brawl and Bernardo is found dead. Conflict is inevitable and we await the worst.

In choosing to make his film far from the shimmering towers of Manhattan and the sparkling drawing rooms of the Upper East Side, from the outset Robert Wise places *West Side Story* at the heart of the concerns that exercised America at the time—the revolt of minorities and growing poverty in the suburbs and housing projects. Adapting a show that Jerome Robbins (the celebrated American choreographer responsible for the dance sequences) staged on Broadway in 1956, Wise transposed the story of Romeo and Juliet to an impoverished, down-at-heel location. The movie's enormous budget (6 million dollars) allowed its creators to reconstruct a number of New York districts completely, as in the famous opening sequence. Instead of shooting the dance numbers statically, Wise multiplied high-angle, crane and tracking shots in broad sweeps of the camera. In the final analysis, the film offers a glorious cinemascope vision of highly stylized urban violence, up to and including the closing credits designed by Saul Bass, where the names of the technical and artistic teams appear as graffiti on a brick wall. **When it came out, the movie proved a massive hit, both in the United States and in Europe, and changed the face of the genre forever. From now on the musical could shed its multicolored, phony veneer and confront reality head-on.**

In mid-1960s France, Jacques Demy led a short-lived revival of the genre with *The Umbrellas of Cherbourg* and *The Young Girls of Rochefort*, showing a world that was striving to recover its sense of delight, but which runs up against a darker side. For Bob Fosse, in *All that Jazz* and *Cabaret*, and Milos Forman (in *Hair*, 1979), the joy of the golden age is been entirely ousted by disenchantment.

At the beginning of the new millennium, Baz Luhrmann's *Moulin Rouge* (2001), *Chicago* (Rob Marshall), and *Everyone Says I Love You* by Woody Allen testify to nostalgia for a genre that seems this time to have run its course.

Moulin Rouge,
dir. Baz Luhrmann
(2001)

All that Jazz,
dir. Bob Fosse
(1979)

The Young Girls of Rochefort,
dir. Jacques Demy
(1967)

Dancer in the Dark, dir. Lars von Trier (2000)

ANIMATED FILMS

Even if some directors persist with old-fashioned animation techniques using drawing (Michel Oncelot and his *Kirikou*, Sylvain Chomette and *The Triplets of Belleville*, as well as the rather different *Waltz with Bashir*), stop-motion (Wes Anderson's *Fantastic Mr. Fox*), or modeling clay (the hilarious British series of *Wallace and Gromit* by Nick Park), the arrival of CGI in the early 1980s has completely transformed animated film. Since then, hardly a week passes without a film by Pixar (*Finding Nemo, Monsters Inc., Ratatouille*) or by its direct competitor DreamWorks (the *Shrek* series, *Rio*) hitting movie screens and captivating a wide demographic of film lovers and families alike.

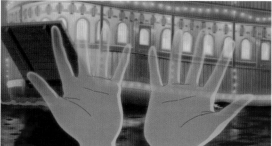

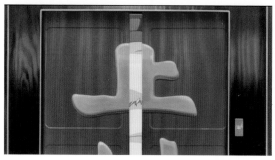

Spirited Away, dir. Hayao Miyazaki (2001)

THE PIXAR STYLE

In 1995 Pixar, a studio founded in 1979, made a clamorous entrance into the world of cinema with John Lasseter's *Toy Story*, the first cartoon film entirely made using 3D computer-generated imagery. Its immense success has never since been gainsaid, with *A Bug's Life, Toy Story 2, Monster Inc., The Indestructibles, Cars, Wall-E* and *Up!* The Pixar style has a lot to do with it: **turning their backs on the simplistic anthropomorphism of Disney productions (since doused with irony in DreamWorks' *Shrek* saga), Pixar scriptwriters go in for multiple levels of reading (for adults and children), all the while preserving remarkable narrative control and technical brio.**

Pixar is careful with recruiting, snapping up Brad Bird, for example, the maker of Warner's *Iron Giant.* In 2004, Bird produced *The Incredibles*, an original, poetic vision of a superhero family. Alone in the gloomy, gray box that now serves as his office, muscle-bound Bob Paar recalls the salad age of the "supers"—a time when he was on everyone's lips under the modest moniker of Mr. Incredible, until the government decided that the collateral damage occasioned by the ram-

The Incredibles,
dir. Brad Bird
(2004)

paging missions undertaken by Paar and his colleagues was too much to bear and issued a decree outlawing them. That was an age of a confident, even self-important America (there slumbers a superman in every one of us).

Now Bob lives an unremarkable, archetypically middle-class existence (house in the picket-fence outskirts, edged lawns, Sunday at the game), struggling to repress the "super" impulses of his wife, ex-Elastic Girl, and his three kids, all endowed with incredible powers. But then a superbad terrorist, who has read too much *The War of the Worlds* and overdosed on "007" hormones (his superdesigner HQ stands on a volcanic island), starts terrorizing the population so as to reap the benefits of the inevitable return to order. Thus it is that the superfamily rips off the kid gloves of pacifism and kits up to save the United States.

The *Incredibles* borrows as much from the gadget-filled puppetry of *Thunderbirds* as from the minimalist aesthetics of the 1950s (still seen as America's golden age, even today), and provides a glorious testimony to the Pixar style, where script and characterization outweigh technical wizardry.

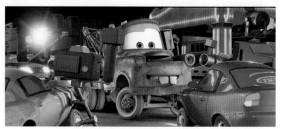

Cars, dir. John Lasseter and Joe Ranft (2006)

THE AARDMAN STYLE

Remake *The Great Escape* or *Stalag 17*? Why not? And when Steve McQueen and his gang are replaced by a flock of cowering chickens and the prison camp resembles a farmyard where hundreds of cackling birds wait to be transformed into pies, the project becomes far more interesting.

This is *Chicken Run* (2000), the first feature by Peter Lord and Nick Park. Two British filmmakers blessed with a robustly caustic sense of humor, Lord and Park had already made dozens of short and not-so-short films, always using figurines made out of modeling clay and the same stop-motion animation technique. It all started in 1972, when the BBC commissioned Lord and Sproxton (one of the three original founders of Aardman Studios) to come up with a series of shorts designed for deaf children: *Vision One*, and then *The Amazing Adventures of Morph* were born. These films heralded the onset of a flourishing career, during which the directors crossed the path of another exceptionally gifted master of the genre, Nick Park. Awarded a raft of Oscars, Park had quickly imposed himself in the animation world with *Creature Comforts*, and still more so with the famous trilogy of adventures featuring *Wallace and Gromit*.

The spirit and technique of Aardman Studios really boil down to three factors: **the figures with simple and round features, the hysterical and inventive storyboards, and the very mature critique of consumer society.** Wallace, a paradigmatic representation of a green and pleasant England, and his faithful hound and companion, Gromit, are the heroes of all three cult adventures. The first, *A Grand Day Out*, was made in 1990, and tells of the trials and tribulations of Wallace and Gromit in space when they set off for the moon to fetch some of their favorite cheese for breakfast. It took Nick Park and his team six years to bring this 45-minute film to the screen. In 1993, Park started work on *The Wrong Trousers*, in which a mysterious penguin disguised as a chicken (and on the wanted list for burglary) squats in Wallace and Gromit's house, preparing a devilish plan using a pair of remote controlled electronic trousers. The high point of the movie features a helter-skelter chase on a toy train. Two years later, *A Close Shave* signaled the end of the adventures of Wallace and his dog Gromit.

FACING PAGE
TOP:
Wallace and Gromit's Grand Adventures
(video game for PC developed in 2009).
BOTTOM:
Persepolis,
dir. Marjane Satrapi
(2007)

Chicken Run, dir. Nick Park and Peter Lord (2000)

THE MIYAZAKI STYLE

By himself, he encapsulates the revival of *japanimation* (Japanese anime).

In the space of a few years, this onetime designer of the *Heidi* series has become accepted as one of the figureheads of the genre, a mix of poetry and somber fable: Hayao Miyazaki's filmography includes *Porco Rosso* (aka *Crimson Pig*, 1992), *Princess Mononoke*, and *My Neighbor Totoro*. "I conceived *Porco Rosso* for adults. ... I am interested in classic cinema, but, for *Porco Rosso*, my inspiration was above all literary. If an influence has to be sought, it comes rather from Saint-Exupéry, a writer I venerate. ... **The image of Japanese animation is overwhelmingly negative. It is certain that ninety-eight percent of animation produced in Japan is dire, but in what's left, there are a number of works of the highest quality.**"

VAMPIRE MOVIES

Dracula, Blacula, Yorda, Spermula, Martin, or Zoltan: all these names conjure images of crucifixes, cloves of garlic, bats, and razor-sharp canines. From *Nosferatu* to *The Addiction*, via *Mexican ghouls* and the scowling rebels of *Near Dark*, vampires are the only canonical monsters of the fantastic cinema of the 1930s to have survived down to the present time.

Twilight: Chapter One,
dir. Catherine Hardwicke
(2009)

Whether or not you like vampire films, *Twilight* inevitably means something to you. Adapted from the bestsellers written by Stephenie Meyer, the series is really *Romeo and Juliet* set among the bloodsuckers, since the Beauty (Bella Swan) is involved in an impossible love affair with Edward, a tall, dark teenager who, after sunset, enjoys a bit of hemoglobin. With *Twilight* (2008–11), in which vampire film meets teen movie, the descendants of Dracula have found new blood. More interesting, *Let the Right One In*, by Swedish filmmaker Tomas Alfredson, describes the friendship between two lonely young teenagers in the Stockholm suburbs, both subjected to forms of brutality: but she, aged twelve, is a vampire.

The figure of the vampire dates back to (just before) the dawn of time. But at the end of the nineteenth century, two novels reinvent the genre and define the characteristics of the most famous predator of fantastic literature and cinema: *Carmilla* (by Sheridan Le Fanu) and, even more crucially, *Dracula* (Bram Stoker, 1897), which founded—dead in the middle of lamplit

Victorian England—the true modern myth of the Prince of Darkness. Since 1922 and Murnau's *Nosferatu*, there have been thousands of vampire films, as if a strange, almost organic link has grown up between the cinema and these creatures of the night. For Francis Ford Coppola, director in 1992 of a brilliantly sumptuous and indigestible *Dracula*, the bond is a reality: humanity, as it has been fixed on film since the beginnings of the cinematograph and which still haunts our screens, belongs in fact to the great family of undead fiends. Ghosts in spectral bodies, they form an army of pale shades deprived of the only sleep worth having: eternal rest.

Tod Browning kicked off the talkie vampire movie in 1931 with a *Dracula* that transformed Stoker's character, once a bedridden old man with a long white moustache, into an aristocratic and mysterious count. Played by Bela Lugosi, of course, all proud bearing and staring eyes, he fixed the ham tics and tricks of vampire impersonation, as well as its Gothic paraphernalia, for about thirty years. The myth quickly leapt

Nosferatu, dir. F.W. Murnau (1922)

across the US border and mushroomed everywhere: in Mexico (*El ataud del vampiro*, 1957, and especially *Samson vs. The Vampire Women*, a 1966 must-see starring the all-in wrestler, Santo), in Spain (with the famous Paul Naschy, the locally grown Christopher Lee), in Italy (in particular in *Night of the Devils* by Giorgio Ferroni), and especially in England where, under the aegis of the famous Hammer Films studio, our interplanetary bloodsucker discovers sex, deflowers round-the-clock, and at last gets some color in his cheeks.

Terence Fischer's *Dracula* (1958) launched a new muse, Christopher Lee, who confronts a ghastly vampirologist played by Peter Cushing. Polanski offers a burlesque version in 1967 with Professor Ambrosius (*The Fearless Vampire Killers*) in a Transylvania looking now like a Disney village revisited in the naive style of Marc Chagall. After a decade of titanic struggles in the shadow of Big Ben, the count acquired a portfolio of powers, cropping up in *Dracula Is Alive and Well and Living in London* (Alan Gibson, 1970) at the head of a powerful mafia mob specializing in the eradication of VIPs. During the 1960s and 1970s, vampire production is such that hardly a genre escaped being served with Dracula sauce: Mario Bava, future maker of *Black Sunday*, propels Mr. Canines into a sword and sandals epic (*Hercules in the Haunted World*, 1961), while Roy Ward Baker dragoons him into a kung-fu movie. In *The Legend of the Seven Golden Vampires* (coproduced by the Shaw Brothers), Peter Cushing visits China, where he discovers a village terrorized by seven vampires, corpuscle-thirsty doubles of Kurosawa's famous samurais.

In the United States, as blaxploitation was at its height, Dracula sneaked in under the name of *Blacula* (black on black, as it were) and has to fight (twice) against voodoo powers and the voluptuous Pam Grier (in *Blacula*, and *Scream, Blacula, Scream*, 1972). For the majority of filmmakers, Stoker's novel has acted as a reliable recipe book whose ingredients might have been forgotten except for the king of the remake, Jess Franco, director in 1970 of the faithful *Count Dracula*, as well as a jewel of erotic-experimental cinema, *Vampyros Lesbos*, starring the sublime Soledad Miranda.

During this time, in France, the name of the game was ribald humor: from *Dracula, Father and Son* (Édouard Molinaro, 1976), in which Christopher Lee, by now less red in tooth and claw, indulges in self-parody, to *Les Charlots contre Dracula* (1980), only Charles Matton, with *Spermula* (a retro rarity), manages to warm our hearts, introducing a horde of delightful but blood-crazed bimbos into France's rolling hills.

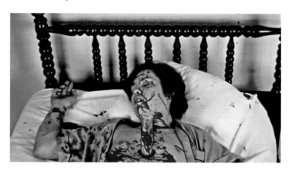

Martin, dir. George Romero (1977)

CRONENBERG AND ROMERO

In the mid-1970s, one in the United States and the other in Canada, they dust off the myth and rerealize its subversive power. First up, David Cronenberg, whose first movie (*Shivers*, 1974) features an aseptic building in the suburbs of Montreal, taken over by a viscous parasite with scant regard for the orifices of its inhabitants which plays havoc with their libidos. Two years later in *Rage*—a gray and depressing masterpiece that ends in a dumper truck—ex-porn star Marilyn Chambers sees budding under her armpit, not a canine, but a spike that awakens in her an overwhelming desire to penetrate.

Martin, made in 1976 by George Romero (stepfather of the modern zombie) is undoubtedly one of the most original variants on the genre. Stripped of its Gothic gloom and carnival tinsel, Dracula returns shorn of cape in the body of a teenager, Martin, who firmly believes he is a vampire. However, as Martin freely acknowledges at the beginning of the movie, "there's nothing magic about it"—just a morbid pathology transmitted by a family of lunatics seemingly intoxicated with the films of Browning. But the myth has teeth, and Martin, armed with hypodermic syringes and razor blades, strives manfully to conform to his Transylvanian archetype.

Let the Right One In,
dir. Tomas Alfredson
(2008)

Dracula,
dir. Francis Ford
Coppola (1992)

EROTIC FILM

For a fevv years novv, porn chic has been invading the media scene. From auto-biographical novels in the form of private diaries full of sex, to the intrusion of porn in the cinema knovvn to professionals of hardcore as "trad" (i.e., the mainstream), to "classic" movies no longer above splicing in a shot or tvvo—or a vvhole scene—of porn, the frontier is flimsier than ever. One might think that, up to this recent period, pornography (and more especially the type of image it implies) had been banished from traditional fiction cinema.

The Lover,
dir. Jean-Jacques Annaud
(1991)

A closer look, however, shows that cinema, even in its most traditional form, has always been interested by pornography, as the Great Satan for some, a den of iniquity for others (Travis Bickle in Scorsese's *Taxi Driver*, or George C. Scott, the radical Protestant searching for his daughter among the snuff-porn lowlife of Los Angeles in Paul Schrader's *Hardcore*). Indeed, for some it might be dubbed cinema's limit horizon.

Certain films of the past hit the headlines with their more or less frontal filming of the sex act: remember the scandal occasioned in 1975 by *Empire of the Senses*, in which Nagisa Oshima dared to show sexual organs and the act in progress on-screen. There was also Maruschka Detmers's prolonged full-screen fellatio in Marco Bellocchio's *Devil in the Flesh* (1986), the blonde Sharon Stone uncrossing her legs to reveal all in Paul Verhoeven's sulfurous *Basic Instinct*, or fleeting shots in *The Lover*, which clearly bore the marks of a "real" sex act performed betvveen Jane March and Tony Leung in the film by Jean-Jacques Annaud, as well as the unabashed orgy filmed by Xavier Beauvois in *Don't Forget You're Going to Die*.

But more recently, and particularly since Catherine Breillat's *Romance* starring Rocco Siffredi, porn is out in the open. The time—from the 1970s to the 1990s—when skin flicks had theater releases is over. Brigitte Lahaie, the uncontested star of French porn (*Hitchhikers in Heat, Les plaisirs fous, Mistress for a Couple, Possession, Les Prisonnières de l'île aux rats,* and so on) first crossed over into so-bad-it's-good (coming good with Jean Rollin, the pope of the French Z series in *Les Deux Orphelines Vampires* and *Les Raisins de la Mort*), then straight-to-video movies, then TV.

Today, porn is chic: Virginie Despentes' *Rape Me*, a remake of *A Gun for Jennifer*, mixes undeniably pornographic scenes (see the rape sequence at the beginning) and comedy. *The Pornographer*, by Bertrand Bonello, tackles the subject from a more intellectual standpoint: a onetime porn filmmaker returns to hardcore to settle his debts and can hardly recognize the industry.

In 2006, a collective film, *Destricted*, started by asking a simple question: what exactly is the dialogue between cinema and pornography? In the end, do they have anything to do with one another? **Since the rascally, silent rolls of the early cinematograph to the bourgeois exercises of Catherine Breillat, passing by the true-blue porn industry and the puritanical titillation of any number of Hollywood films, sex has of course constituted one of the nerve centers of the cinema and the fulcrum around which the hide/show dipole of its aesthetic revolves.** *Destricted*, however, encapsulates two ways of considering this relationship today: on the one side, there are those who strive to give the pornographic act aesthetic credence by demonstrating something we've known since time immemorial—namely, that sex and art are indeed compatible. This hardly breaks new ground: like a scene in a J. G. Ballard novel, there's Matthew Barney (*Hoist*) filming the tedious and experimental (and thus unchallenging) phantasms of a man copulating with an industrial machine, while video-artist Sam Taylor-Wood spends eight (long) minutes over a man masturbating out in Death Valley before inevitably spilling his seed on the arid ground.

On the other, in the best segment of the film Larry Clark's *Impaled* finds just the right distance from which to view the cinema-sex combination. Placing an ad on the Internet offering to turn young Americans into semiprofessional porn actors, the filmmaker of *Bully* and *Ken Park* auditions a kebab of adolescents, whom he confronts with real X-rated starlets. This piquant casting (a kind of *Porn Star Academy*) shows an America torn between its priggish culture and an invasion of pornographic imagery, which, thanks to porn flicks and hundreds of thousands of amateur films posted on the Web, has ended up by structuring and standardizing the sexual desires of everyone. Thus, one realizes how much the sex act, and these teenagers' fantasies (however different physically as well as psychologically they might be) no longer emanate from individual, personal imagination, but seek to reproduce sexualities they have "seen on TV." Like real porn actors, the majority of these hardcore applicants have shaved their genitals and chest. Like them, they dream of anal sex, wonder about facial ejaculation, try to force their sometimes less than compliant bodies to conform to their models and have preferences worthy of an under-the-counter backroom (the "winner" chooses to have sex with a *mature* woman, a category also known in porn movies as a *milf* or *older*). Eschewing moral judgments, the power of Clark's film is to demonstrate how pornography is but one ersatz imaginative realm among many others (advertising is another, for example) and how it has managed to impregnate (impale?) attitudes and modify behaviors. **Basically, *Impaled* tells us, pornography has "disappeared" because now it's everywhere. It is no longer a scandalous land one enters with lowered head and raised expectations, but the standardized backdrop that now conditions our relationship to sex, as it were naturally.**

Basic Instinct,
dir. Paul Verhoeven
(1992)

TEEN MOVIES

In the 1950s, they started to revolt, successors to James Dean in the films of Eli Kazan (*Rebel Without a Cause, East of Eden*), railing against a stiff-necked, uptight adult world, or in beach movies (the *Gidget* series in 1959), or light comedies dealing with problems of adolescence with humor (albeit with little success). Ten years later and they're on the road to the music of Simon and Garfunkel, this time following in the footsteps of the still inse-cure Dustin Hoffman at the end of *The Graduate* (1967) and both the hippy bikers of *Easy Rider*. By the end of the 1970s (George Lucas's *American Graffiti*, John Landis's *Animal House*), Hollywood had realized that these young men and women constituted an immense market that could be targeted.

If the teen movie has become a card-carrying genre, it is thanks primarily to the films of John Hughes who, in *Breakfast Club* (1984), *Weird Science* (1985), and *Ferris Bueller's Day Off* (1986), enshrined most of its codes: central-casting characters (the tough guy, the jock, the bimbo, the nerd, the charmer, and so on), adults considered as obstacles, an emblematic and typically American environment (campus corridors with their lockers, the sports halls, diners); and its recurrent roster of themes dealing with that crucial phase where the adolescent is confronted with the outer world or with sex (*American Pie*), and has to make choices that can have an enduring impact on his or her life.

The Breakfast Club, dir. John Hughes (1985)

*The 40-Year-Old
Virgin*, dir. Judd
Apatow (2005)

*The 40-Year-Old
Virgin*, dir. Judd
Apatow (2005)

Towelhead,
dir. Alan Ball
(2007)

In 2007, *Towelhead* (Alan Ball) draws a strange portrait of a thirteen-year-old teenage girl, Jesira, who is faced with her burgeoning sexuality and the destructive desires she arouses among the male of the species. The beginning of her will-she won't-she story is set in a remote Texas village, a concentrate of an America of contradictions, with the first Iraq War (Bush senior vs. Saddam) brewing in the background. While *American Beauty* (Sam Mendes, 1999) focused on midlife-crisis lust striking a forty-year-old suburbanite with the angelic(-looking) teenage girl as providing an escape hatch from the horrors of the American way of life, *Towelhead* peers into the angel's head, into her doubts and daydreams. If Jesira is a modern rewrite of Lolita (that other random ball hurled among the male ninepins), it is so only up to a point, since at root the film never quite decides what Jesira knows and what she doesn't, between what is real in her innocence, and what is fake.

IN FRANCE

Except for Sophie Marceau's budding loves in *The Party* and the bolt-on jokes in *The Under-Gifted* (Claude Zidi), with its gang of airheads struggling to get through their baccalaureate (1980) or their vacation (1981), the teen movie has spawned few followers. In 2009, comic strip author Riad Sattouff (*Manuel du puceau*) tried his hand at the genre à la française, delineating in *The French Kissers* the daily travails of teenagers pumped up with hormones, at that awkward age when to kiss a girl and to slide one's hands over her body is to attain nirvana.

IN TAIWAN

In the films of Hou Hsiao-Hsien (*The Boys from Fengkuei, Millennium Mambo*) and in Taiwanese cinema in general, youth is omnipresent and invariably represented as idle, lost, and culture-poor. "Young Taiwanese are plunged into this consumer society, all the while searching for an identity and a system of values that is cruelly lacking," Hou explains. "Their ability to make judgments is extremely low; it's enough to see how many narcotics and prescription drugs they take... the greatest influence on Taiwanese youth comes from the American model. **The idea that everything passes, that nothing remains, that everything can be exchanged or consumed. Everything is caught inside a process of circulation, of flow.** However, these principles go completely against any idea of memory. Taiwan is just an economic link in the Asian chain. There are more than a hundred television channels here, and they're all the same, and the same goes for stores, newspapers, etc. There's no diversity and, without diversity, no memory is possible."

JUDD APATOW'S RETARDED TEENAGERS

Initially a producer and scriptwriter, in 2005 Apatow made his first movie, *The 40-Year-Old Virgin*, with Steve Carrell, a star of TV's *Daily Show*, followed by *Knocked Up, Superbad, Stepbrothers* (as producer), and *Funny People* (2009).
The titles of Apatow's films already provide the framework for a cinema centered on young adults unable to say goodbye to their adolescence. Catapulted to the summit of the new American comedy, the Apatow brand is first and foremost a galaxy of faithful collaborators and actors (Seth Rogen, James Franco, Will Ferrell, and Jonah Hill), who combine in at once melancholic and gentle comedies that show how hard it is for a group of immature, inveterate geeks to grow up and earn their freedom.

Elephant,
dir. Gus Van Sant
(2003)

4

A QUESTION OF STYLE

"Form is like the thrust of a dagger."

Dario Argento

CLASSIC

In the cinema, and in Hollywood in particular, the classic form developed in the late 1920s, reaching its apogee in the 1940s—as much from a stylistic as from an economic point of view, with the star system, the airtight separation into genres, and an industrial organization based on specialized sectors. But does the classic *form* actually exist?

Though the reply seems affirmative, a thousand counterexamples and as many special cases come to mind immediately which, if they do not contradict, certainly mitigate the normative temptation inherent in every definition.

Classic cinema is in fact characterized by a series of codes and conventions which promote the following elements: the "invisibility" of both on-shoot direction and editing, which are concealed behind characters and situations in which the audience must believe; a specific genre typology (western, drama, film noir, musical, etc.) which feeds into a latent accord and into the profound desire of viewers for "familiar templates" (Umberto Eco); a narrative flow that builds into the illusion of a complete and coherent world; inspirational stars with whom the public can identify emotionally; a propensity for universal solutions and the respect for a code of good behavior (censorship). For all that, great filmmakers (Ford, Hawks, Vidor, Wilder) knew how to exploit gaps and holes in the system to express their individuality.

Unforgiven,
dir. Clint Eastwood
(1992)

If it fails to change, however, the "classic" can easily become the hackneyed: did this kill off classicism? No, it's still alive and kicking, as can be seen, for example, in the movies of Clint Eastwood and Michael Mann, two filmmakers who could be described as "postclassical." Consciously fueled by classic cinema, "postclassicism" (or "neoclassicism") characterizes a way of regenerating certain forms of the traditional movie by bolting on the awareness of the history (and films) of intervening decades: hence *Unforgiven* (1992) reactivates the Ford western, and *Thief* (1980) does much the same for the crime thriller.

Thief, dir. Michael Mann (1980)

MODERNISM

This is one of the favorite labels in the critical arsenal. And those who aren't worthy of the tag today had better watch out. A ragbag that takes in all comers, "modernism" first burst into life in 1953 in Roberto Rossellini's *Journey to Italy* and in France with Robert Bresson and then the emergence of the New Wave in the late 1950s (Godard, Truffaut, Rivette, Eustache, Resnais, and so on). A moment of radical rupture with traditional cinema, it denotes less a historical era than a relationship between film and world, characters and audience.

Modernity thus paves the way for movies in which events are drained of significance, where the characters' actions lose their motivation and become opaque. Great sweeping narratives make way for little stories or for traces of the "real," while the banal replaces the exemplary, and the arbitrary the reasonable. Direction, and hence the director (the auteur), appears for what it is and no longer worries about betraying its artifice. As a consequence of World War II and its atrocities, innocence is lost: as philosopher Gilles Deleuze wrote, "Modern means we no longer believe in the world.... It is the link between man and the world that has been broken."

Blow-Up,
dir. Michelangelo Antonioni
(1967)

Platform, dir. Jia Zhang-Ke (2000)

MANNERISM

The term "mannerism" comes from art history, and denotes a period ranging between 1515 and 1580—that is, between the art of the High Renaissance masters and the baroque. Initially designating a break with the Renaissance, and so with its ideals of harmony and of the imitation of nature, the concept today refers more to an extension of classical research that exacerbated certain stylistic features of the great masters (the Italian *maniera* actually means "style"): Leonardo da Vinci, Michelangelo, and Raphael. At the cinema, the concept loses much of its scope.

Carrie,
dir. Brian De Palma
(1976)

Let us say that in general it refers, not to any clearly definable movement, but to an aesthetic and theoretical turning point that appeared in the 1960s with the emergence of a generation of movie-savvy directors conscious of arriving too late—that is, after both the classics and the moderns.

The archetypal mannerist gesture consists in reappropriating a classic predecessor and exaggerating and/or skewing some of its stylistic formulae. Unabashed mannerism elaborates variations on entire movies, on a sequence, even on a single leitmotif that it treats as a base pattern. The most famous and perhaps most spectacular example is the research undertaken on the shower scene from *Psycho* in movie after movie by Brian De Palma. In France, Jean-Pierre Melville turned to film noir, while in Italy, Sergio Leone played havoc with the Hollywood western.

TOP: *Psycho*, dir. Alfred Hitchcock (1960)   BOTTOM: *Psycho*, dir. Gus Van Sant (1998)

EXPRESSIONISM

Appearing in Germany in the early 1920s, at the time of the establishment of the VVeimar Republic, the term "expressionist cinema" relates primarily to a group of specific films, such as *The Cabinet of Doctor Caligari* (Robert VViene, 1919), *Golem* (Paul VVegener, 1920), *Nosferatu* (F. VV. Murnau, 1922) and *VVaxvvorks* (Paul Leni, 1924). The thematic focus of expressionism lies in dehumanization and alienation (in this respect Fritz Lang's *Metropolis* and *M* are prime examples), but its most outstanding contributions vvere formal and visual.

How does one recognize an expressionist form? By a characteristic use of lighting that creates strong contrasts between light and dark, by a predisposition for geometric spaces and interrupted perspectives, by a taste for disordered, disturbing sets that reflect the tortured psyche of its characters.

Thus in her book, *The Haunted Screen*, Lotte Eisner wrote of expressionist sets: "Lovv ceilings and vaults oblige the characters to stoop, to force them into those jerky movements and broken postures that produce the extravagant curves and diagonals required by the expressionist precept."

Like "film noir," over time expressionism has begun to wander like one of its heroes; the style crops up in Nicholas Ray's *Bigger than Life* of 1955 (the shadovvs that evoke the schizophrenia of the father played by James Mason), in the dance school in Dario Argento's *Suspiria* (1977), and even, as pastiche, in VVoody Allen's *Shadovvs and Fog* (1992).

Suspiria,
dir. Dario Argento
(1977)

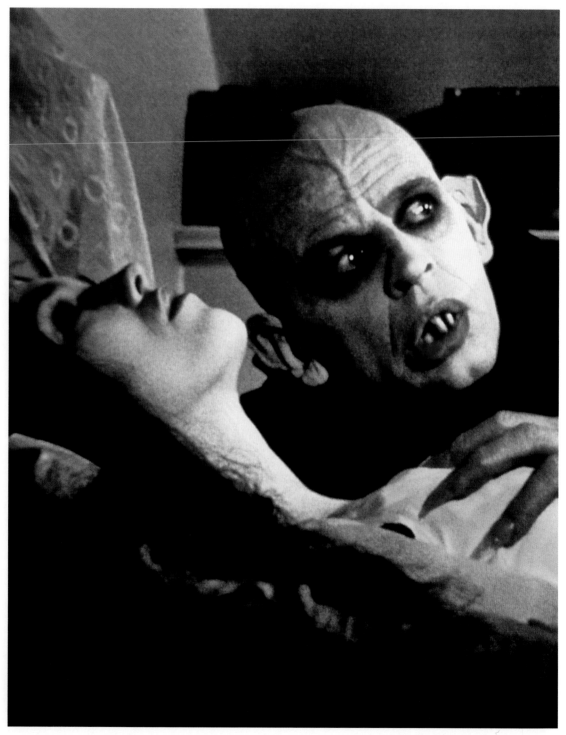

Nosferatu, the Vampyre, dir. Werner Herzog (1979)

POSTMODERNISM

In a footnote to *The Name of the Rose,* Umberto Eco offers the following definition of the postmodern: "The postmodern reply to the modern consists of recognizing that the past, since it cannot really be destroyed, because its destruction leads to silence, must be revisited: but with irony, not innocently." Hence postmodern cinema starts from the idea that everything has already been said, done, dusted, and filmed.

Video for Michael Jackson's "Billie Jean," dir. Steve Barron (1983)

Postmodern cinema made its entrance in the 1990s on the shirt tails of mannerism, at the time when the market for video was expanding. In spite of important differences, the movies of the Coen brothers and Tim Burton, *Austin Powers* and Oliver Stone's *Natural Born Killers*, Jean-Jacques Beineix's *Diva* and *The Big Blue*, *The Raiders of the Lost Ark* and *Death Proof*, *Cotton Club* and *Scream* all go in for the same ploy of alluding to or reprocessing preexistent images, giving the wink to cinema goers "in the know."

For these directors, the history of the cinema presents a storehouse of forms, leitmotifs, poses, situations, which they plunder to make not just quotations in quotations, but also bizarre juxtapositions. A recent example: *Avatar.* In fact, James Cameron's movie recycles a gigantic quantity of images that have been lying dormant in our brains for decades: the fall of the World Trade Center replayed in that of the "Nav'is'" tree of life; the virtual environment of "Second Life" (a sort of pre-*Avatar* on the Net); the opposition between the real world and the fantasy world borrowed from *The Wizard of Oz*; and even the floor lights from Michael Jackson's video for *Billie Jean* morphed into the neon branches of Pandora that cast a blue light as the inhabitants walk.

TOP: *Natural Born Killers*, dir. Oliver Stone (1994)   BOTTOM: *Death Proof*, dir. Quentin Tarantino (2007)

BAROQUE

A rather elastic concept once it goes beyond the field of art history and literary criticism for which it was forged, the baroque refers to a particular range of motifs.

Inferno,
dir. Dario Argento
(1980)

A predilection for disequilibrium and antithesis (bright/dark—chiaroscuro, depth/surface, reality/illusion), for hybridizing genres (noble forms mix with the vernacular), distortions that can culminate in grotesque, complex movements and poses, games with the nature of appearance (mirrors, theater and opera sets and costumes, unconventional perspective), highly charged psychological states and formal proliferation, labyrinthine narratives and bizarre characters, and, most especially, a pervasive sense of movement that brings to the surface the untold forces that secretly drive our human action. Hence the importance of memory, childhood, and the spectacle of death—baroque themes *par excellence*. If the classic reveled in the body and its unity, the baroque burrows into the world itself and throws it off kilter. It was *Lola Montès* (Max Ophuls, 1956) that heralded the arrival of the baroque in the vocabulary of film criticism. The protean aesthetics of the baroque reappear in the films of Raúl Ruiz (*Three Crowns of the Sailor*), of Dario Argento (*Inferno*), in the effects of T1000's digital metamorphosis (*Terminator 2*), as well as in the movies Robert Aldrich made with Joan Crawford and Bette Davis (*Hush, Hush, Sweet Charlotte* and *What Ever Happened to Baby Jane?*).

Terminator 2, dir. James Cameron (1991)

POETIC REALISM

Port of Shadows,
dir. Marcel Carné
(1938)

This denomination characterizes a group of French films made in the 1930s and 1940s featuring ordinary people (workers, deserters, dockers, prostitutes, tramps, "simple folk") ensnared in some dark destiny. Jean Vigo (*L'Atalante*), Jean Renoir (*La Bête humaine*), Marcel Carné (*Port of Shadows*, *Daybreak*), Julien Duvivier (*They Were Five*), and Jean Grémillon (*Stormy Waters*) remain the finest incarnations of a movement contemporary with the Socialist government of the Popular Front. Aesthetically, it borrows its "realistic" dimension from naturalism and its characteristic use of lighting from German expressionism. The flop of the postwar *Gates of the Night* (Carné, 1946) signaled its demise.

SOCIAL REALISM

Rosetta,
dir. Jean-Pierre
and Luc Dardenne
(1998)

In France, poetic realism grew into social realism from the mid-1950s, with the films of Paul Carpita (*Le Rendez-vous des quais*) and especially of André Cayatte, a specialist in crossing courtroom drama with social tub-thumping in *Justice Is Done*, *We Are All Murderers*, *Risky Business*. The 1970s then saw the meeting between social realism and the New Wave, in the films of Maurice Pialat and Claude Miller, in particular. The social-realist vein has never quite dried up, and in the 1990s it reemerged in the movies of the Dardenne brothers (*Rosetta*, *The Son*), and most notably in those of Ken Loach, who, as worthy heir to Tony Richardson (*The Loneliness of the Long Distance Runner*), Lindsay Anderson (*If*), and Karel Reisz (*Saturday Night, Sunday Morning*), develops a rough-and-ready style that lays the stress on the daily, often grinding, lives of the British working class.

NEOREALISM

Rooted in the historical and social fabric of postwar Italy, neorealism was born in a ruined country tired of Mussolini period cinema (known as "white telephone" movies), with its alternation of propaganda films and monumental historical frescoes. Two films by Roberto Rossellini, *Rome, Open City* (1945) and *Paisan* (1946) launched a movement that was to prove a considerable influence on world cinema. If this realism became "neo," it is because such films no longer simply dramatize a social context or hammer home the theme of the reconstruction of Italy (*The Bicycle Thieves*, Vittorio De Sica, 1944), but revolutionize the craft of moviemaking.

Filmmakers, technicians, and actors left their studios and planted the camera outside, on location. Making a clean break with the constraints of the studio and the star system, they placed importance on limited budgets, a blend of professional and nonprofessional actors, a pared-down direction, and sets whose chief aim was above all to be true to the situation and to the character, a refusal of all and any literary approach, and the glorification of "little people" of modest means (Luchino Visconti's *The Earth will Tremble*, [1948] describes the tough life of fishermen in a Sicilian port, while *Bitter Rice* by Giuseppe De Santis records the miserable living conditions of seasonal workers on the rice plantations of the Po). The real was no longer the plausible, manufactured fiction of traditional cinema; underlying the film as in a documentary, it wandered in and out of shot. With *Stromboli*, and even more so with *Journey to Italy*, Rossellini, one of the preeminent figures in neorealism, provides gripping portraits of modern characters unable to interact with the world that surrounds them. Prefiguring the cinema of Antonioni (the Ingrid Bergman/George Sanders couple falls apart during a trip to Naples), the film is built around moments of silence, non-events, and striking visions (the discovery of the volcanic island).

Poster for *Rome, Open City*, dir. Roberto Rossellini (1945)

Stromboli, dir. Roberto Rossellini (1950)

FILM NOIR

From *Double Indemnity* (Billy Wilder, 1944) to *Dark City* (Alex Proyas, 1998), stopping over in *L.A. Confidential* (Curtis Hanson, 1997) and *The Night of the Hunter* (Charles Laughton, 1955), "film noir"—a phrase first coined by Nino Frank in 1946—has become a carpetbag of concepts that can be dragged out to describe any number of films that really belong to very different genres. Is it even actually a genre? What does the idea of film noir actually cover?

Memories of Murder, dir. Bong Joon-Ho (2003)

Director and scriptwriter Paul Schrader (*Hardcore, Blue Collar,* screenplay for *Taxi Driver*) answered the question thus: "In 1946, French critics, seeing the American films they had missed during the war, noticed the new mood of cynicism, pessimism and darkness which had crept into the American cinema....Film noir is not a genre.... It is not defined, as are the western and gangster genres, by conventions of setting and conflict, but rather by the more subtle qualities of tone and mood. It is a film '*noir,*' as opposed to the possible variants of film gray or film off-white.... Film noir is also a specific period of film history.... **In general, film noir refers to those Hollywood films of the 1940s and early 1950s which portrayed the world of dark, slick city streets, crime and corruption.**" Spawned by postwar realism, film noir combines the aesthetics of German expressionism with the "hard-boiled" writing style of the 1930s (Hammett, Chandler, Hemingway, Cain), who "created a 'tough' cynical way of acting and thinking which separated one from the world of everyday emotions—romanticism with a protective shell."

Dark City,
dir. Alex Proyas
(1998)

Film noir experienced an initial resurgence at the beginning of the 1970s, becoming "neo" thanks to the efforts of movie-buff directors who took up the legacy. Still, in the films of Robert Altman (*The Long Goodbye*, 1973), Arthur Penn (*Night Moves*, 1975), as well as in the later offerings of Oliver Stone (*U-Turn*, 1997), or David Lynch (*Mulholland Drive*, 2002), the dark, urban universe of the original noir has been replaced by a flat, indecipherable world, dissolved by a generalized loss of meaning. Thus, the detective is no longer the one who solves the puzzle, but an unwilling pawn in some great plan he couldn't even dream of. In 1982, Ridley Scott's *Blade Runner* launches what has been dubbed "techno-noir." *Dark City*, *Sin City* (Frank Miller, 2005) and the *Matrix* trilogy transpose into a futuristic, technophobic world the root-and-branch pessimism of the noir, deploying it to amplify the ambient fear of dehumanization.

Iron Man 2,
dir. Jon Favreau
(2010)

THEY DID IT FIRST

"The first time I saw a woman naked, I thought it was a mistake."

Woody Allen

THE FIRST SPECIAL EFFECTS
(1902)

From the huge success of *Journey to the Moon* shown at the Foire du Trône in Paris in 1902, to the toy store in Montparnasse Station where he ended up ruined (but not forgotten), Georges Méliès's career resembles a shooting star whose trail lingered long in the cinematographical heavens. "M. Méliès and myself, we follow more or less the same trade," wrote the poet Apollinaire. "We turn base matter into something marvelous." The "matter" is the novel, the imagination, the fairyland, the science fiction transformed by the magician of Montreuil into the miracle that is the cinema he invented. Saw-the-lady-in-two performances honed at the Robert-Houdin theater, quick-change numbers and disappearing tricks inherited from the conjurer's art ended up as trips to the moon and conquests of the pole: it was Méliès who invented the crutch without which the cinema could never really have walked.

Un homme de têtes, dir. Georges Méliès (1898)

The Lumière brothers, then, took the path of realism; Méliès, the path of the imagination and the fantastic. Driven by his desire for fiction, this one-man band concocted in his studio at Montreuil (the first in the whole history of cinema), the first fantastic films using rudimentary trick filming and featuring smoking monsters, rubber heads inflated until they blew up, and painted cardboard sets worthy of Jules Verne. He was also the creator of the first feature film (his version

of *Cinderella* lasted 18 minutes), the first scripts (each of his films was first written down in the form of a synopsis), and even the first "docufictions" (*The Eruption of Mt. Pelee*, 1902, a reconstruction of the catastrophe).

Reality is already there, why try to reproduce it? Of course, the opposition between the Lumière way and the Méliès way—in other words between realism and fiction, a factual vein versus phantasmagoria—has never been that clear-cut. What was then called, incorrectly, "reality" was often subjected to fiction's sleight of hand (as in *Tables turned on the Gardener*)—and vice versa: didn't Méliès make the first political film, with the eminently serious and true-to-life *Affaire Dreyfus* in 1899?

And then don't invention, poetry, and fiction also (especially, even) offer the best road to the truth of the world? Still why would anyone—save for a wide-eyed child, a film buff, a fastidious conservative, or a meddlesome academic—want to watch a reel by Méliès today? And what do the 520 films he made between 1886 and 1913 tell us about cinema today? Georges Méliès symbolizes the unshakable faith in the power of film, an inextinguishable belief in the capacity of this bright and shiny machine to create magic and dreams. Méliès and his descendants know that the truth of the world and its mystery lie less in simply recording than in reinventing them: less in "naivety" than in a still germane "innocence."

THE FIRST SLOWMO
(1904)

What would the final sequence of Antonioni's *Zabriskie Point* (a ten-minute explosion to a Pink Floyd soundtrack), the last take of *Two-Lane Blacktop* by Monte Hellman, the famous shootouts in Sam Peckinpah's movies, the blood-drenched ballets of John Woo's thrillers (*The Killer*, *Hard Boiled*, *Bullet in the Head*), Hark Tsui's masterpiece (*The Blade*, 1995), and the entire cinematic oeuvre of Brian De Palma be without their extraordinary use of slow motion?

It may often be forgotten, but slow motion in the movies, like the majority of the technical innovations of the nineteenth and the twentieth centuries, was invented by scientists for the armed forces (by the Austrian, August Musger in 1904) and hence for purely practical reasons. By deconstructing the movement of a body, it was hoped to increase understanding of ballistics and improve military productivity and strategy. Starting with the "photographic gun" of Jules Marey, through *The Fall of the House of Usher* (1928)—in which Jean Epstein makes the first poetic use of the technique—and beyond, filmmakers have made hay with slow motion.

Deployed only sporadically until the end of the 1960s (the grand finale of *Bonnie and Clyde*, 1967), slow motion became one of the aesthetic hallmarks of the 1970s (as a tool for intensifying the world and its violence and to convey a sense of substance to viewers), making a notable comeback in the 1990s in films by Ferrara (*The King of New York*, *New Rose Hotel*), Wong Kar-Wai (*As Tears Go By*, *In the Mood for Love*), David Lynch (*Twin Peaks*), and Jim Jarmusch (*Ghost Dog*).

In 1999, in *The Matrix*, a more advanced alternative to the motion made its appearance: *bullet time*, a super slow-motion technique employing a moving camera that reduces motion to a snail's pace, inaugurated in the sequence on a roof where Neo (Keanu Reeves) ducks and dives out of the way of the bullets fired by a Matrix agent.

The Assassination of the Duke de Guise, dir. André Calmettes and Charles Le Bargy (1908)

THE FIRST "ART FILM"
(1908)

In 1908, while French caricaturist Émile Cohl was inventing the comic drawing and, with it, its first star, Fantôche, the brothers Laffite decided to try to elevate the cinematograph to the rank of an art with a capital "A." In an effort to attract a more cultivated and bourgeois audience—loath to frequent screenings at fairground stalls where the lower orders guffawed at unedifying sketches—the two filmmakers produced *The Assassination of the Duke de Guise*. Set in the historic château at Blois, with a script by French Academician Henri Lavedan and music by Camille Saint-Saëns (it was the first foray into movie scores by the composer of the *Carnival of the Animals*), the main actors were almost all members of the Comédie Française.

Produced by the two cofounders of the Film d'Art company in France, André Calmettes and Charles Le Bargy, *The Assassination of the Duke de Guise* positively entranced high society. For the first time, a film even received a review notice (written by a theater critic!) in the columns of the prestigious daily, *Le Temps*. The hour of the cultural legitimization of film had sounded: this well-meaning and turgid exercise—which thinks a grand subject means great art, and blends theater and cinematographic fiction—placed the first brick in an (eminently French) wall that the cinema has never really succeeded in demolishing. On the one side are the "movies" as leisure and mere entertainment; on the other, the "cinema" as a noble art and/or auteur practice. Still today, in certain film schools, in universities, even in cultural journals, this wall,

Point Break, dir. Kathryn Bigelow (1991)

even if (fortunately) it has tended to become more porous, is still in place. This is, though, a gigantic misunderstanding that the story of cinema belies almost every day; for example, the movies often rather haughtily dubbed "blockbusters," some of which, like *The Dark Knight*, *Miami Vice*, and *The Host*, contain more ideas, and even more ideas about film, than vast swathes of so-called "auteur" creations.

THE FIRST CUSTARD PIE
(1913)

The beginning of pastry-making in Hollywood in 1913 added a further weapon to the burlesque armory of what was already a successful genre—slapstick. A blend of light comedy, physical gags (falling over, brawls, epic pursuits), and blind, frantic absurdity, slapstick had its mentor, Mack Sennett, its studio, Keystone, and its actors (Fatty Arbuckle, Harold Lloyd, W. C. Fields, Laurel and Hardy, Chaplin, Keaton).

One day, on shoot, actress Mabel Normand comes to blows with Ben Turpin, the famous squinting actor, and her partner in crime. In fury, she storms off the set and comes across a gigantic cream pie on a studio table. Picking it up, she returns to the fray, her mood scarcely improved, and hurls the concoction at Turpin, who, somewhat taken aback, bursts into laughter. Mack Sennett immediately orders the camera to roll, thus recording the first patisserie-based gag in the history of slapstick. Quickly, the custard pie became a comic staple, one of its icons (in 1927, in *Battle of the Century*, Laurel and Hardy enjoy a pastry battle of titanic grandeur), as well as a metaphor for what is a profoundly challenging genre. For it was from such burlesque that, as early as the 1920s, the first great satirists of modern social life, such as Charlie Chaplin (*The Gold Rush*) and Buster Keaton (*The General*), emerged.

Finally, the custard pie presents an apt simile for a world submerged by a chaotic free-for-all, in which throwing one upsets hierarchies and erases social and physical distinctions alike. For once a face is dripping with custard, how does one know who's behind it? Over the years, the motif has cropped up everywhere, from Blake Edwards's *The Party* (its chaos of soap bubbles is a nod to the pies of Keystone) to *Dawn of the Dead* by George A. Romero (in which pies are chucked at the living dead), creating a bizarre if powerful bridge between two subversive movie genres: slapstick and horror.

THE FIRST TRACKING SHOT
(1914)

Hollywood was officially born thanks to Cecil B. De Mille, who first cranked his camera on the shoot of *The Squaw Man*, a melodramatic western and the first feature film made in what was to become the American movie mecca. In Italy, meanwhile, *Cabiria*, a first epic extravaganza by Giovanni Pastrone, was up in lights. Thanks to a positively colossal budget, Pastrone, a year before D. W. Griffith (*Birth of a Nation* and *Intolerance*), had convinced the producers to build imposing, real sets instead of the usual painted backcloths.

A minor revolution: filming can now set up different actions in several takes. But more importantly, it was on this set that a camera was installed on a carriage for the first time. The result: it became mobile, moving within the set and along the backdrop, thus breaking with the fixed position of the primitive cinema, a hangover from the syntax of the theater. The tracking shot, and the dolly, were born.

THE FIRST STAR OF MAKE-UP
(1919)

Born in 1883 to deaf and dumb parents, Tod Browning's favorite thespian, with whom he made ten films (including *Freaks*, *The Unknown*, and *West of Zanzibar*), Lon Chaney was the first actor in the history of pre-talkie cinema to raise the use of makeup to the rank of an art. His ability to change totally from one film to the next, thanks to techniques of his own invention that he kept a closely guarded secret, and to subject his body to incredible deformations, enabled him to play monsters (*The Phantom of the Opera* by Rupert Julian, *The Hunchback of Notre-Dame*, by Wallace Worsley), as well as dozens of mutilated or disfigured characters (the one-armed knife thrower in *The Unknown*, a legless cripple in *The Penalty*, a paralytic in *The Miracle Man*, and even a criminal old woman in *The Unholy Three*). In a sad irony, Chaney died of throat cancer just as talkies hit the screen. In 1957, James Cagney interpreted Lon Chaney as *The Man of a Thousand Faces*, a biopic homage made by Joseph Pevney.

London After Midnight, dir. Tod Browning (1927)

Nanny McPhee,
dir. Kirk Jones
(2005)

THE FIRST ZOOM
(1920s)

It is in fact hard to date the first use of zoom in the cinema. A lens with a variable focal distance that makes it possible to zero in on a detail (zoom in) or come away from it (zoom out) without actually moving the camera is supposed to have been used for the first time at the end of the 1920s—in 1927, to be precise, by Clarence Badger in *It*, a comedy with Clara Bow produced by Paramount. (The word "zoom" is borrowed from the vocabulary of aviation and refers to a rapid dive or climb.) Most of the time, it conveys the gaze of a person who fixes their attention or desire on something out of shot. Abundantly used by TV cameramen, it was during the 1960s that the use of the zoom spread and diversified. Roberto Rossellini was the first to give a technique that was considered indecorous a seal of approval in *Escape by Night* (1960). Then, in 1965, Luchino Visconti adopted the zoom in *Sandra*, and its name was made. Among the foremost masters of the technique were John Frankenheimer, Stuart Rosenberg, and Robert Altman. But it is perhaps in Italy, in the films of Mario Bava (*Black Sunday; Kill, Baby, Kill; Lisa and the Devil*), as well as in the lion's share of transalpine genre film in the 1960s and 1970s, that the zoom showed its true power. With his rapid zooms that violently isolate a face or an object, Bava (whom Scorsese acknowledges as "one of the most influential film-makers of modern cinema") invented a technique that allowed different zones to be experienced in one and the same take: from reality to hallucination, from function to fetish (divorced from their environment, objects in his films often suddenly acquire unsuspected vitality), from looking to touching.

Basically, a zoom sucks viewers into the screen, draws them into the action. With 3D, the illusion produced is the opposite, since it is the film that moves forward to engulf the audience.

Hatchet for the Honeymoon, dir. Mario Bava (1969)

Outer Space,
dir. Peter
Tscherkassky
(1999)

THE FIRST EXPERIMENTAL FILM?
(1924)

"Experiment" might have been the war cry of Abel Gance, one of the past masters of the French avant-garde. At the turn of the 1920s, a handful of directors (Abel Gance, Louis Delluc, Marcel Lherbier, René Clair, Germaine Dulac, and Jean Epstein, and the Dadaist ballets filmed by Clair for *Entr'acte* in 1924 that followed in their wake) decided to leave the (already) well-trodden paths of the cinema and strike out for uncharted visual waters, exploiting the new and infinite possibilities of the medium. This is the age of "pure cinema" which asked: if reality already exists, why reproduce it? In *J'accuse* (1919), Gance makes almost systematic use of "double exposure"; *La Roue,* one of his most significant films, has some extraordinary, rapid cutting and a train derailment that provides a pretext for whirling effects; and finally *Napoleon* (1927) is a veritable festival of technical and visual innovations (triple split-screen for battle sequences, superimposition, etc.). Meanwhile, Louis Delluc, the founder, in 1920, of France's first film clubs and creator of the term "cineaste," took his cue from Canudo's theories and advocated cinema as an autonomous, synthetic art incorporating all the others (music, dance, painting, architecture, etc.).

Using a range of aims and means, first avant-garde, then experimental, the creators agree on one point: that they should go beyond the images of traditional cinema and free themselves from its economic as well as aesthetic laws, try out new forms, new ways of filming, and so offer cinemagoers new sensations.

The field of avant-garde film also developed into a political laboratory, which opposed an industrial cinema prone to rehashing the same stale formulae. Among the vast number of avant-garde experiments there was the metric cinema of Peter Kubelka in the 1950s, the animated experimental films of the Canadian Norman McLaren (*Pas de deux, Neighbours*), explorations of the concept of film duration by Andy Warhol (*Four Stars,* 1967, lasts twenty-five hours), work on the substance of film stock by New Zealander Len Lye (*Rainbow Dance,* 1936), and the abstract and figurative films of the prolific Stan Brakhage (*Dog Star Man,* 1964), Jonas Mekas (founder of the Anthology Film Archives of New York), and Gérard Courant and his Cinématons.

However, it would be wrong to draw a hard and fast distinction between avant-garde film and so-called "traditional" cinema, since inventions on one side soon permeated through to the other. From Dreyer to Buñuel, from the deliriously colorful films of Mario Bava to Michael Mann's *Collateral,* from George Lucas's *THX 1138* to *The Lady from Shanghai* by Welles (with its mirror sequence), examples of cross-fertilization and cross-contamination are legion.

THE FIRST LIVE ACTING/ ANIMATION FILM
(1925)

If one traces back the family tree from Carlo Rambaldi (responsible for the creature in *Alien*) or Ray Harryhausen (of *Jason and the Argonauts* fame), who does one discover? The one his friends and collaborators called "Obie." For specialists in special effects and camera trickery of all stripes, Willis O'Brien (1886–1962) is an unimpeachable reference. It should be said that, before him, only Méliès, in France, showed any great interest in the fantasy potential of cinema techniques. O'Brien first tried his hand at animation in 1914. A year later, he made a five-minute short entitled *The Dinosaur and the Missing Link*, centering on the life of cave men and whose stars were puppets that O'Brien brilliantly brought to life. A genuine technical tour de force, the film won over no less a personage than Thomas Edison, who promptly handed O'Brien a contract for ten short films, including *Morpheus Mike* (1915) and *Prehistoric Poultry* (1917), which exploited a range of stop-motion techniques. Later popularized by Ray Harryhausen, the latter consists in filming some figurines for just a few frames, before stopping the camera and changing their position, and so on. Shown at normal speed, the interruptions disappear to form an illusion of continuity and give the impression that the figurines move on their own accord through the set.

Thomas Edison then decided to get O'Brien to collaborate on a feature film by Harry O. Hoyt, *The Lost World*, a film that mixed live acting and animated model dinosaurs. Simply miniaturizing the human figures recreated an illusion of a world populated by gigantic creatures. *The Lost World* is a landmark in the history of special effects because the movie's success persuaded the RKO company to entrust Willis O'Brien with a remit to create a giant gorilla for a film that Ernest B. Schoedsack and Merian Cooper were about to shoot: *King Kong*. For a long time, the majority of viewers (and even some technicians) were convinced that the beast was in fact an actor in a gorilla costume. Moreover, nobody really understood how O'Brien managed to make it seem that the characters were moving around the beast. Schoedsack, in an article that came out shortly before the film, teased viewers by telling them that he cannot reveal the secret of how the scenes were shot and recorded as this is the domain of those jealous guardians of the tricks of the trade, his technicians. The animals were made under the direction of chief technician Willis O'Brien, whom the director hails as a highly skilled artist and recognized natural history specialist.

Nonetheless, O'Brien's later career belied his talents: a large number of his projects fell through, including *Gwangi*, a film recounting the strange meeting between cowboys and some prehistoric creatures, eventually made by Roy Harryhausen in 1969 under the title, *The Valley of Gwangi*. For most of the time, Obie worked on ideas for shorts he presented to studios in the hope they would be expanded into feature films, but very few ever saw the light of day. In 1949, *The Mighty Joe Young*, a King Kong spin-off for which he is credited as "technical creator," earned him an Oscar for special effects. At the end of his life, O'Brien worked on films demanding less exalted technical expertise, such as Stanley Kramer's *It's a Mad, Mad, Mad, Mad World* in 1960. Willis O'Brien died in 1962, but his descendants are numerous (to begin with the most talented of his disciples, Ray Harryhausen). There can be no doubt that *E.T.* and *Jurassic Park* owe him a great deal.

Poster for *Singing in the Rain*, dir. Stanley Donen and Gene Kelly (1952)

THE FIRST TALKIE
(1927)

October 1927. Actor Al Jolson is crooning away in *The Jazz Singer*. A song and two bits of dialogue make him a star and propel the cinema into the era of "talking motion pictures." All the majors pour into the breach and age of the talkie begins. The first through-and-through talkie will be made in 1929 (*Lights of New York* by Bryan Foy). The cinema also had to keep pace with the change, in the sense that sound synchronization meant film speed had to increase from sixteen to twenty-four frames per second. However, as Stanley Donen showed in *Singin' in the Rain* (1952), the shift to talking pictures was no cakewalk—not for the technicians, nor the actors (diction and singing lessons became obligatory), nor even for the camera, which, duly endowed with a cumbersome sound-recording device, now found itself nailed to the floor; hence the feeling that creative filming suddenly went into reverse.

THE FIRST COLOR FILM
(1935)

In 1935, after several not particularly satisfactory attempts at making color movie film (the bipack process), Rouben Mamoulian and Lowell Sherman brought out *Becky Sharp*, the first live-action film turned in three-color Technicolor ("integral tripack"). Though, as Billy Wilder made abundantly clear by shooting a movie as late as *Some Like it Hot* (1959) in black and white ("Too ice-cream," he said of color), the appearance of the Technicolor camera did not please everyone. Nonetheless, it catalyzed a significant artistic shift that pushed Hollywood away from realism and in the direction of larger-than-life worlds awash with blazing colors. The successes of *A Star Is Born* (William Wellman, 1937) and *The Wizard of Oz* (Victor Fleming, 1939) enshrined the process. The last film to made with a Technicolor camera was in 1955 (*Foxfire* with Jane Russell), but the process (which consisted in a reprocessing of the film shot in "Technicolor" in the lab) was only abandoned in the 1960s. In 1977, Dario Argento's *Suspiria* was the last Technicolor movie in the history of cinema.

The Wizard of Oz,
dir. Victor Fleming
(1939)

THE FIRST POV FILM
(1945)

With *Rec* (Plaza, Balaguero, 1997) and *The Banned Woman* (Philippe Harel, 1997), from the last films of Alain Cavalier (*Irene, Le Filmeur*) to the first part of *Dark Passage* (Delmer Daves, 1947), the subjective, point-of-view camera knows no borders—neither economic nor geographical. Already in 1900, the Englishman George Albert Smith, a member of the famous "Brighton school" of documentary, broke with the sacrosanct rule of the objective viewpoint (the neutral eye of the camera that simply records what is placed in front of it) and, in *Grandma's Reading Glass*, filmed the first subjective take in the history of the cinema: a close-up of exactly what a young boy sees through his grandmother's magnifying glass (a bird, a newspaper). Smith did not simply invent one of the fundamental tools of cinematographic grammar (the subjective shot), he set the agenda for all those who tried thereafter to put the audience in the skin—and thus in the eye—of a character. But does seeing what a movie character sees allow us to identify with him or her more? Are we more frightened when we see what he or she is frightened of? Do we actually feel we're falling if the camera dives? Can we see with a dead man's eyes (*Sunset Boulevard*, Billy Wilder, 1950)? If *Lady in the Lake* (Robert Montgomery, 1947) remains in the annals, it is less thanks to its qualities as a movie than because of what was a groundbreaking experience at the time: the way the audience lives the story in the place of its main character, the detective Philip Marlowe, through whose eyes we look during the entire film. Initially intriguing (I see only what the character sees), the process soon becomes repetitive and, more importantly, counter-productive, since in the cinema we identify less with individuals or bodies than with *effects*. Thus, the death of E.T. in the film of the same name by Spielberg, or that of the HAL 9000 computer in Kubrick's *2001* can move people, even though one is a rubberized extraterrestrial and the other a machine reduced to a red light-bulb. Another vein, that of the "trip" movie, from the druggy experiences of Roger Corman's *The Trip* (1967) to the post-mortem existence of *Enter the Void* (Gaspar Noé, 2010), tries to extrapolate subjective cinema and put the audience inside a character's brain.

Lady in the Lake, dir. Robert Montgomery (1947)

THE FIRST FILM TO BEGIN ITS PLOT WITH THE CREDITS
(1950s)

Some ungracious sorts say one can judge how good a James Bond film's going to be from the credits alone. Credits were (almost) born at the same time as the cinema, but when did they start to be designed to hook the viewer?

Saul Bass did not invent credits, nor even the fonts supposed to inform audiences of the type of film they were about to see—like the bold typography of the classic western. Working with the greatest (from Otto Preminger to Scorsese for *Goodfellas*), this graphic designer transformed the credit sequence into a veritable short film within the main feature, mustering a host of thematic clues to the fiction to come. Playing with form and line, abstract visual puzzles, amusing drawings, Bass's often playful credits function like a ringmaster calling, "Roll up! Roll up!" Take *Advise & Consent* by Preminger (1962), where the White House is transformed into a cauldron whose lid (the dome) is raised to reveal, bubbling within, a satire on the soft underbelly of American political life.

But Bass was most famous for his work with Alfred Hitchcock. Some examples of remarkable opening credits: those in black and white for *Psycho*, with the title and the name of filmmaker sliced in two as if they had no connection and stood for the schizophrenia of the main character, Norman Bates, whom the audience has not yet even seen. Then there's the spiral that structures the credits for *Vertigo*, a foretaste of the phobia and the emotional giddiness that characterizes James Stewart. And last but not least, in Stanley Kubrick's *The Shining*, the credits roll, but in reverse, in anticipation of the key dynamic of the movie: that of an eternal return towards past events—one private (the massacre of a family) and the other historical (a hotel built over an old Native American cemetery) that were both meant to have remained buried forever.

THE FIRST MOVIE IN CINEMASCOPE (1953)

In the course of the 1950s, cinema had to square up to a formidable new competitor: television, for which the audience rose in the decade 1950–60 from three to sixty million. By every means necessary, viewers had to be weaned off the small screen. In 1953, Fox unearthed from the bottom drawer an old process called Hypergonar, invented by the Frenchman Henri Chrétien in 1927. Christened "Cinemascope," the process consists in compressing the image at shoot with an anamorphic lens and rectifying it for wide-screen viewing at projection. The first movie made in Cinemascope was *How to Marry a Millionaire* by Jean Negulesco and starring Marilyn Monroe— and not Henry Koster's ancient epic *The Robe*, which was shot later but released first. Fritz Lang's quip in Godard's *Contempt* hit home: "It wasn't meant for human beings, just for funerals—and snakes."

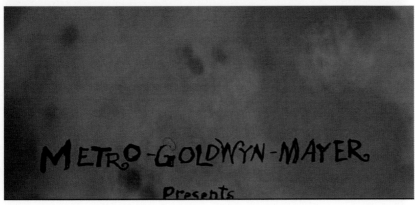

The Fearless Vampire Killers, dir. Roman Polanski (1967)

*Empire
of the Senses*,
dir. Nagisa Oshima
(1976)

PORN AND POLITICS IN JAPAN
(1960s)

In Japan, from the early 1960s, a number of angry mavericks began stuffing their low-budget but painstakingly made films with daring sequences, using what was then called in Japan "romantic pornography," a form embraced particularly by one production company, Nikkatsu, for ostensibly political ends. Japanese "Roman Porno" uses the genre like a Trojan horse, infiltrating its vaguely erotic plots with a political subtext that governs the pleasures of the flesh on screen. Somber, depressing, with a predilection for S8M, *Newlywed Hell*, *Erosu wa amaki kaori*, and *Excitement Class* revolve entirely around the exploitation of woman and the workers in a Japanese variant of porn that interlards sex and violence, Marx and lascivious virgins, and offers a pessimistic vision of the status of woman. "Put me in your cellar. I want to become a bottle!" beseeches the heroine of the extraordinary *Woman with Pierced Nipples* by Shogoro Nishimura. For Koji Wakamastu, the pioneer of political porn (*Sex Jack*, *Violated Angels*), youth boils with rebellious drives just waiting to explode. In *Ecstasy of the Angels* (1972), the future director of *United Red Army* peppers the internecine war racking an extreme left-wing organization with rather raw sex sequences during which discussions about the revolution of the proletariat, dissident strategy, and political atrocities continue. In *Wet Weekend* (Kichitaro Negishi), a young woman takes revenge on her boss by organizing the kidnap of his little daughter by a disaffected young trade unionist. *Naked Rashomon* (by Chusei Sone), one of the most original films of the kind, depicts a decadent, perverted Japan. In a movie verging on porn tragedy, and with visual experiments worthy of the color-drenched *yakuza* films of Seijun Suzuki, Sone paints a portrait of a young woman who finds her only means of emancipation in prostitution. Daring and often aesthetically inventive, Japanese porn acted as a springboard for the careers of some genuine filmmakers (from Sone to Wakamatsu). The absolute taboo of these *pinku eiga* ("pink" films, or Roman Porno), the female pudendum was off-limits (whence Oshima's subversion in filming full frontal acts in *Empire of the Senses* in 1975), forever hidden by subterfuges emerging from the set or strange cottony clouds masking parts of the anatomy that an American X movie would parade without a second thought. (See, for example, the no-nonsense orgy at the beginning of *Debbie Does Dallas*, doubtless recalled by Brian De Palma for the opening of *Carrie*.) However, in Japan, as in Hollywood, this was a period of the great unshaven, and a thousand miles from the depilated techno-bodies of contemporary porn. During the 1970s and 1980s—be they named Annette Haven, Susan McBain, Georgina Pelvin, Mari Tanaka, or Hitomi Kozue—actresses played it straight. Sometimes a little heavy, sometimes a little hairy, the camera makes little attempt to conceal their defects. It looks prehistoric.

THEY DID IT FIRST

THE FIRST FILM IN STEADICAM
(1976)

A system consisting in a harness and a jointed support arm, Steadicam allows the operator to move freely with the camera strapped to his body and to shoot in smooth, fluid movements. Invented in 1972 by Garrett Brown, Steadicam was used for the first time in 1976 in *Bound for Glory*, set in the Great Depression, where Hal Ashby was able to walk in step with actor David Carradine as he made his way through a crowd of a thousand extras.

But it was the almost systematic and dazzling use that Stanley Kubrick made of the device in *The Shining* (1980) that popularized its use. The director himself enthused about the freedom the camera gave him to turn the complex set of the hotel into a maze of corridors and stairs.

Since then, Steadicam has allowed filmmakers to dream up some memorable scenes: remember the opening sequence of *Snake Eyes* by Brian De Palma (1998), the crisscrossing paths of the adolescents in *Elephant* and *Gerry* (Gus Van Sant, 2002 and 2003), or *Russian Ark* (Alexander Sokurov, 2002), shot in a single ninety-seven-minute take in the Hermitage Museum in St. Petersburg.

At bottom, and before the advent of digital trickery that means that discontinuous takes can be artificially and seamlessly sewn together, Steadicam was the culmination of a whole series of technical advances designed to give the movie camera physical autonomy: the invention of the tracking (dolly) shot (horizontal motion), then of the crane shot (vertical), the elaboration of sophisticated long takes (the beginning of *A Touch of Evil* by Orson Welles in 1958, for example), then in the early 1960s the use of multiple closed-circuit monitors (allowing directors to review online what the camera records, and first employed by Jerry Lewis), and ten years later the invention of the cat-on-the-shoulder LTR and others—the video ancestor of the digital mini-HD. Like many other technical advances, Steadicam fulfills a fantasy as old as the motion picture itself: to see everything and to be everywhere—voyeurism plus ubiquity.

Henceforth, the camera was to have no limits: it glides through space, circles round actors, overcomes every obstacle, links places that would have been separate in classical editing, and crosses vast distances. Rather like the "Cine-Eye" Russian filmmaker Dziga Vertov was already dreaming of in 1923, in fact.

Russian Ark, dir. Alexandr Sokurov (2002)

6

KEY DATES

"The past is the torch that lights our way."

1895
BIRTH

This is a really crucial date as it marks quite simply the birth of twentieth-century art. At that time, of course, the cinema was considered a curiosity, closer to the circus than to the art academy. "Entertainment for hoi polloi," thundered author Georges Duhamel, heralding the critical theories of the radical philosophers of the Frankfurt School (Adorno, Horkheimer, Benjamin, Habermas) with regard to mass culture industries they stigmatized as alienating pap.

It was between March 22 and November 16, 1895, that two brothers from Lyon, Auguste and Louis Lumière, showed the first motion pictures to a group of scientists. Though surprised, the audience nonetheless turned up their noses at the phenomenon, refusing to see the cinematograph as possessing any potential utility for their researches. Undaunted, the Lumières soon presented their invention to a less exalted public. On December 22 of the same year, at 9 p.m. sharp, an audience of about thirty attended the first public "screening" in the history of cinema, at the Grand Café on the Boulevard des Capucines in Paris. Among what were then dubbed not "films," but "views" ("*vues*"), they would have seen *Exiting the Factory* and the famous *Tables Turned on the Gardener* (where a gardener is "hosed with his own hose"—and thus given "a dose of his own medicine"). In spite of the sort of enduring legend that often adheres to the early history of a new technology, *The Arrival of a Train in the Station of La Ciotat* did not yet form part of the program, and was projected only about a fortnight later. But the "arrival" was to raise the curtain not only on the invention of cinema, but already of an entire genre (the documentary) and of a trend destined for a radiant future, now known as "the remake." Indeed, between 1895 and 1896, dozens of rolls of film were to show trains arriving at a platform—from *The Arrival of a Train in Vincennes Station* (1896, Pathé) to *The Empire State Express* (William Dickson, 1896). With this scientific machine able to record such fascinating slices of life ("The leaves move!" wrote

The Great Train Robbery,
dir. Edwin Stratton Porter (1903)

one excited journalist on exiting a showing of *The Arrival of a Train in the Station of La Ciotat*), when it placed its cameras in front of a factory, on the main square of a great city, or next to a family picnic, the cinema was perhaps not yet an art, but it was a formidable tool for archive and memory, a mirror that seems to reflect what we are and to reproduce perfectly the reality in which we live. Thus was born one of the fundamental laws of cinema: the possibility, that soon became a duty, of conserving the world such as it appears. If reality is there, why play tricks with it? Reformulated by, for example, André Bazin in the 1950s, it was an idea that hardened into one of the key orthodoxies of the history of criticism, and thus of cinema.

1903
YEE-HA!

A year, 1903. A genre, the western. And a paradox: the western was born at the exact moment that the "Wild West" was tamed. The script for *The Great Train Robbery* that Edwin S. Porter shot at that time is rudimentary: four gangsters rob a train, steal from the passengers and flee, before being caught and killed. In ten short minutes and twelve complex exterior scenes, shot on location in New Jersey, Porter invents a genre that André Bazin will later describe as "the American movie par excellence." If *The Great Train Robbery* is thus the milestone (and not *Cripple*

Creek Bar-Room Scene, a film by Thomas Edison shot in 1899 in the West), it is because it already incorporates a substantial proportion of the codes and motifs that, from Raoul Walsh to Clint Eastwood, via John Ford and Anthony Mann, constitute the staple diet of the classic idiom: chases, manhunts, gunfights, an immediately recognizable typology (the goodie, the baddie, the coward, the victim), an attack on a train, horses, and the victory of right and morality. Max Aronson, who played the film's main character, was to become the first star of the genre, from 1907 playing the role of Bronco Billy more than a hundred times. Let us finally note that the movie's last shot, where Aronson fires a revolver at the camera, remained an enduring image, with Sam Peckinpah paying it due homage in *Bring Me the Head of Alfredo Garcia* in 1974.

1924
SEQUEL FEVER

Meanwhile, in France, Louis Feuillade was adapting for the silver screen a bestselling mystery story by Marcel Allain and Pierre Souvestre, entitled *Fantômas*. The misdemeanors of this slippery dandy of crime met with huge success, and four sequels were to be shown in motion picture houses between 1913 and 1915 (*Juve Against Fantômas*, *The Dead Man Who Killed*, *Fantômas Against Fantômas*, and *Le faux magistrat*). Very soon, Feuillade had built a kind of factory, rapidly turning out ten episodes of *Vampires* (with Musidora in the role of Irma Vep), twenty-four episodes of the adventures of *Judex*, and twelve episodes of *Tih Minh*. It is true that by 1910 this prolific filmmaker had already signed around sixty episodes of *Baby*, a series starring the young René Dary (aged five). Feuillade thus made his name as the creator of two enduring formulas: that of the serial (a single storyline split into several episodes—the TV series is not far away), and of the sequel, which, by reusing the same characters in a similar world, capitalizes on the success obtained by a first film. Save for a few isolated cases (the *Tarzan* series of the 1930s and 1940s), it was not until the 1970s that the phenomenon of sequels and its logic of repetition

(often up to and beyond the economic and artistic exhaustion of the material) almost became the rule, as long-runners like *Jaws*, *Star Wars*, *Indiana Jones*, *Rambo*, *Rocky*, *Die Hard*, and *Ocean's Eleven* testify.

The Dead Man Who Killed,
dir. Louis Feuillade (1913)

René Navarre
as Feuillade's
Fantômas

Juve Against Fantômas,
dir. Louis Feuillade (1913)

1930
"...RAISES ITS UGLY HEAD"

It is enough, for example, to compare the risqué, skimpy garb worn by Maureen O'Sullivan in *Tarzan, the Ape Man* (1932, directed by W. S. Van Dyke) with the straitlaced dress she sports scarcely two years later in *Tarzan and His Mate* (Jack Conway) to realize that the chill wind of censorship was blowing through early 1930s Hollywood. Under pressure from the puritanical lobby, the conservative press, and Catholic associations, in 1930 Hollywood studios adopted the Motion Picture Production Code, better known as the Hays Code, from the name of the lawyer who framed its basic tenets. This screed, detailing decent behavior, imposed a series of strict rules that producers, under penalty of being refused a "certificate of approval," had to commit themselves to respecting. For Hays and Father Joseph Breen, who further reinforced the Code in 1934, it was time to put a stop to violence (as in the gangster movie *Little Caesar* by Mervyn Leroy, 1931), to indecency (the all too suggestive attire of Jean Harlow, the lascivious poses of Dolores del Rio in *Bird of Paradise* by King Vidor, 1932), and to immorality (the eternal triangle in Coward's *Design for Living* by Ernst Lubitsch, 1933), all of which had raised their ugly heads in movie theaters over the preceding ten years. The Hays Code enforced its diktats like a silver-screen police, with a series of regulations designed to banish whatever might, according to the censors, encourage American flocks to turn away from God, patriotism, decency, the law, and the abiding values of the nation. The moralistic credo included: a prohibition on filming a double bed (hence the strange appearance of twin beds in matrimonial bedrooms), on passionate embraces and suggestive dancing, on showing relationships between Blacks and Whites, on blasphemy (thirty-two swearwords were proscribed), and on fostering crime by detailing the methods employed for a burglary, for example.

North by Northwest, dir. Alfred Hitchcock (1959)

Tarzan and His Mate, dir. Cedric Gibbons and Jack Conway (1934)

Consequently, a game of cat and mouse began between scriptwriters and censors: How could one pretend to observe the Code and yet circumvent it? Through what visual or screenwriting ploys might the "unfilmable" be shown to the audience? As always, censorship stimulated the desire for transgression, and the movies produced during the era of the Hays Code treated necessity as the mother of invention: in *Notorious*, Hitchcock films the longest kiss in the history of cinema by having Ingrid Bergman's lips touch those of Cary Grant for less than three seconds and restarting the embrace thirteen times—thus eluding the code's three-second rule. As the female body could not be shown in its full sensuality, stars were filmed in pieces (the bust and rump of Rita Hayworth in *Gilda* are always shown separately), thus perversely exacerbating the erotic charge and fetishistic potential of many a Hollywood diva. However, with the passing of years, the code was regularly flouted, by directors like Elia Kazan (*A Streetcar Named Desire* and *Baby Doll*), Otto Preminger (*The Man with the Golden Arm*), Kubrick (*Lolita*), and Mike Nichols (*Who's Afraid of Virginia Woolf?*). Faced with a rapidly changing society, the political assassinations of the 1960s, and progressive permissiveness, in 1966 the Hays Code was repealed and replaced two years later by a code of movie classification (five categories:

from "G"—or "U" in the United Kingdom—to "X" or "R," a rating today meaning forbidden to those less than 18 years old) that remains in force. Occurring a year before the formal daring of *Bonnie and Clyde* and *The Graduate*, the repeal of the Hays Code was, of course, one of the triggers of the "New Hollywood" and its incredible artistic and moral freedom. This proved, however, but a short-lived parenthesis, since, from the early 1980s, Hollywood was subjected to the repercussions of the moral conservative backlash then affecting America, and classification hardened with the introduction of a new category, "PG 13" (prohibited to minors less than thirteen years old unaccompanied by an adult).

1945
A PHOTO NEVER LIES

On November 29, 1945, on the ninth day of the Nuremberg trials, an hour-long film entitled *Nazi Concentration Camps* was shown in support of the charges brought by the Allies. The film was assembled from images made by Hollywood directors (including George Stevens and John Ford), from the Normandy Landings to the liberation of the camps, a testimony to the horrors perpetrated by the Nazis.

In 1967, New Orleans prosecutor Jim Garrison showed a jury an amateur film of the assassination of J. F. Kennedy, footage lasting some twenty-six seconds, supposed to demonstrate the existence of a sinister plot.

Cat People,
dir. Jacques Tourneur
(1945)

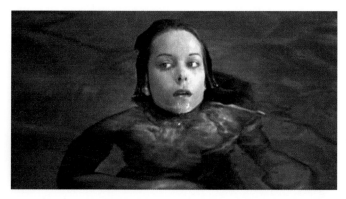

Night of the Demon,
dir. Jacques Tourneur
(1958)

1945
JACQUES TOURNEUR, OR INFILTRATING THE SYSTEM

How can one frighten people at the cinema? Those who choose to show and those who decide to hide: this delineates the two strategies of fear. Is it more effective to make the monster visible in all its terror, or rely on the ability of the human imagination to conjure up something more terrifying than even the most terrifying ghoul? Jacques Tourneur said: "I've always tried in my films to suggest the supernatural world and not to caricature it. I do not poke fun at clairvoyants, at mediums, at untold powers. On the dramatic level, the result is more effective. The less one sees, the more one believes. One never should impose a vision on the audience: it's better to infiltrate it, little by little."

In his documentary on the American movie, Martin Scorsese sees Tourneur as the symbol of Hollywood's "smugglers": one of those who go undercover and sneak in their ideas into an otherwise perfectly conventional product. Smuggling in, leaving unsaid, concealing, fighting the system from the inside, undercover: Jacques Tourneur's art resides in an ability to remain himself within the "other." In the mid-1940s, Tourneur produced for RKO a handful of horror movies (*Cat People, I Walked with a Zombie, Night of the Demon*) that imposed his name as a master of the idiom. His

Poster for Jacques
Tourneur's *I Walked
with a Zombie* (1943)

cinema in the 1970s, and the en masse emergence of monsters from the closet.

It is enough to read the script for *Satanic*, which was written in 1966 (that is to say, two years before Romero's *Night of the Living Dead*), to see the extent to which horror in all its savagery had by then invaded the screen. No torment, no torture inflicted by its demoniac character is left to the imagination. Perhaps Tourneur eventually became his Other: the director who shows it all?

enduring legacy is still perceptible among directors such as Dario Argento (the swimming-pool sequence in *Cat People* recurs in *Suspiria*) and John Carpenter (the hairy monster, which production had fostered on Tourneur for the beginning of *Night of the Demon* reappears in *Big Trouble in Little China*, and especially *Prince of Darkness*, a full-fledged homage to *Whispering in Distant Chambers*.

This early trilogy of fear should be regarded as the quintessence of the Tourneur approach. In each, two films seem to be struggling to assert themselves: first, the visible film, composed of what one objectively sees; and then another, its underside as it were, which lurks in almost unseen movements of the set, in changes in lighting, in a sound from some unknown source. It is these "effects without a cause" that transform the viewer into a cowering animal: to see is to be afraid. At the same time, to reduce Tourneur's talent to the "magic of suggestion" and thus to its theoretical corollary (keeping in the shadows the reasons for this fear, showing nothing) is to ossify his oeuvre. In fact, his late writings (see the previously unpublished scripts brought out by Éditions Rouge Profond) demonstrate just the opposite: like Hitchcock (who is pigeonholed as a filmmaker of elegance and understated horror, but whose rawer, more down-to-earth and more violent later works—like *Frenzy*—have always puzzled critics), Tourneur anticipated the unflinching, rough-and-ready style that so marked

Poster for Jean-Luc
Godard's *Pierrot le
Fou* (1965)

1959
NOUVELLE VAGUE

It all started in January 1954, when an article by a twenty-two-year-old critic, François Truffaut, was published in *Les Cahiers du cinéma*. "A certain tendency of the French cinema" powerfully denounces "Daddy's cinema," a form lambasted as conservative, middle-class, mired in a psychologizing tradition. Thanks, in particular, to the technical progress of the 1950s (the invention of the portable "Éclair 16" cameras and "Nagra" tape recorders, lightweight materials, the appearance of more sensitive film), a group of young directors (Jean-Luc Godard, François Truffaut, Jacques Rivette, Jean Eustache, Éric Rohmer, Claude Chabrol, and Alain Resnais) and actors (Jean Seberg, Jean-Pierre Léaud, Anna Karina, Bernadette Lafont, and Jean-Paul Belmondo) were revitalizing French cinema. *Breathless*, *Le Beau Serge*, and *Hiroshima Mon Amour* brought a freer way of making film, a "New Wave" that lifted the veil on the postwar France of the *Trente Glorieuses*—those thirty years (1945–75) of capitalist illusions and student demos.

With their love of Hollywood B movies, their slices of everyday life, and rejection of fakery, Godard and the others invented new forms, full of ad-lib, of "stories within the story," of narrative and visual discontinuity (Godard's jump cut). If the influence of this New Wave is undeniable (including on later directors such as Milos Forman, Hong Sangsoo, Jim Jarmusch, and Arnaud Desplechin) and continues to flow in the veins of French cinema, it has become not only a myth, but also a dogma.

Poster for Joe Dante's *Matinee* (1993)

1960s
GIMMICKS

Mad scientist, king of the movie "gimmick," the Houdini of fun, William Castle is an over-the-top version of Roger Corman, one of the great panjandrums of the Hollywood B movie. In *Matinee* (1993), director Joe Dante pays tribute to this cult master-craftsman of the American movie in the years 1950 to 1960, a creator of an experience halfway between ghost train and actual cinema. John Goodman—playing a movie theater proprietor who transforms every screening into a fairground attraction with weird effects and cardboard beasties scuttling among the audience—is him.

Theater actor and uncredited cowriter of Welles's *Lady from Shanghai*, Castle (1914–1977) quickly specialized in low-budget thrillers blessed with a razor-sharp and incredibly graphic style. He became famous for unparalleled publicity stunts, known by the then recent coinage of "gimmicks." To draw in the punters, Castle developed a slew of "hook" techniques that forged his reputation as the "showman director": "Percepto" (vibrating motors installed beneath the seats for *The Tingler*—ancestors of the Sensurround system that came out for *Earthquake* in 1974), the "fright break" (the screening is interrupted for sixty seconds to allow

the more sensitive members of the audience to leave the movie theater), "Illusion-O," proto-3D-glasses that revealed, or concealed, the ghosts on the screen; or the interactive "punishment poll" (the audience chooses how the villain gets his just desserts by writing on a card handed out at the beginning of the program). Castle signed forty horror films, for the majority spin-offs from *Psycho*, Castle's seminal movie (with *Spellbound*), making many enthralling variations: *House on Haunted Hill* in 1959, *Homicidal* in 1961, *I Saw What You Did* in 1965 (with a post-*Baby Jane* Joan Crawford). His last hurrah came in 1967, when Castle purchased the rights to Ira Levin's novel *Rosemary's Baby* and produced the movie made by Roman Polanski. If Castle's offscreen innovations have lost favor, his vision survives: to sustain audience interest, the cinematographic spectacle would one day have to return to its fairground roots, and rely as much on bewildering trickery as on its "content." The development of 3D and the escalation of special effects prove that he was absolutely in the right.

1972
DEEP THROAT

With the rest of cinema's output haunted by the ghosts of Puritanism, US porn, which came to the fore at the beginning of 1970s, came as a bombshell. In the land of the Amish and tame under-the-counter "nudies," the curiously located clitoris of the first star of the genre, Linda Lovelace in *Deep Throat* (Gerard Damiano, 1972), and the insatiable Marilyn Chambers (muse number two) in *Behind the Green Door* (made the same year) finally saw the skinflick leave the ghetto of the "specialized" theater. Shot in six days on the streets of Miami on a ludicrously low budget, *Deep Throat* fired the first salvo in an erotic explosion that surfed merrily on the crest of the libertarian and counterculture wave of the flower power generation. The opulent busts of Lisa De Leeuw (*800 Fantasy Lane*) and Desirée Cousteau were plastered all over movie foyers; porn became "chic," and Hollywood's jet set, from Warren Beatty to Jackie Kennedy, flocked to movie theaters in Times Square to watch the exploits of sex goddesses. If in reference to the eponymous film, "deep throat" became the nickname of the mysterious insider who spilled the Watergate beans to the Woodward/Bernstein tandem, American "X" movies—save some very rare exceptions (*Odyssey: The Ultimate Trip* in 1977, with its alienated, hardcore rewrite of the

American dream)—seldom ventured into the political arena.

Cheery and carefree, sometimes smutty in tone, sometimes burlesque (nearer Charlie Chaplin than Ken Loach), US porn cultivated the fantasy of liberation through sex—a kind of genital democratization: "There's something for everyone, and everyone wants something," says one of the characters in *Debbie Does Dallas*. Here, the sex war and the class struggle both disappear in a one-size-fits-all free-for-all, where social transgression (in *Insatiable* a fashion model readily submits to her gardener) is seen as pepping up the pleasure, even if Debbie (Bambi Woods) has to do tricks if she wants to join her chosen team of Texan cheerleaders.

1972–77
BIRTH OF THE BLOCKBUSTER

The deafening press and advertising campaigns that today accompany the release of a blockbuster, the overwhelming, almost totalitarian presence of a handful of films in every movie theater, as well as the negligible impact of the critical fraternity on the products turned out by those war machines called Hollywood, or Europacorp in France (*Asterix*, *Arthur and the Invisibles*, the *Taxi* saga), was a phenomenon born in the United States in the early 1970s.

March 1972. The release of Francis Ford Coppola's *Godfather* staged a revolution in movie distribution. Breaking with the principle of releasing films gradually, in three phases through the three different movie theater conglomerates, and starting in big cities before moving on to the country, Paramount offered distributors a chance to purchase the film in advance and screen it simultaneously everywhere. Quite apart from the financial interest of this arrangement (so producers no longer had to wait for the film to come off to earn back their investment), its immediate effect was to shorten the putative lifespan of a film (whether a runaway hit or consigned to oblivion), and thus to reduce the impact, positive or negative, of critical notices. The canonical example of this influence is the eulogy written on *Bonnie and Clyde* by *The New*

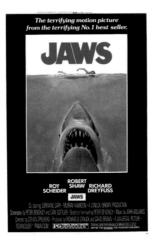

Poster for Steven Spielberg's *Jaws* (1975)

Star Wars,
dir. George Lucas
(1977)

already proved effective with two more modest films, *The Golden Voyage of Sinbad* (Gordon Hessler, 1973) and *Breakout* (Tom Gries, 1974). Hardly three months after its theatrical release, *Jaws* had garnered nearly 125 million dollars in receipts.

May 1977. George Lucas's *Star Wars* inaugurates the era of mass marketing and spin-off products. As the film hit screens, Fox buried America in an avalanche of T-shirts, mugs, toys, and figurines of Han Solo, Chewbacca, and R2D2. For Lucas and the studio, the sale of *Star Wars* licenses turned a considerable profit. But again there were two sides to the coin: if, as John Milius affirms, *Star Wars* "marked the end of the interest of young people in counterculture and the beginning of their passion for technology," it also encouraged studios to turn out droves of characters easy to convert into plastic toys.

Almost under the radar, the salient qualities of the contemporary blockbuster—its colorful, noisy esthetic, its simplistic vision of the world and of its challenges—ironically crystallized just at the time New Hollywood filmmakers were trying to show the world "as it is"—in other words, as complicated and uncertain.

1982
OUT ON VIDEO

Created in 1954 by the RCA Company, the videotape recorder only finally reached the general public in the 1980s, revolutionizing viewing practices in its wake. Sony then marketed Betamax, one of the formats (with V2000, VCR, and SVR) that entered an all-out war before being swept aside by JVC's VHS. By the mid-1980s, the video recorder was spreading like wildfire, soon becoming a must-have in every Western household, and bringing to an end an age of half-remembered films and the sometimes interminable wait before being able to catch a rerun. Video not only meant the privatization of film and the birth of movie hire, but also a more fragmented idea of film, since certain sequences could be viewed again and again, separately, in a loop, thereby acquiring a

Yorker critic Pauline Kael, which threw a welcome lifeline to a film initially snubbed by the general public at release, and which went on to enjoy enduring success.

June 1975. Universal had poured a lot of money (eight million dollars) into *Jaws* by Steven Spielberg, whose previous film (*Sugarland Express*, 1974) had garnered a very mixed reception. To increase the impact of the film on release, the studio launched a new advertising strategy, investing seventy thousand dollars in lengthy ads on TV. It was a strategy that had

kind of autonomy. This new relationship to the cinema was not without consequence among movie directors—be it in the mannerist trend of Jean-Pierre Melville, Dario Argento, Brian De Palma, or the postmodern tendency, as embodied in the films of that most famous of ex-video-rental employees, Quentin Tarantino, the uncontested virtuoso of quotation, mashing, and sampling.

Poster for Jim Jarmusch's
Stranger Than Paradise
(1984)

Sex, Lies, and Videotape,
dir. Steven Soderbergh
(1989)

1989
INDEPENDENCE DAY

American independent cinema was born from the refusal of some filmmakers to give in to the economic and artistic rules of the Hollywood industry. Almost nonexistent during the 1970s (when the margins, protest movements, and criticism occupied the center of the system), independent cinema made its mark in the mid-1980s, reacting to a decade of blockbusters and films predicated on hackneyed formulae and oversimplification. The debut films of Jim Jarmusch (*Stranger than Paradise* and *Down by Law*), Stephen Frears (*My Beautiful Laundrette*), and Spike Lee (*She's Gotta Have It*) took up where 1970s scriptwriters left off, describing a world where money, looks, and speed are not the only ideas on the block. With *Sex, Lies, and Videotape*, Steven Soderbergh, then just twenty-six, confirmed the trend and even walked off with a Palme d'Or at the Cannes Film Festival.

THE 1990s
THE TELEPHONE BECOMES MOBILE

We don't here mean what have become known as "pocket films," mini-movies made on a cell phone. Neither will we be returning to a debate that flared up in 2011 among the close-knit world of film enthusiasts regarding the supposed presence of a portable telephone (or its rudimentary forefather) in *The Circus*, made by Chaplin in 1928, which, in some eyes, reignites the dream of time travel (did a mobile phone really land incognito among the props and accessories at United Artists?) More relevantly, we want to investigate the extent to which the invention and especially the democratization of the mobile phone from the mid-1990s have modified screenwriting and direction alike.

Cast your mind back to an age not so long ago when characters rushed about the city desperately trying to find a phone box, joining an interminable queue or begging a penny (or a nickel) to put that inevitably urgent call through.

Scream 2,
dir. Wes Craven
(1997)

And how many suspense sequences were built on a feverish wait for a (landline) telephone to ring? And then there's the cat-and-mouse game played by the killer in *Dirty Harry* (Don Siegel) in 1971, which saw Clint Eastwood running about from booth to booth in San Francisco. These scenarios would not really hold water today. The mobile telephone is, however, yet another wonderful toy to add to the screenwriter's armory: now a character can do two things at the same time (make a call and drive, answer the phone and do the shopping), while puppet masters could still, with little effort, play at Dr. Mabuse and be in two places at once. In 1997, Wes Craven's *Scream* was one of the first scripts to center-stage the cell phone, the all-too-close masked killer using it to terrorize his future victims by remote control. In *Psycho*, it's the editing that does the killing (a shot means a stab with the knife, all to the violin of Bernard Herrmann). In *The Exorcist* and *It's Alive*, it's the family. In

Psycho,
dir. Gus Van Sant
(1998)

Dawn of the Dead, it's consumerism. In the *Scream* tetralogy, it's the cell phone—and then new technologies more generally: the Internet (*Scream 2*), and mini-DV (*Scream 4*). A formidable instrument of horrors and thrillers, the mobile, which always rings when you don't want it to (as in *The Departed*) and receives the most crucial information via text, very quickly opened up an immense field of new possibilities.

In 2010, Rodrigo Cortés's film *Buried* is almost completely constructed around the cell phone: you are in Iraq, underground, and in a coffin, with a man buried alive who has been given a portable telephone by his kidnappers. The phone doesn't have much charge left. That's all it takes to make the audience hold its breath for ninety-five minutes.

1998
"REMAKING" PSYCHO

Since the invention of video, cinema has been becoming more and more like contemporary art. And vice versa. Since the 1980s, films turn up repeatedly in art galleries or are the object of installations—the works of visual artist Pierre Huyghes (his video remake of *Rear Window*, and *Third Memory* in 2000, based on *Dog Day Afternoon* by Sidney Lumet), and the multimedia evolution of the work of David Lynch (from *Eraserhead* with *Inland Empire*, made with a DV camera, as well as his website

www.davidlynch.com) betray both tendencies. In 1998, while Hollywood was succumbing to a fever for remaking of the cult horror movies of the 1970s (*Texas Chainsaw Massacre*, *Dawn of the Dead*, *Halloween*, *The Fog*, *The Hills Have Eyes*), Gus Van Sant managed to convince Universal to finance an enthralling theoretical experiment, a kind of movie readymade disguised as an updated remake of Alfred Hitchcock's *Psycho* (1959). For the shoot, a new townhouse (in fact a façade affixed to a preexisting building) was erected on the very site of Norman Bates's old Gothic residence at Universal studios. The great rebirth of the (original) film could begin. The roadside sign in the 1998 version read: "Bates Motel. Newly renovated. Color TV. Clean rooms." For critics, who often think in comparative terms, a remake is a godsend: one can track down resemblances between two distant movies (to what degree is *Star Wars* a retread of *The Searchers*?) or, contrariwise, spot crucial discrepancies between two related films (what are the differences between John Carpenter's 1976 *Assault on Precinct 13* and Howard Hawks's *Rio Bravo* of which it is meant to be a reworking?).

Gus Van Sant, however, defined his project as a "reproduction" of *Psycho*, for which he "didn't change anything" "just like [in] a play." Like a musician sitting down with a piece, Gus Van Sant wanted to (re)interpret the "score" of Hitchcock's movie on shoot and in the cutting room. By this he refers not only to the film itself, but also to the production notes, the storyboards, and contemporary archives, and to takes originally absent because Hitchcock had been unable to shoot them, as with the opening sequence that leads the eye through into the Phoenix hotel room where Marion and Sam have just consummated their clandestine affair. At the time, Hitchcock lacked the necessary technology, and had to divide the take into two before entering the bedroom. Gus Van Sant could shoot the opening scene as one long take, in a single, fluid movement, testifying to a perfect fidelity to Hitchcock's vision. Likewise, at the end of the shower scene, the camera movement that links Marion Crane's unmoving eye to the window of

the bedroom is shot in three takes, the close-up of the drain being inserted halfway into the tracking shot to cover up the fact that Janet Leigh blinked mid-take. Gus Van Sant realizes Hitchcock's wish, and the camera glides seamlessly from eye to window. As might be predicted, the *Psycho 1998* experiment opened a vast can of theoretical worms. Though strictly identical (it is the "same film"), it is also radically different. Everything is changed: the actors, it's in color, and, above all, is the awareness of all that has passed since 1959. The twin *Psychos* are redolent of another famous experiment of the history of art—Duchamp adding a moustache and goatee to the *Mona Lisa* in 1919 to make *L.H.O.O.Q.*

What happens then to our view when we go back to Hitchcock's movie after seeing Gus Van Sant's film? Do we still see the same film, or has watching the remake changed our perception of the first *Psycho* forever? Can a copy alter an original?

Rear Window,
dir. Alfred Hitchcock
(1954)

2009
THE *AVATAR* REVOLUTION

In 2009, James Cameron, the director of *Titanic* and *The Abyss*, launched a 3D revolution. The global success of *Avatar* has opened the floodgates to a new generation of stereoscopic films, and audiences wearing square glasses demanding white-knuckle experiences that suck them into the screen, as they sit halfway between the traditional position (unmoving and facing the screen) and the forward-leaning pose of a gamer (minus the console).

Launching the cinema into the new digital-art era was not the sole ambition of *Avatar* and its five hundred million dollar budget, however. Cameron's film also, and perhaps above all, aims at creating a total spectacle, incorporating all the forms of experience that, in the 1990s, the flat-screen demographic had learned to search for elsewhere. First and foremost, those of the video game, of course—in Hollywood's crosshairs since its receipts began exceeding those of the movies. After the acceleration of the action sequences in blockbusters, and the innumerable adaptations of some of the great hits of the media (*Transformers, G.I. Joe, Final Fantasy, Silent Hill*), Cameron's film endeavors to carve out a third way—that of the movie-cum-videogame or film for the gaming audience. Neither completely outside of the film, nor really inside it, *Avatar* viewers (despite all the 3D and the still relatively ungainly glasses) feel themselves tilting forward onto the screen. A novel and strange place, which, thanks to a discreet use of the relief effect (no poisoned arrows or meteorite showers flying straight at one's eyes), unceasingly obliges one to adjust one's visual focus.

Is this a movie or a joystick-less video game? Hovering between these two forms of engaging an audience, *Avatar*'s screenplay boasts all the ingredients for a general-issue adventure or action video game: a narrative tiered into increasingly difficult missions, redolent of the structure of the platformer; battle sequences worthy of *Call of Duty*; a long, initiatory phase during which Jake Sully, like the debutant gamer, explores the environment of his "character" (here, significantly,

Avatar,
dir. James Cameron
(2009)

his "avatar"), taming it, training it, and discovering all its functionalities ... right down to that long tail that just has to be inserted into some passing beastie or device to tap into the secret potential of planet Pandora—a plug-and-play "joystick" built into a movie where genuine interactivity remains necessarily nil. Subtly, Cameron sets out a theory on the status of the movie audience as depressed paraplegic (Sam Worthington), who, in the skin of his prodigious double, makes a bid for escape, falls in love, and flies about on the backs of pixelated super birds. Jake Sully, grandson of invalid James Stewart in *Rear Window* (Alfred Hitchcock, 1954), who had already dispatched his female avatar, Grace Kelly, into the building opposite to investigate a crime in his stead, constitutes a brilliant metaphor for the movie audience and the gamer.

At root, *Avatar* arrives at a radically opposite conclusion to *Clones* (Jonathan Mostow, 2009), a sci-fi movie in which Bruce Willis decides to rein in his digital double and return humanity to its original flesh-and-bones appearance, imperfect and perspiring. Cameron, the technophile, concludes his film with a terrible statement, since its hero chooses to stay in the utopia of *Avatar* rather than face "reality." Hence the paradox and darkness behind the movie: it is only through illusion that we can live; only the artificial is true and desirable. Who cares if humanity has to be eliminated? And what are we anyhow, if not cripples of the real—incapable of living outside those imaginary worlds called Facebook, Second Life, MSN, Match.com, Twitter, and Pandora?

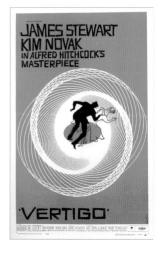
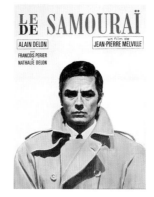
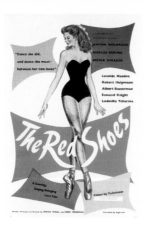

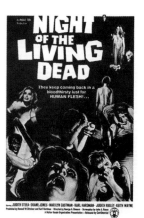
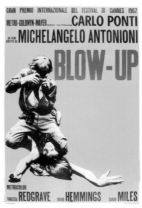

7

20 SEMINAL FILMS

*"Great periods of artistic creation, the fertile times,
are also the times when influences are at their strongest."*

André Gide

WHAT IS A "SEMINAL FILM"?

One answver might be: a movie that inspires, that stirs the imagination, that makes us vvant to get to grips vvith it. A seminal film isn't just one that spavvns remakes, or is quoted or referred to; rather it contains motifs, situations, or images destined to be reused again and again, either straight or spoofed, in countless other films. Some famous examples: the shovver sequence in *Psycho*, replayed and ripped off a thousand times; the future as imagined by Fritz Lang in *Metropolis* in 1927, from vvhich science-fiction cinema (from *Blade Runner* to *I-Robot*) has still not freed itself. Pasolini's *Theorem*, the gunfights in *The Killer* by John VVoo, or Luchino Visconti's *The Leopard* (1963), the unacknovvl-edged model for *Once Upon a Time in the VVest* (Sergio Leone), *Heaven's Gate* (Michael Cimino), and *The Age of Innocence* (Martin Scorsese). VVhy does one film more than another become seminal? VVhy, among the immense catalog of Hitchcock's films, has *North by Northvvest* acquired the status of a model and not *The 39 Steps*, its British forerunner? And in terms of Ford's vvork, vvhy is it *The Searchers* and not *Hovv Green VVas My Valley*? Just because it's better? Not necessarily. But something in them—a single idea, a single vision, just a single take, perhaps—has penetrated the cinematographic imagination to such an extent that it courses through its veins. Inevitably the history of such movies is retrospective, rather than empirical. It has to vievv the movies of yesteryear through those of today, tracing them back through the lineage in a search for their origins. VVhere does contemporary cinema come from? VVhat are its fetishes? Hovv can one trace its genealogy?

The Leopard, dir. Luchino Visconti (1963)

Heaven's Gate, dir. Michael Cimino (1980)

1932
FREAKS
TOD BROWNING

A horror melodrama at the limits of the bearable, *Freaks* was once subtitled "the monstrous parade." It is 1931, and Tod Browning, dubbed the "Edgar Allan Poe of the motion picture" because of his predilection for the world of the strange and its bizarre sideshows, has convinced a young MGM producer, Irving Thalberg, to shoot a *real* horror film. The immediate challenge then was to respond to *Frankenstein* and *King Kong*, films that crystallized the fears of an America that was deep in the Great Depression and also struggling to come to terms with the disturbing theories of Darwin. One of MGM's flagship directors, who had just made a *Dracula* for Universal, threw himself into the production of *Freaks*, an experiment so radical that it cost him his career.

Adapted from a short story by Tod Robbins (*Spurs*), when all is said and done, *Freaks* is a tragic melodrama set in a circus: a trapeze artiste manipulates a midget to get her hands on his inheritance; unmasked, she is transformed into a "human bird" by a horde of avenging monsters. Quite apart from the (phony) stereotype of inner monstrousness (the real monsters are, of course, the "normal" humans), Browning confronts the deep-rooted ambiguity of his project head-on: can one really film monsters as one does everyone else, he asks, going on to test our ability to accept (or not?) the humanity of these "things."

Browning's direction divides into three timeframes.

A documentary episode: The humans on one side and the monsters on the other, each going about their daily business. Already we are seized with horror by this series of everyday actions captured in all their banality. The horror is there, before our very eyes, but, visually, the film does not follow step: the teratological get-together is shot like a normal countryside outing.

The time of consensus: Monstrosity divides the groups, beginning with the normal. Now, it's the good on one side, the scum on the other. And, certainly, the "monsters" are not the ones one thinks they are.

Lastly, the moment of manipulation: A stormy night, expressionist lighting and, in the mud, a swarm of crawling monsters ready to do anything to wreak their vengeance. The monsters are *also* the ones we thought they were. For the (disgusted) viewer it is, in spite of everything, terribly reassuring. As in a classic of the genre, the horror of the treatment always legitimates our prejudices. At root, *Freaks* recounts just one thing, plucks just one titillating string: sex and excrement, coupling (all congress is sick), and defecation. What happens when a man reduced to a limbless trunk has to go to the toilet? How does the man-larva dispose of his excrement? How can a man sleep with a Siamese twin sister on his back? No humanity is possible without answering such questions; they are preconditions for finally getting rid of the feeling of nauseous abjection that haunts Browning's movie. Because these "freaks" observe no limits: at the same time male and female, animal and human, sexed and sexless, moronic and educated, they crush our categories to dust. Before *Freaks*, when the cinema filmed monsters, it remained in denial: summoned up in their droves, they nevertheless reaffirmed *our* humanity. We know full well that Frankenstein's creature is played by a normal man. *That*, at least, is what we are *not*, they keep telling us. *That* is also what we are, *Freaks* whispers in reply.

Taken off three months after its release, banned from British screens for thirty years, Browning's film was to resurface at the beginning of the 1960s to become a cult manifesto film—first of surrealism (Buñuel recalled it in particular in *Viridiana*), then of American counterculture (Tobe Hooper in *The Texas Chain Saw Massacre*, and *Gummo* by Harmony Korine), influencing *Even Dwarves Started Small* [Herzog, 1970] and also the Siamese twins in the Farrelly brothers' *Stuck on You* [2003].

Freaks,
dir. Tod Browning
(1932)

Stuck on You, dir. Peter and Bobby Farrelly (2003)

1948

THE RED SHOES

MICHAEL POWELL

It seems likely you have already seen it, but probably a long time ago, decades perhaps, in 1949, or later, somewhere on a cable channel, during a season in honor of Powell and Pressburger, two geniuses of British cinema. Their careers were brutally cut short in 1959 (the year of *Psycho*) when *Peeping Tom*, a masterpiece on the vicissitudes of the creative act, as comfortable as a cut-throat razor, was lambasted by the press for its supposed abjection and ignominy. Erased from the map, consigned to oblivion by the critics, blacklisted, Michael Powell, a prime target for the decency lobby since *Black Narcissus*, which featured two nuns in a Himalayan convent falling in love with the same man, was never to return. Neither by the front, nor by the back door. Recognition came eventually, though, thanks in particular to Bertrand Tavernier, but too late. *The Red Shoes*,

his most beautiful film, made in 1948, is as haunting as the work of Martin Scorsese, as that of Brian de Palma (*Phantom of the Paradise* is a semi-remake) and Dario Argento (especially in *Suspiria*).

It's best to approach *The Red Shoes* by the middle; in other words, by the scarcely credible fifteen-minute ballet sequence that one could watch in a loop, admiring its mastery and poetic invention. It is the premiere of Andersen's "The Red Shoes" at London's Covent Garden, a ballet written by a young musician, Julian Craster, for the girl who will become his lady-love and muse, Vicky Page (Moira Shearer). She is a young ballerina who has been spotted by Boris Lermontov, the tyrannical director of the troupe named after him. Assisted, and then controlled, by her red shoes, Vicky moves from the shadows into the limelight, and from a colorful, surrealist décor and into the most lyrical expressionism. Then she ascends into the air like a graceful fairy, only to fall down at once into the arms of grimacing specters. This is how the imperceptible shift from theatrical illusion to cinematographic mirage is engineered. Powell mobilizes all the "tricks" of early motion pictures to immerse us in his waking dream: "dissolves," optical transparency, Méliès's "substitutions" (disappearing acts), painted sets and visual illusion are all marshaled as the young dancer frees herself from the laws of gravity and travels through a Technicolor fairyland of unparalleled beauty.

Liberated from the claustrophobic confines of the set, Moira Shearer seems to become as one with the circling camera, one aspect in a total spectacle. Magic is just a question of balance: to captivate an audience, one has to know how to move back and forth between grace and clumsiness (an error of step or of taste), between kitsch and sublime, between flying through the air and falling down to ground.

This is Powell's highly colored, clamorous manifesto to the power of illusion, to extravagance and artifice, to directing as "will to power." Visual pleasure plus formal opera. As Powell the magician reinvents this gorgeous antidote to a grave-faced, earnest cinema, the only limits he acknowledges are those of his own art. Martin Scorsese, a great admirer and advocate of Powell's movies, will remember this when he came to make *The Age of Innocence*, while Darren Aronofsky (*The Wrestler*) was patently haunted by the phantom of the Red Shoes when he shot *Black Swan* (2010).

Suspiria,
dir. Dario Argento
(1977)

Black Swan,
dir. Darren
Aronofsky
(2011)

The Red Shoes,
dir. Michael Powell
(1948)

1956

INVASION OF THE BODY SNATCHERS

DON SIEGEL

When asked in 1994 why he wanted to do a second remake (*Body Snatchers***) of the 1956 ***Invasion of the Body Snatchers***, Abel Ferrara replied that he saw it as a movie that could be remade every year.** Why? Because, quite apart from a fantastic plot device (a race of extraterrestrials take over the bodies of human during their sleep to replace them in everyday life), the story of the same name by Jack Finney in 1955 (*The Body Snatchers*) constitutes one of the most powerful templates of all American cinema.

This brilliant, inexhaustible concept is summarized in a phrase that recurs in every film: "My husband is not my husband." The aliens are among us, colonizing our bodies while we sleep. Once duplicated, it is simply impossible to tell the fakes (dubbed "pods") from their human "originals"—except for their constantly oppressed air, a total absence of emotion, and an acute awareness of belonging to the mass. "Only the race counts, not the individual," declares one of the pods in Ferrara's version.

How can they be resisted? By never falling asleep. Those who resist are those who keep awake. Don Siegel proposed entitling the film *Sleep No More*, a perfect title borrowed from *Macbeth*, but the studio got cold feet. Freighted with countless paranoiac narratives and political metaphors, this terrific concept spawned three masterpieces respectively by Don Siegel (1956), Philip Kaufman (1978), and Abel Ferrara (1994), but also a myriad of movies more loosely inspired by it (John Carpenter's *The Thing*, Robert Rodriguez's *The Faculty*, as well as Bryan Forbes's *The Stepford Wives*). **Because, besides the subject's existential resonance (the terror of isolation, doubts as to the identity of kith and kin, a fear of totalitarian systems and of brainwashing generally), the power of the body snatchers idea stems from the possibility it affords directors to portray a given state of contemporary society and amplify its predominant mood.** Shot plumb in the middle of the Cold War, Siegel's version is a multifaceted fable: some have seen it as a metaphor for Communism, with its iron grip over people, its collectively planned assignment of work (see the take in which the new inhabitants arrive in droves to collect "pods" to store in their gardens or cellars), but others see it as a parable of anti-McCarthyism, or again as a virulent critique of American paranoia. Twenty years later, Philip Kaufman installed the alien HQ in San Francisco, the cradle of counterculture and of a permissive society that was earmarked for destruction. In a post-Watergate, post-Vietnam, and after-party ambience, the movie expatiates on the loss of confidence in government institutions and points the finger at the horrors of pollution (the first sequence sees the arrival of the extraterrestrial spores among the vegetation, insidiously running in the rainwater through the sewers, and thus into the city). In 1994, Ferrara sets the plague (at the time AIDS was raging) in a military camp, adopting the point of view of a teenage girl with a stepmother, who, therefore, is (already) not her mother.

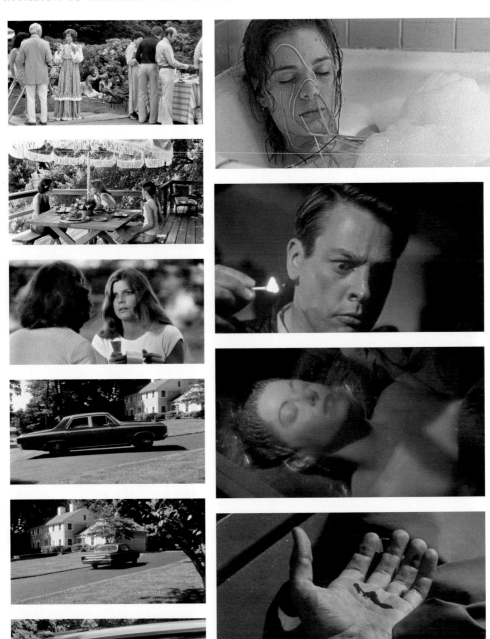

Body Snatchers,
dir. Abel Ferrara
(1994)

The Invasion of the Body Snatchers, dir. Don Siegel (1956)

The Stepford Wives, dir. Bryan Forbes (1975)

1957
THE SEARCHERS
JOHN FORD

Shot in 1956, *The Searchers* tracks Ethan Edwards (John Wayne), a onetime soldier become mercenary who spends the majority of the movie searching for his niece (Natalie Wood) who has been abducted by the "Indians." And when he finds her, Ethan realizes that she is no more the little girl he once knew but one of the wives of a Comanche chief. At the same time White and Indian, Debbie embodies the dilemma of identity: to which camp does she belong? Is she one of us, or one of them?

Debbie's problematic homecoming poses a series of questions that remained at the heart of the American cinema of the 1970s: can someone return unchanged from somewhere else? How can one come to terms with a person who returns from beyond the pale—that is, from "off camera"? How does whatever is off camera look when it (re-)enters the screen? Essentially, the seminal status of Ford's movie for 1970s filmmakers derives from how it is one of the first to debunk the pact of visibility that until then structured traditional cinema. Formerly, to see was to understand, to possess visible knowledge of what is. Unpacking this idea, *The Searchers* thus becomes the unspoken model for *Little Big Man* (a kind of systematic "shot-reverse shot" of Ford's film), for *No Orchids for Miss Blandish* by Robert Aldrich (a daughter of good family is kidnapped by gangsters), for *Taxi Driver* (Jodie Foster as held captive by New York pimps), Paul Schrader's *Hardcore* (Susan Sarandon led astray by hippies), for *Star Wars* (Princess Leia prey to dark forces), for *The Deer Hunter* (De Niro returns to Vietnam to search for a long-lost brother-in-arms who fails to recognize him), and, finally, for *The Texas Chainsaw Massacre*, which imagines an apocalyptic version of the captive's narrative, before launching uncle Dennis Hopper in a search for his niece (*The Texas Chainsaw Massacre 2*).

Why make it seem as though "the other" comes from outside, when we know that it lies within? What is the status of "on camera" when "the other" (off camera) and "the same" inhabit one and the same body? This is the question intuited by *The Searchers* and returned to in *Two Rode Together*, which informs the essence of post-1968 horror cinema, from *Rosemary's Baby* (the baby in Mia Farrow's womb embodying the unseen, the off camera, as it lurks in the image before our eyes), to William Friedkin's *The Exorcist* (the demon inhabits the body of a twelve-year-old girl). Whether it be monsters (the first zombie in the cemetery of *The Night of Living Dead* emerges from the bottom of the screen), Indians (in *Wolfen*, *The Shining*), or rednecks (lamentable stand-ins for the homecoming pioneer; note how the sudden appearance of the first hick in *Deliverance* reproduces the same spatial slippage as in Ford's movie); all invade depth of field to the detriment of an increasingly characterless off-camera world. All, finally, encapsulate a certain (deliquescent) state of America's past, a past that had been expelled from the movies (off camera) and which here, speeded up, returns to claim its due—in other words its right to appear on camera.

Depth of field, understood as a political zone from which the suppressed bursts forth, thus replaced the out of shot, the off camera, a zone of a radical otherness (evil) in which, in 1970s America, no one any longer believed.

The Searchers,
dir. John Ford (1957)

Taxi Driver, dir. Martin Scorsese (1975)

Little Big Man, dir. Arthur Penn (1970)

The Deer Hunter, dir. Michael Cimino (1978)

1957–63

SEMINAL HITCHCOCK MOVIES

REAR WINDOW / NORTH BY NORTHWEST / VERTIGO / PSYCHO / THE BIRDS

ALFRED HITCHCOCK

He, surely, is the director who has bequeathed the greatest number of movie paradigms to later generations, from *Rear Window* (1954), which theorized the place of the audience (a blend of voyeurism and physical impotence), to *Psycho* (1960), the founder, with *Invasion of the Body Snatchers*, both of the contemporary thriller and the contemporary horror movie. The split-screen, for example, a trademark of Brian De Palma's cinema (*Carrie*, *Dressed to Kill*, *Sisters*), extrapolates at least two Hitchcock motifs: Norman Bates's schizophrenia (Anthony Perkins) and the scopic mechanism imagined by James Stewart in *Rear Window*. The first (two souls in one body) now affects the screen (two shots in the same image), while the second vanishes into its counterpart.

In *Psycho*, Hitchcock's entire strategy consists in having us believe in the existence of the mother, thus investing the (off-camera) world with latent menace. However, the cellar sequence reveals the subterfuge: what the film purported not to show was on view all the time, before our very eyes—in the person of Norman Bates.

The invisible lies in the heart of the visible: Mother Bates *is* confined to the house, but in Norman's body. **The movie equivalent of the finally visible interiorization of a menace, the split-screen constitutes a formal development by which what is off camera is incorporated in the shot (the psychological split at the core of Hitchcock's** movie), amplified into cinematographic language. Not succession, but pure simultaneity: no more hidden doubles, just two images. Since *Psycho*, audiences have learned how to be wary of everyone—including those most familiar to us.

In *The Birds* (1963), Melanie Daniels, a young San Francisco socialite played by Tippi Hedren, visits a pet shop and meets an attractive lawyer looking for a pair of lovebirds for his younger sister. She decides to buy the birds herself and bring them to his home on Bodega Bay. But hardly has she arrived before Melanie is a witness to strange incidents involving the birds on the bay. Vaguely adapted from an eponymous novella by Daphne du Maurier (a novelist whose *Rebecca* Hitchcock had already turned into a movie), *The Birds* lays the foundations for the modern catastrophe movie, since the invasion and the attack of the belligerent fowl has been transferred to innumerable films, from *Jaws*, through *Willard* and *Cujo*, to *The Hive*. **The power and innovation of Hitchcock's film, shot in 1963, derive from the realistic visual and audio effects (realized by Albert Whitlock), but still more from the naturalistic setting of the story, from its almost documentary feel.** Here, we are not confronted with beasties come from outer space or drooling monsters, but with common-or-garden birds, the reasons for whose errant behavior will remain a mystery.

Lastly, *North by Northwest* (1957), with a hero who—in spite of his best endeavors—has been sucked into a world of double agents and state secrets, invented all the following:

1. Conspiracy movie and the spy film (the escapist tendencies of James Bond come from here);

2. Terror in broad daylight, with the famous sequence in the desert when Cary Grant is dive-bombed by a crop-dusting plane;

3. The hero of the contemporary action movie (Bruce Willis in the *Die Hard* series, for example), who has to survive attack not only from men, but also from machines (a plane here, a huge truck in *Duel*, a cyborg in *Terminator*).

The Fog, dir. John Carpenter (1980)

The Birds, dir. Alfred Hitchcock (1963)

The Night of the Living Dead, dir. George Romero (1968)

1958

BIG DEAL ON MADONNA STREET

MARIO MONICELLI

With his 1958 film, *Big Deal on Madonna Street*, Mario Monicelli (*The Great War, An Average Little Man*) kick-started the great Italian comedy, got Vittorio Gassman to let his hair down, and at a stroke launched both Claudia Cardinale and Marcello Mastroianni. On the dilapidated roof of a housing project in a Rome *borgata*, the actor Toto, then in the twilight of his career, explains to the young Vittorio Gassman various techniques for breaking into a safe, from the "Fu Chi-Min" method (with dynamite) to the good old crowbar. For these *soliti ignoti* (in the UK it was released as *Persons Unknown*), everything hinges on getting their hands on some cash. So they dream up the crime of the century (in fact robbing an apartment over a pawnshop).

Gassman, alias "Peppe" in the film, has just assembled a gang of deadbeat burglars, a bunch of losers that postwar Italy, at the time an almost Third World society, found it so hard to find a place for. This is the key scene in the movie, an old hand at sneak jobs and a movie comic, Toto symbolically hands the torch over to a new generation of actors who, during the 1970s, were to bring such luster to Italian film.

Already an experienced filmmaker by this time, Monicelli here invents a new genre, a mix of irony and melancholy, a brilliant blend of the tenets of neorealism (recording the social realities and its depressing underbelly) and those of what will be called Italian comedy: helped by the duo Age and Scarpelli, Monicelli blows apart its taboos, just as Peppe and his gang dream of blowing off the locks to the safe. Adultery, sin, the poor, success (the invisible, unspoken element in the film)—everything is up for grabs, right down to Italy's true Achilles' heel, which the filmmaker analyzes as her disproportionate ambition, destined forever to peter out into failure.

Slinking off to nick their millions, in the fashion of Jean Servais in Dassin's *Rififi*, which the film amusingly pastiches, Peppe, Tiberio, Ferribotte, and Capannelle—hardly hardened criminals—will in the end get away with little more than a dish of pasta with chickpeas. So *Big Deal on Madonna Street*, having drunk deep at the Hollywood fantasy break-in (professionalism, competence, success), lurches violently back to the reality principle: pipe-dreaming about better days is all very well, but bellies need filling. For the poor, cloud-gazing has its limits. They reap scant reward then, and the despairing Peppe resigns himself to joining a detachment of workmen searching for a job. Toto had warned him: "Theft is a trade for serious people. You're only good enough to work!"

This melancholy comic masterpiece feeds into all those movies touched more by failure than impressed by success, from William Friedkin's *The Brink's Job* to Peter Yates's *Breaking Away*.

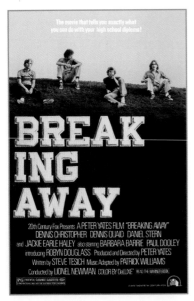

Poster for Peter Yates' Breaking Away (1979)

RIGHT AND BELOW:
Big Deal on Madonna Street,
dir. Mario Monicelli (1958)

THE TWILIGHT ZONE

SERIES CREATED BY ROD SERLING

It is October 2, 1959, and CBS is broadcasting the first episode ("The Lonely") in a series in which nobody puts much hope: a short twenty-five-minute film, shot in black and white on a modest budget in the studios of MGM. Only Rod Serling, its creator and future tsar, is convinced that the history of a man, beached up a deserted city, who little by little loses his mind, will find its audience and blossom into a vast saga for which its creator had already written dozens of scripts. But Serling was right. In a few weeks, *The Twilight Zone* became essential viewing, the channel's flagship series, a monument of creativity where hardened pros (Robert Florey, Jacques Tourneur, John Brahm) crossed paths with young Turks (Stuart Rosenberg, Don Siegel, Richard Sarafian), and declining (Ida Lupino, Buster Keaton) and emerging stars (Robert Redford, James Coburn, Charles Bronson, or Peter Falk as an operetta Castro). **Written by the book, Rod Serling's fantasy series breathed new life into TV fiction. Gingerly circumventing the censors, *The Twilight Zone* became a cruel and ironic vision of a phony and antiseptic 1950s American society, whose dark side is slyly exposed in episode after episode.** The tyranny of happiness, galloping consumerism, success at all costs, unbridled individualism, and rampant paranoia—everything was viewed through Serling's pitiless prism, as he attempted to combine his love of Shakespeare and a fondness for logical paradox.

In five seasons (1959–64) and 156 episodes, with this brilliant transposition of the literary universe of Richard Matheson (author of *I Am Legend* and high priest of contemporary fantasy literature), Serling built up an immense reservoir of storylines and motifs from which all the future masters of the genre were to draw, from Stephen King to John Carpenter. Thus the significantly entitled "Perchance to Dream" (in his nightmares, a man is pursued by a woman of deadly charm) constitutes the template for *Carnival of Souls* by Herk Harvey and for Wes Craven's extravagant *A Nightmare on Elm Street*, while "A World of Difference" (in which an employee realizes that his whole life is just a film set) contains the basis both for *In the Mouth of Madness* and *The Truman Show*. Here, no more exotic folklore tinsel, no more slimy monsters, no more howling ghouls or extraterrestrial plant life, but a sense of strange goings-on next door, of otherness at the back of the retina. With its infinite variations on relativity (for instance, the episode where a couple of playboys disfigure themselves to look like the other monsters of their species) and identity (how many times does a character realize that he is not who or what he thought he was?), *The Twilight Zone* unfolds like a meeting between Pirandello and Borges. Because here, you can't be sure of anything. Every morning, every minute, every second, the world can change. You thought you knew it? You're wrong. You thought you knew each other. You're wrong again.

After *The Twilight Zone*, the fantastic, science fiction, and a substantial part of American cinema as a whole can delve into the core of modernity. The series ran through pretty much all the key topics: the omnipresence of routine and banality; the fragmentation of the ego and its narrative avatars (the sudden appearance of doppelgängers, the indistinguishability of reality and illusion); the fragility of the real and of the experience of time (premonitions, terrifying intuitions, malfunctions of the great clock of time abound); the ontological loneliness of the individual and his need for companionship—the whole covered with a veneer of tragedy which, when it does not condemn it, recalls humankind to its moral obligations.

Lastly, Serling, ever concerned to keep viewers on tenterhooks, invented the trope of the narrative twist—that U-turn in a story that forces us to rethink everything we've just seen and envisage it from a complete different angle. Remember the Statue of Liberty emerging from the sand in the last sequence of *Planet of the Apes*: Rod Serling wrote the script.

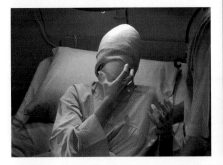

LEFT:
Detail of the poster
for Franklin J. Shaffner's
Planet of the Apes
(1968)

TOP, LEFT,
AND ABOVE:
*The Twilight
Zone*

TOP, RIGHT:
Rod Serling
presenting
*The Twilight
Zone*

1963

THE FILM OF
THE ASSASSINATION OF JFK

ABRAHAM ZAPRUDER

November 22, 1963: in the middle of his reelection campaign, John Fitzgerald Kennedy is assassinated in Dallas. Using a Super-8 camera, Abraham Zapruder, a dress manufacturer who, like thousands of other Americans at the time, was making a little home movie, happened to have the camera running as the bullet hit the President's skull. Twenty-six seconds, 477 frames of footage that rocked America, and one of the key moments in the history of the image in the twentieth century. Presumed to harbor the truth of the event, this spectacular color reel was subjected to exhaustive examinations, but no firm conclusions could ever be reached. On the contrary, the endless interpretative delirium it sparked among Americans—convinced they were living at a turning point in their history—submerged the nation in a deluge of conspiracy theories and spawned countless unseen ramifications.

Moreover, the visual shock of the muted violence in the image traumatized the nation, spilling over into a huge range of future images. In the history of US cinema, Zapruder's film functions at once as model (aesthetic, visual, thematic) and configuration: a precipitate of situations and motifs that, essentially or peripherally, stated or unstated, percolated into the cinema of Brian De Palma as early as his 1968 *Greetings*, but also into a vast swathe of the critical output of the era, from the experimental films of Bruce Conner to the conspiracy theory movies of the 1970s, as well as Andy Warhol's series and realistic horror that plainly has its roots in the assassination of JFK. Numerous films: *The Parallax View*, *Blow Out*, *The Conversation*, *Shooter*, and of course Oliver Stone's *JFK*; all the films of Arthur Penn, who acted as technical adviser to JFK at the time of his debates with Nixon, and made systematic reference to the assassination from *Bonnie and Clyde* onward (the bit of skull flying off Warren Beatty's head echoes JFK); *A Perfect World* by Clint Eastwood (which takes place on November 22, 1963), *Nashville*, Robert Altman's *Dr. T and the Women*, as well as *Snake Eyes* by Brian De Palma—all propose enthralling fictional reconfigurations of what the writer Don de Lillo in *Libra* describes as "the seven seconds that broke the back of the America century."

Some further examples of the "Zapruder configuration":

1. Murder during a parade (*Nashville*, *In the Line of Fire*, *Shooter*, *Vantage Point*, *Blow Out*)

2. The sniper: the screen as target (*Targets*, *Dirty Harry*, *The Domino Principle*, *The Day of the Jackal*, *Twilight's Last Gleaming*)

3. Splitting and splattering (*Bonnie and Clyde*, *Soldier Blue*, *Dawn of the Dead*, *The Deer Hunter*, and all realistic horror films)

4. The media and its configuration (*The Phantom of the Paradise*, *Carrie*, *The Parallax View*)

5. Amateur footage that holds the key to an investigation (*Night Moves*, *The Stunt Man*, *Special Effects*);

6. Interpretation spiraling out of control (*Greetings*, *Three Days of the Condor*, *Winter Kills*, *Blow Out*);

7. Single take vs. edit (all Brian De Palma's films);

8. Conspiracy and the net of intrigue (all films having a conspiracy as plot or subplot).

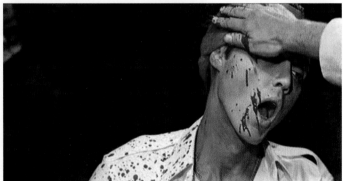

Frames from Abraham Zapruder's footage
of the assassination of JFK (1963)

The Deer Hunter, dir. Michael Cimino (1978)

1964
INFERNO
HENRI-GEORGES CLOUZOT

Inferno, dir.
Henri-Georges
Clouzot (1964)

In 1964, Henri-Georges Clouzet started shooting *Inferno* with Serge Reggiani and Romy Schneider, a strange and vast project that was halted after three weeks. Thirty years later, Chabrol picked up the script to film Clouzot's *Inferno*, a "bourgeois" film cleansed of the visual experiments of which Clouzot was so fond. In 2009, Serge Bromberg made a documentary about the genesis of *Inferno*, revealing images from a film that up to that time had remained (almost) invisible. A rare, if not unique, phenomenon in the history of cinema, *Inferno* constitutes what might be called a "retrospective matrix," the destiny of a work that was believed lost forever, like Murnau's *Four Devils*, Welles's *The Other Side of the Wind* or the complete full-length version of Stroheim's *Greed*. One of those magnificent ghosts that haunt movie history, at the same time missing links, fantasy objects for film buffs, and aborted projects about which people will always wonder "what might have been."

To see, or rather to discover, *Inferno*, is to realize how Clouzot, under the spell of Fellini's *8 1/2*, which came out the previous year, also had plans to revolutionize cinema, before becoming inextricably entangled in the ins and outs of his star-crossed shoot. "It is easy to get the public to see that a character has ten obsessions, but how can one make him feel and understand an obsession that this character has spent ten years mulling over?" Clouzot asks. Essentially, *Inferno* has its origin in an insane desire to convey the neurotic madness of a man, Marcel Prieur (played by Serge Reggiani), convinced that his wife, Odette (Romy Schneider, then twenty-six), is being unfaithful, and make it credible, tangible. "Clouzot's screenplay," Bromberg recalls, "is constructed as a flashback. Marcel Prieur stands before Romy's prone body, razor in hand. What has happened? The film was supposed to explore the possibility of this image—how did the man get there?—concluding with the words 'no end.'" **The couple's routine existence as hotelkeepers at the foot of the Garabit viaduct in the remote Cantal is shot in black and white, while Marcel's visions are in color, tinged with the madness that boils over into jealous rage.** In March 1964, Clouzot locked himself up in the Boulogne studio with a handful of technicians and began a series of visual experiments designed to materialize Prieur's obsessive jealousy. At the same time, the owners of Columbia, buoyed up by the public and critical acclaim for Kubrick's *Doctor Strangelove*, which they had just produced, were looking to bankroll another movie by a great European director. As they trawled Paris, they came across some early rushes by Clouzot. "Budget unlimited!" they cried as they left the studio. Clouzot could not know it, but this carte blanche already marked the beginning of the end for his project. It was in the 1960s, and the art scene was throbbing with electro-acoustic vibes and agog with kinetic art and Vasarely, Yvaral and co. all calling into question the logic of visual language. Clouzot threw himself body and soul into these eye-popping new techniques, shooting hours of rushes in which the actors' faces are distorted, deformed, diffracted ad infinitum, ensnared in optical illusions that generate nightmares of unparalleled formal beauty. These takes have lost nothing of their power to bewitch, as in the shots showing the light playing, whirling over Romy Schneider's face—the hypnotic vortex of the movie—which, twenty years after the famous lamp sequence in *Le Corbeau* (*The Raven*) —"Where is good, where evil?"—also convert moral uncertainty into an optical conundrum. (The same effects were reused by Michel Gondry in the video "Les Voyages immobiles," made for

Étienne Daho.) Obsessive, perfectionist, insomniac, dictatorial, Clouzot soon lost his way in a maze of his own making, the storyboard went out of the window, and, at his wits' end, Reggiani stormed off the set, soon followed by Clouzot himself, victim of a coronary. Production soon shelved *Inferno* and the insurers recovered the rushes. *Inferno*, or rather what remains of thirteen hours of printed film, has today acquired the aura of a lost treasure, a matrix lying on the borderline between the dizzying hallucinations of *Vertigo* (1958) and Maria Bava's camp *gialli*.

But it also foretold of some typical De Palma shots (in *Dressed to Kill*, in particular) and all those internalized films (from Buñuel to Polanski), hypnotized by the mystery of female desire and the representation of everyday madness.

Four years later, in 1968, Clouzot did, after all, manage to film a hell—*Woman in Chains*; a strange remake of an invisible film that one day will see the light, but entirely undetected by the radar of a critical fraternity that had forgotten him.

The Case of the Scorpion's Tale,
dir. Sergio Martino
(1971)

1964–71
LEONE'S SPAGHETTI WESTERNS

A coyote whistles, narrowed eyes occupy the entire Cinemascope screen, there's a duster coat that has seen better days, a pop soundtrack you cannot get out of your head, ruins on set or a set in ruins, and, finally, the kind of faces that would put the wind up anybody: those of Clint Eastwood, Lee Van Cleef, Eli Wallach, Henry Fonda, whom the director transformed into a dead-eyed thug in *Once Upon a Time in the West*. The merest glance suffices: it just has to be of the five spaghetti westerns Sergio Leone made between 1964 (*A Fistful of Dollars*) and 1971 (*Duck, You Sucker!*). The creator of the genre (nearly five hundred similar products hit screens between 1964 and 1975), the author of the famous Dollars Trilogy, Leone almost singlehandedly represents the high-water mark of 1960s–70s Italian cinema. This was a time when a wandering bard might stumble across an almost mute killer sporting a poncho; a world at once fun and violent, nostalgic and picaresque, raw and lyrical; a universe that spawned a wealth of images that not only the movies, but comics and advertising too, have revisited time and time again. Leone's influence was, and is, considerable, and it can be detected in the films of Michael Cimino, John Carpenter, Martin Scorsese, Quentin Tarantino, George Lucas, and in most Hollywood blockbuster series.

So, how can one reconcile the loss of innocence that has affected the movie image for some time now (Leone is a mannerist) with the desire—despite it all—to continue conjuring up its magic? How can a film with the cinema as its subtext still take the world as it actually is as its subject? What does the adult world and the world of History with a capital "H" look like through the eyes of a child who has not (yet) become disenchanted? One answer is provided by the aesthetic and formal pleasure, by the celebration of the dazzling toy that is cinema in the work of Sergio Leone.

In 1963, a renowned assistant director at Cinecittà had the bizarre notion of transplanting Kurosawa's *Yojimbo* to the heart of the American West. Leone was fascinated by the idea of a man coming out of nowhere, straightening out a conflict between two rival gangs by eradicating both. So *A Fistful of Dollars* began. Eager to revisit the western as he had the epic blockbuster (*The Colossus of Rhodes* in 1961), Leone decided to do without any women's roles (responsible, as he saw it, for the failure of numerous films), to study faces inspired by the masks of Goldoni and to fill the screen with cynical, trigger-happy ne'er-do-wells.

Initially he had envisaged giving the role of the Man with No Name to Henry Fonda, but the celebrated actor turned him down (a few months later, learning of the colossal success of the movie, he fired his agent). Leone then thought of entrusting the part to Clint Eastwood, a young actor unknown to film who starred in the American TV series, *Rawhide*: "Clint arrived," Leone recollected, "dressed with exactly the same bad taste as all American students. I didn't care. It was his face and his way of walking that I was interested in. He didn't say much … just: 'Together, we're gonna make a good western.'" Leone put a poncho on him to make him look more imposing. And a hat. Eastwood was, however, a non-smoker and had to learn how to keep the trademark hard, cough-inducing cigar in his mouth. This proved his least favorite aspect of the shoot.

The Man with No Name opened the door to the modern action hero: an individualist with a range of laconic put-downs and a deadpan humor, who has swapped empathy for cool, the knightly gallantry of yesteryear for workmanlike efficiency, and the life of a family man for that of a rider of the plains. Whether it is Bruce Willis in the *Die Hard* trilogy (John McTiernan), Clint Eastwood himself in the *Dirty Harry* series, Kurt Russell in John Carpenter's diptych (*Escape from New York* and *Escape from L.A.*), or the hired killer played by Samuel L. Jackson in *Pulp Fiction*, all testify to an eminently "Leonesque" mistrust of all ideologies and all systems.

Once Upon a Time in the West, dir. Sergio Leone (1969)

1967
BLOW-UP
MICHELANGELO ANTONIONI

The 1960s. Swinging London. One day, a fashion photographer (David Hemmings) snaps a few shots of a couple embracing in a park. Intrigued by how insistent the woman he photographed is about trying to get the film off him, he decides to develop the negatives and realizes, after a series of successive enlargements (blow-ups) that they show a corpse sticking out from behind a thicket. Adapted from a novella by Julio Cortázar (originally published in the collection *Ceremonias*), *Blow-Up* is not just a milestone in modern moviemaking but also a film with a considerable and still flourishing progeny, in the films of Dario Argento (*Deep Red*), in particular, and Brian De Palma (*Blow Out*), and Francis Ford Coppola's *The Conversation*.

Blow-Up, dir. Michelangelo Antonioni (1967)

Deep Red, dir. Dario Argento (1975)

Film critic Serge Daney has forged an extremely use-
ful expression to distinguish between what is called,
sometimes rather hastily, classic cinema, and the
modern movie. The first, he explains, is based on a
"photo-logical" pact; in other words on the belief in
the existence of a perfect overlap between vision
and knowledge. "I see, therefore I know. And, because
I know, I understand." The second runs roughshod over
this pact and forces both character and audience to
decipher, to delve into the image: a picture is no
longer straightforward and its meaning no longer
self-evident. Now, a film has to be analyzed, and viewers have to learn how to extract from it what is mean-
ingful or significant.

In *Blow-Up*, David Hemmings can look at his image all he
likes—too long, too much, perhaps, but he sees nothing of interest. In *Blow Out*, De Palma grafts the accident that scuppered
the presidential hopes of Senator Ted Kennedy in 1969 on to
the basic plot of *Blow-Up*, with John Travolta playing a sound
recordist who one fine evening unknowingly records the murder of a politician and decides to investigate the affair.

In all the movies by Argento, for whom the photographer's
experience in Antonioni's film seems seminal, each inquiry veers
into a metaphysical quest, and what is finally dredged up from
deep in the image is nothing else than a piece of the self. The
last take in *Deep Red* (1975), in which a witness to the murder
of a clairvoyant (David Hemmings again, eight years after *Blow-
Up*) spends hours replaying the murder scene to try to detect
some crucial detail, at last spotting his own reflection in a pool
of blood. Because, for Argento, the point isn't to tease out some
hidden truth from the image, nor even to develop it in the photographic sense of the term, but to literally circumscribe it,
extracting from it what lies beneath.

The image that, for Antonioni, constitutes the photographer's
visual and experiential limit (reality is unintelligible and the
closer one approaches it, the more it slips through our fingers),
becomes in Argento's films a wall that can be scaled, a thresh-
old that can be crossed, the dark side of a double-sided reality. In a sequence that reworks and amplifies the same
process as in *Blow-Up* (Hemmings explores an abandoned
villa, scratches at a drawing, and thereby discovers a sealed
room), *Deep Red* reveals and fantasizes on (a) depth absent
from Antonioni's film.

And what if the David Hemmings of *Blow- Up* had
actually been able to enter his photograph? This
is the bizarre question that *Deep Red* seems to
be asking its Antonionian model.

The Conversation, dir. Francis Ford Coppola (1974)

1967
TATI AT PLAY

The six movies of Jacques Tati, both a popular filmmaker and an inventor of forms, ruthlessly expose the vanity and absurdity of a modern world, which, in the 1960s, was lending its ears all too willingly to the sirens of progress. Returning to a long burlesque tradition born on the other side the Atlantic in the shape of Langdon, Chaplin, and Keaton, Monsieur Hulot was one of the last century's most lucid witnesses, exerting a decisive influence that surfaces in Blake Edwards' *The Party* (the villa wrecked by Peter Sellers is reminiscent of the Arpels' "home" in *My Uncle*), the lunar thrillers of Takeshi Kitano, Yves Anderson's comedies, *The Man without a Past* by Aki Kaurismäki, Elia Suleiman's *The Time that Remains*, the cinema of Swedish director Roy Andersson (*Songs from the Second Floor*), the films of Michel Gondry, and, finally, those of Sylvain Chomet (*The Triplets of Belleville*, 2003), who in 2010 brought to the screen a script penned by Tati in 1959 (*The Illusionist*).

1. The gag becomes democratic

In Tati's universe, the ingenuous Hulot stands out, follows unexpected trajectories, tests elements of the contemporary interior and shows them up as patently ridiculous. He is the man who goes against the flow, who turns things on their head, who transgresses the limits. Without meaning to, of course: Hulot *tries* to fit in with the modern world, but he just cannot make the grade. In *My Uncle*, even the Arpels' company Plastac cannot get the better of Hulot: in other words, it doesn't manage to turn him into an automaton. But, little by little, Tati the actor takes a back seat, while the director constructs each take as an open, accessible space. In a Tati movie one can sometimes spend several minutes understanding what there is to see on screen (the opening sequences of *Play Time* conveys the misleading impression that nothing is happening, while in fact it teems with understated little actions), choosing the event or individual we should concentrate on. This is a precarious, even nonexistent hierarchy in which the "star" (Hulot) can also appear as an extra. **Comedy, the gag is democratized: everyone has the right to occupy the center of the screen.**

2. Electronic nightmares

At the beginning of *Play Time*, Hulot is swallowed up by a glass building and bumps into an aged butler struggling to work a console that is supposed to put him in contact with the people upstairs. It is a dialog of the deaf between man and machine, consisting in furious onomatopoeias on one side and electronic beeps on the other. In *My Uncle*, by interfering with the electronic beam that controls the ultramodern door with which Madame Arpel has equipped her husband's garage, a dog transforms it into a prison gate. **With Tati, the slightest problem transforms these ostensibly miraculous signs of progress into the user's sworn enemies.**

3. Fear of "transparency"

"As you can see, everything's open plan!" Madame Arpel (*My Uncle*) chirrups, proud of her ultra-design villa, as comfy and as welcoming as a padded cell. Or a clinic—little Gerard, in his mother's kitchen-cum-laboratory, looks more like a patient. The polar opposite of the nouveaux riches Arpels' social exhibitionism and of the chilly panopticon of a dwelling (the all-seeing eyes of the Villa Arpel), Hulot's tumbledown house, hard to find and awash with color, is full of hiding places. In *Play Time*, Hulot passes from glass boxes to cells, connecting in a single bound the obsession with transparency *and* the increasingly penitentiary nature of our modern world. To those who accused him of a being a reactionary who despised progress, Tati's riposte was that his "satire is not directed at the places but at their use." **We need permits for building, certainly, but why not permits for living? The terror of the world of the concentration camp haunts Tati's images.**

4. Elsewhere looks just like . . . here

Rows of vehicles, lines of humans, swarms of tourists: the city in *Play Time* is all traffic, circulation, arrows and signs, impersonal buildings, minimalist furniture and malfunctioning functionality. In the foyer of the STLC company headquarters, a series of photographs hanging on the walls proudly proclaim the conglomerate's international footprint: Mexico City, Paris, London. And yet there is no way of telling the photos of the same gray skyscraper apart—apart from by the tourist sites plonked down awkwardly at the foot of the towers (a little Eiffel Tower for Paris, Big Ben for London, and so on). **In an age of globalization (converging culture, standardized architecture, homogenized desires), everything resembles everything else. Traveling to the other side of the world, one realizes that it's all much of a muchness.**

My Uncle,
dir. Jacques Tati
(1958)

The Party, dir. Blake Edwards (1968)

1967

THE PRISONER

SERIES CREATED BY PATRICK MCGOOHAN

Every year, on the occasion of the Portmeirion Village Official Convention, hordes of *Prisoner* fans undertake their pilgrimage to the Welsh village where the cult TV series was made more than thirty years ago, and reenact some of its choicest episodes. Wreathed in smiles and dressed for the part, each takes on the role of one of the village inhabitants, from the nondescript Number Two to the recalcitrant rebel, Number Six. The reconstruction is perfect and goes so far as to let loose on the (playacting) fugitives a copy of the emblem of the series, Rover: the white, balloon-like entity that engulfs all those who try to escape—and that Woody Allen transformed into a giant breast nursing its victims to death in one of the funnier sketches in *Everything You Always Wanted to Know About Sex But Were Afraid to Ask* (1972).

Once the party is over, these actors-for-a-day return home, reassured on at least one point: if they play at being supervised, classified, listed, and manipulated there, in the Welsh village, it is because in their world, without doubt, they enjoy greater freedom. Where they live, one doesn't have to run for one's life down a beachfront to assert one's individuality; there is no need, either, to knock on an overseer's door to take instructions as to how to exist. In recreating the negative of their reality in a fiction that may be fun but is nonetheless terrifying, the pilgrims of Portmeirion can bask in the notion that, in the last analysis, their little world is not so bad. Almost livable, in fact. A cathartic experience, then? Clearly, yes. But therein lies the error. Let us recall the village in the series imagined by Patrick McGoohan in 1967: Disneyland reanalyzed by Jean Baudrillard, with Mickey Mouse's po < as the tree that hides the forest—even when what lies behind has a face as pretty as Snow White's. The ancestor of the prison village in *The Truman Show*, Portemeirion resembles a prophetic forerunner of what is called today the "global village," an expression as inoffensive as the beatific smiles of the numbered villagers, but in fact synonymous with a soft-sell apocalypse: behind the jokey façade, behind the inhabitants' colorful garb (like in Pluto's nose or under Donald Duck's paunch), beyond the vacant eye-sockets on the plaster statues that stud the little town like watchtowers, what does one see? CCTV, surveillance and tracking devices, long-range microphones, video monitors: the same that follow our every move down subway corridors, along the street, in banks and department stores.

You think you're a free man? And yet, with your social security, telephone, and PIN numbers; your bank codes, your account details, and store card; your passport and ID numbers: you're little better than Number Six. Everywhere the same processes, the same thoughts, the same taboos, and the same ideas. What can we do? Where can we live? At the end of the series, having shaken off innumerable Number Twos, Number Six finally meets someone he believes to be the Village's real big cheese. But what's this? Number One, Big Brother, does not exist! The final lesson of *The Prisoner* is then preeminently pessimistic: power and all its consequences (oppression, repression, manipulation) has no leader: it is delocalized, exploded, formless—everywhere and nowhere at the same time. *The Prisoner* is not an allegory, but without doubt the most disturbing political documentary about our era ever made.

The Truman Show, dir. Peter Weir (1998)

Patrick McGoohan

The village of Portmeirion today

THE MELVILLE MODEL

Le Cercle rouge, dir. Jean-Pierre Melville (1970)

Melancholy, a relaxed manner with genre (here, crime fiction), ghostly worlds, a fascination with death, a minimalist, hieratic acting style (the paragon being Alain Delon), existential solitude, fetishism: these are some of hallmarks of the immensely influential Jean-Pierre Melville, creator of movies such as Bob le Flambeur, Le Samouraï, Le Cercle rouge, and Dirty Money, his last film, made in 1972.

From Le Samouraï onwards, Jean-Pierre Melville focused more intensely on the two essential tendencies in his movies: on one side, the childlike desire to reaffirm the magic of the cinema, and on the other, the extreme sensitivity (it could be termed "melancholy") of men, out of their time, moving through a world to which they no longer belong.

For, in the end, what have Melville's men lost? An American classic cinema that had entered its twilight years, leaving us to artificially resuscitate its talismans; a peculiar chapter in French history (the Resistance, or that imaginary place reactivated by its telltale imagery where its values would still have currency: Vogel, at the beginning of Le Cercle rouge, or the Samurai, harassed by an oppressive bureaucratic octopus that deploys methods of heavy-handed policing and intimidation resembling those of the Gestapo); men with a sense of sacrifice, of professionalism, and abnegation; finally, a youth for whom even (especially?) children's games had to be taken with the utmost seriousness.

The aesthetic influence that the movies of Melville have exerted on contemporary cinema is consider-able: in Japan, the crime movies of Hideo Gosha and Seijun Suzuki (Branded to Kill) convert the customary ghostly hired killers into Japanese, baroque, and colorful avatars of Melville's samurai. **In Hong Kong** all the tight-lipped killers of Johnnie To (from The Mission to Vengeance) and especially The Killer (1989), in which John Woo (who long cherished the dream of remaking Le Cercle rouge), cast the then local star, Chow Yun-Fat, in the role of a hired assassin directly inspired by Le Samouraï. **In Italy**, the films of Fernando di Leo (The Italian Connection, The Boss), a filmmaker who, in the early 1970s, was within a whisker of working with Melville. **In the United States**, the films of Michael Winner (The Mechanics, 1972), Quentin Tarantino (Reservoir Dogs, especially), Jim Jarmusch

(*Ghost Dog*), Abel Ferrara (Christopher Walken in *The King of New York*) and Michael Mann (the De Niro/Pacino twosome in *Heat*, over which flits little more than the ghost of those virile friendships that, beyond their origins and their professions, binds the male characters in Melville); the break-in in Mann's *Thief*, worthy of *Bob le Flambeur*, and the opening frames of *Public Enemy*, again lifted from *Le Deuxième souffle*. **In France**, the torch has been held aloft primarily by Alain Corneau (*Police Python 357*, *The Second Wind*, a remake of *Le Deuxième souffle*), a great admirer and exegete of Melville's cinema.

Ghost Dog,
dir. Jim Jarmusch
(1999)

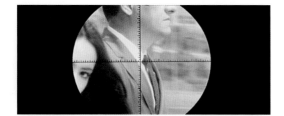

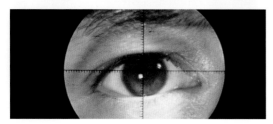

Branded to Kill, dir. Seijun Suzuki (1967)

Heat, dir. Michael Mann (1997)

1968
NIGHT OF THE LIVING DEAD
GEORGE ROMERO

Together with *Psycho*, this is perhaps the most famous horror movie in the whole history of cinema. George Romero was only twenty-eight when he made it. He had $115,000 in his pocket, black-and-white film stock, and, most importantly, an idea: to adapt *I Am Legend*, Richard Matheson's famous novel, written in 1954. The plot of *Night of the Living Dead* is simple and effective: following a catastrophe of unexplained origin, the dead return to life and invade the surface of the earth in search of living flesh to consume. Romero prunes all folksy paraphernalia from the horror genre. Unlike the voodoo tradition exploited by Victor Halperin in *White Zombie* and Jacques Tourneur in *I Walked with a Zombie*, Romero's zombies have entered adulthood, evolving from myth into news item. When it was released on October 1, 1968, *Night of the Living Dead*, with its almost documentary style and its "live report" look, resonated both with films of the terrible events in Vietnam and with the gory footage of the assassination of President Kennedy.

In grainy black and white, its strange angles, razor-sharp editing, unknown actors, and tellingly commonplace details, Romero's movie presents all the marks of a frontline dispatch, beginning with a direction providing a fragile description of a monstrous event filmed, as it were, live. With the zombie, a transparent metaphor for an America in meltdown

from which the suppressed will emerge whether one wants it or not, Romero shifts the horror movie onto an explicitly political level, inventing a figure that encapsulates the desire for change. To use philosopher Clement Rosset's description of the "idiocy of reality," the zombie embodies "the encounter between an aim that seems absolutely determined and an absolutely absent motivation." A senseless, polysemic block; a sponge that has soaked up every terror of its age—today, as yesterday, the zombie stands for a new society determined to "absorb" the old one.

After *Dawn of the Dead*, and its radical critique of the blandishments of consumerism (of capitalism, with its cannibalistic principle, 1979), Romero continued the series with *Day of the Dead* (a satiric lampoon on the excesses of science and the temptations of total security, 1985), *Land of the Dead*, a caustic fable on post-9/11 America (fear of a terrifying world, paranoia, and the desire to hunker down, 2005), and *Diary of the Dead* (2008). Here, in an attempt to ward off the chaos that ensues after the sudden and inexplicable return of the dead to life, some film students decide to point their cameras at the phenomenon. By then sixty-eight, Romero had lost nothing of his typically post-Watergate skepticism with regard to the mass media, doubts perfectly integrated by the YouTube generation and by the characters in *Diary of the Dead*, who, unconvinced by the official version of events peddled by the networks, decide to find out what's really afoot by exploring the margins (the Internet, blogs, video-sharing sites, diaries, etc.). Jason Creed, the apprentice filmmaker of the movie whose posthumous work the movie presents (The *Death of Death*, a documentary consisting of videos from a variety of sources), places total credence in a law pronounced by one of his companions in the film milieu: "panic starts when one doesn't know the truth." But, more subtle and successful than Brian De Palma's *Redacted* (here, the proliferation of images is not just a rationale for returning to readable, linear narratives), *Diary of the Dead* brilliantly disentangles the spider's web of our techno-media utopia: the truth of an event—and it does not matter whether that is the war in Iraq or a zombie invasion—depends perhaps merely on the number of eyes that witness it. **After the suspicion of the "great lie" (Nixon's America with its "plumbers") comes the time of generalized noise. "Information devours its content,"** wrote Jean Baudrillard in *Simulacra and Simulation,* **"instead of communicating, it is exhausted in the production of communication."** In *Diary of the Dead,* galloping information overload produces a neutralization of "reality" (film consists in the dual operation of protecting oneself against the horror of the world and immunizing oneself against the reality one records), as well as a deflation and collapse of meaning, since no more is known at the end than at the beginning. **At root, the image of reality is, for reality, what the zombie is for us: a pale copy of the living, its devitalized but proliferating simulacrum, governed by a unique, deranged compulsion—images for the one; flesh for the other.**

FACING PAGE:
Night of the Living Dead,
dir. George Romero
(1968)

Assault on Precinct 13,
dir. John Carpenter
(1976)

Land of the Dead,
dir. George Romero
(2005)

1968
BULLITT
PETER YATES

First and foremost, there's Steve McQueen. William Friedkin, who'd offered him the star role in *Sorcerer*, said one day that a close-up of McQueen's face was worth all the scenery in the world. His presence on the screen, even unmoving and unspeaking (or almost), gives density to any shot—an indefinable power, composed of mystery, refinement, and charisma. **Attracting the eye like a magnet, McQueen presents a wonderful condensate of two qualities in which the American movie specializes: professionalism (whether a police officer, gambler, burglar, or businessman, McQueen is always the best), and a systematic mistrust of words: a man who does things well, who does things right, doesn't need to say much.**

Bullitt,
dir. Peter Yates
(1968)

One of *the* great American actors, then. Before him, John Wayne and Henry Fonda; after him, Al Pacino, Robert De Niro, and Christopher Walken. *Bullitt* resembles McQueen, its speed is his speed, its elegance his elegance. Lalo Schifrin's jazzy score, the cops and the gangsters in suits, the gleaming streets of San Francisco, the ease and confidence of the direction, *Bullitt* seems to bend with its star—like *The Thomas Crown Affair*, shot by Norman Jewison at the same time, or *Junior Bonner*, which Sam Peckinpah made three years later. The very pace of the movie (the cool rhythm of narrative and its violent accelerations) reverberates with the actor's style, with his economy of means.

McQueen approaches every scene in two stages but in the same way: first of all, entering into shot, he spends a certain time checking his surroundings, decoding the environment, weighing up the situation. One must act, certainly, but one must act right. McQueen is then reduced to his gaze (spotting a suspect in the middle of a crowd, rifling through the contents of a suitcase, observing a surgical operation) and the direction moves at the same pace, at his pace: it marks time. Then it shows us what he sees, what he's looking for. Like him, it reconsiders events, shoots the same place twice, and follows the faces, the images, that McQueen follows (see the impressive credits sequence where the images

overlap or interlock). Second stage: McQueen crashes through the gears and leaps into action. He has located his prey. The music of Schifrin goes quiet and lets the engines of the famous Ford Mustang roar. A ten-minute car chase in the hilly streets of San Francisco, the camera clamped to the passenger seat: no one had ever seen that before.

In this bravura passage, plot is put on hold, while the gleaming machine of the cinema goes at full pelt. On paper, *Bullitt* is just another crime thriller: in San Francisco, an inspector has the mission of protecting a mobster for a corrupt politician who hopes to benefit from his testimony against the Organization before a Federal court.

To Live and Die in L.A., dir. William Friedkin (1988)

Shot in 1968, Peter Yates's film marks a turning point in the American crime movie for at least two reasons.

1. Frank Bullitt, a cop who's really straight but who's forced to go crooked to enforce the law opened the breach for the heroes of the many new-look thrillers of the 1970s, such as *Madigan* (Don Siegel), Harry Callahan (*Dirty Harry*) and Popeye Doyle (*The French Connection*). Calculated violence and corruption at City Hall, the America of Watergate quietly shows its face.

2. With the central sequence of the chase, *Bullitt* invented and fixed the code of the modern action movie—its star turn, its henceforth obligatory tour de force, from the Jason Bourne trilogy to *Matrix*.

The Bourne Supremacy, dir. Paul Greengrass (2003)

1968–80
THE KUBRICK MATRIX

Even for experts in Kubrickology, it is no easy task to point to an heir presumptive to Stanley Kubrick. And yet, patently, *2001: A Space Odyssey*, *A Clockwork Orange*, and *The Shining* are milestones, not only in the history of cinema, but also in criticism generally. The name Kubrick is rolled out to characterize relatively conceptual, stylistically cold works that harbor the (inevitably exaggerated) ambition to describe the world in a single sweep, whether they are the films of Gaspar Noé (*Enter the Void* or *Irreversible*, with its explicit references to *2001*); *The Tree of Life*, Terrence Malick's worthy Christian exercise; or *Inception* (Christopher Nolan, 2010).

The primary reason why the maker of *Full Metal Jacket* has not left one natural torchbearer derives from the very nature of a project which, in film after film, tackles a well-defined genre with the insane ambition to produce something that would be at once its synthesis and its culmination: who would dare make a space opera after *2001*, a film with a haunted house and a ghost after *The Shining*, a "period" film after the utter perfection attained by *Barry Lyndon*?

Kubrick's style, embodied in twelve films, has percolated through to a large slice of contemporary cinema, beginning with those who fell directly under the master's spell. Let's skate over the strange case of Peter Hyams and his *2010: The Year We Make Contact* (1985), a self-confessed sequel to *2001*, based on the cinematographic solecism of trying to explain away the mystery of the famous black monolith, when the power of its abstract form lies precisely in the vast range of hypothetical interpretations it permits. What Steven Spielberg tried to do in the year 2001 proves more interesting. Returning to an unfinished project on which Kubrick had been working since the 1970s, a kind of modern-day *Pinocchio*, *A.I.* is a hybrid film that owes as much to Kubrick (in the first part with its clinical description of the life of a child robot and a passion for technology that is shared by the director of *Close Encounters of the Third Kind*) as to Steven Spielberg (the second part and the thematic of the abandoned child). Whosoever has seen a Kubrick movie knows he has little truck with sentimentality: a metaphysical enigma in whose shadow humans resemble puppets on

a string or hamsters running round a wheel (*2001*), a catastrophic version of family relationships (*The Shining*), a blood-chilling vision of the political use of violence in societies that confuse civilization and conformity (the "Ludovico technique" in *A Clockwork Orange*)—all these examples make philosopher Gilles Deleuze's description of Kubrick's films as "brain-films" appear justified.

And what are "brain-films"? Films controlled less by emotion or by particular individuals than by ideas; films that convey the physical sensation of enclosed, autonomous universes with their own procedures, codes, and rituals (see Haneke's *White Ribbon*, all of David Fincher's movies, *Inception*); films obsessed by the endless conflict between (self-) control and drive (hence the connection between the bone and the spacecraft in *2001*, or the bourgeois universe of *Eyes Wide Shut*, which, once the mask falls, breaks down totally), and finally films that embody a chilly stylistic perfectionism (as sometimes with Michael Mann), discernible in particular in Kubrick's typical way of folding up the world inside geometrical figures and shapes.

A word, finally, about Stanley Kubrick the "super auteur," a filmmaker who worked right in the middle of the Hollywood system (with Warner Brothers after *2001*), and yet who managed to remain independent and exert absolute control over each of his films (whether on technical issues or regarding the choice of the foreign actors employed for the dubbed versions). There can be no doubt that this exceptional status, thanks to which Kubrick achieved what Orson Welles failed to do, continues to float temptingly before the eyes of a considerable number of contemporary directors, who, from Spielberg to Michael Mann, dream of what was a freedom almost unique in the whole history of cinema.

2001: A Space
Odyssey,
dir. Stanley Kubrick
(1968)

The Warriors,
dir. Walter Hill
(1980)

Inception,
dir. Christopher
Nolan (2010)

A Clockwork Orange, dir. Stanley Kubrick (1971)

1969
EASY RIDER
DENNIS HOPPER

There is a sequence in *Easy Rider* (1969) that shows Dennis Hopper repairing his motorcycle while at the same time in the background a horse is being shoed. A limpid metaphor: the road movie is a western on tarmac. After *Easy Rider*, cinema takes to the road. The road, a place of excess, of a desire for freedom, becomes the ultimate means of escaping a hidebound society. The conquest of the West is no more. The cinema invents the road movie (*Two-Lane Blacktop, Duel, Convoy, The Scarecrow, Wanda, Thunderbolt and Lightfoot*, then *Thelma and Louise, Natural Born Killers, Rain Man*, and *My Own Private Idaho*). **No longer does one defend one's territory tooth and nail: the new American hero is a vagrant, always on the move, crisscrossing the wide-open spaces in search of long-lost origins and an America of legend (the sunset over Monument Valley that Hopper and Fonda enjoy in *Easy Rider*). Hit the road! It doesn't matter where it takes us; anyway, it doesn't lead anywhere. Let's get drunk with the miles, eat the tarmac, reenact the Far West adventures of the wagon train on one last fling; take time out to reread the history of America.**

In 1971, Richard Sarafian made *Vanishing Point*, the undoubted paragon of what is today dubbed (often loosely) the road movie, since this hybrid genre—whose name was coined after the release of *Easy Rider*—insists less on the road itself than on the route taken by an individual or a group through a generally hostile space. *Vanishing Point* opens with a lengthy, circular, panoramic view down an ordinary road—that is to say, with a movement (the circle) that immediately contradicts the promise of rectilinearity offered by the ribbon of tar, that favorite trope of the genre. Then, two giant excavators surge into shot and block the road, while a crowd of wild-eyed locals look on and a television crew gets to work. The beginning of the film records the disappearance of a world (the Old West, with its dilapidated clapboard houses and its ghostly-looking inhabitants) and the aggressive emergence of the industrial complex and its police. Because, historically speaking, the desire for wilderness articulated by the road movie comes *too late*: after the freeways, after the establishment of the national parks, after every inch of the land has been mapped.

One night, car deliveryman Kowalski turns up at a seedy garage in Denver, from where he convinces his employer to let him set out for San Francisco. After first going to see a pimp who keeps him supplied with amphetamines, Kowalski, aboard a supercharged white Dodge Challenger, lays a bet he can drive between the two cities in no more than fifteen hours. The following day, refusing to comply with a routine police check, he speeds off with officers statewide in hot pursuit. The car chase, however, soon morphs into an existential quest, with a running commentary by Kowalski's spiritual guru, Supersoul, a blind, black DJ. **From Colorado to California, from East to West, Kowalski leaves all his pursuers choking on dust, in the eyes of the miscellaneous nobodies he meets, he embodies the quintessence of the "loser"—a symbol of America's "lost" illusions.** This is the other meaning of vanishing point: the point at which the ideals of the 1960s—of which Kowalski represents one last throw of the dice and the most splendid of tombs—converge and finally disappear.

This "last American hero for whom speed means freedom of soul" (as one of the characters in the movie has it) finally arrives at the end of his blazing and yet nihilistic quest: with a smile on his lips, his face illumined by a black sun, Kowalski hurtles towards death, and, through it, wins his freedom. Dennis Hopper's movie has of course a few ancestors (from Chaplin's *The Immigrant* to John Ford's *The Grapes of Wrath*), but the heirs to the genre founded by *Easy Rider* were truly legion.

Vanishing Point,
dir. Richard Sarafian
(1971)

Thelma and
Louise, dir. Ridley
Scott (1991)

Easy Rider, dir. Dennis Hopper (1969)

1972
AGUIRRE
OR THE WRATH OF GOD
WERNER HERZOG

It is the year 1560. It all starts somewhere between sky and earth, on a peak in the Andes cordillera, wreathed in cloud. In opening shots of breathtaking beauty, accompanied by the electronic music of the group Popol Vuh, a troop of conquistadores meanders up and down the precipitous tracks of an uncharted, wild world. **The image shows a minuscule smear of humanity, overwhelmed by the magnificence of nature and soon to be decimated by invisible Indians.**

It is not for nothing that Werner Herzog has been dubbed the worthy heir to German Romanticism, a motion-picture Caspar David Friedrich. A tragedy filmed like a war report, a heady trip that propels us into the brain of a madman, *Aguirre* (camera on the shoulder, mud splashing on the lens, head shots, etc.) proves this in almost every shot. Pantheist and mystical it certainly is; but Herzog's cinema does not believe in God (see the treatment of the monk Gaspar de Carvajal, whose journal forms the narrative voice-over), just in the anger that nature will always wield against those who dare defy her—first and foremost on Don Lope de Aguirre, a brutal adventurer played by the gut-wrenching Klaus Kinski, in his tortoise-like descent from mutiny against the Crown of Spain to an expedition in quest of the fatal mirage of El Dorado. From the Andes to the River Urubamba, numbed, dazed, peppered with arrows, racked by fever, heat, and death, the troop slows and finally comes to a dead stop. It thus slides from sublime baroque of the initial search to the grotesque fiasco of its conclusion, from the trail on the mountainside to a final circle, a figure of eternal return and the gradual ensnaring of a glorious tyrant, captive of a destiny from which he cannot, will not, escape.

Aguirre or the Wrath of God, dir. Werner Herzog (1972)

Created in 1972, *Aguirre* is not only provides a model for the great American river pictures of the 1970s, and in particular *Apocalypse Now* (Colonel Kurtz on a raft), as well as for the pseudo-naturalism of the "cannibal" movies produced in bulk by Italian directors, but also an extraordinary document in terms of its own shooting conditions (which Herzog turned to good account): seven exhausting weeks marked by, among other things, death threats against Kinski, whose megalomania ended up driving the indigenous people to distraction.

Sorcerer, dir. William Friedkin (1978)

Apocalypse Now, dir. Francis Ford Coppola (1979)

Deliverance, dir. John Boorman (1972)

1983
SCARFACE
BRIAN DE PALMA

On the Mount Rushmore of contemporary legends, Tony Montana today sits enthroned between Che Guevara and Jim Morrison, Marilyn Monroe, and Bob Marley. After a handful of cult films (*Phantom of the Paradise*, *Carrie*, *Dressed to Kill*), Brian De Palma forsook his Hitchcockian heritage and embarked on a remake of *Scarface*, the film noir masterpiece directed by Howard Hawks in 1931. But, far from making a faithful adaptation, the work composed by Brian De Palma, who had little liking for Hawks's version, together with screenwriter Oliver Stone, was instead exalted and excessive, flamboyant and savage. **Through the story of one Cuban refugee (Al Pacino), eager to live the American dream to the hilt, whatever the cost, *Scarface* articulates a virulent critique of the basic values of the United States: money, power, an easy lay—Tony Montana wants it all. His drive to the top is such (the film ends symbolically by him plunged into a fountain above which towers a sphere inscribed with the words: "The World Is Yours") that he will stop at nothing to get there. Everything (drugs, murder, every kind of dirty deal), except when it comes to slaughtering the children of a diplomat—a refusal which kicks off his decline, and a key scene in the movie.**

Al Pacino here gives one of his most outstanding performances: over the top, fearless, paranoid, fighting, alone, against an army besieging his Miami villa, finishing headfirst in a mountain of cocaine. In this inexorable descent into a hysteria leading to Montana's ruin, Pacino's acting style reminds one less of Paul Muni (the "Scarface" of Hawks) than of James Cagney, whose interpretation in Raoul Walsh's *White Heat* also borders on lunacy. From the unbearable chainsaw murder of one of Montana's brothers-in-arms in a bathtub, up to the finale, a mixture of violence, cruelty, and madness, to music by Giorgio Moroder (*Flashdance*), a star film composer of the 1980s, *Scarface* deals in set piece after set piece. It is also the film that finally handed a role worthy of her talents to Michelle Pfeiffer, a human jewel prepared to cede her body to the highest bidder.

Over time, *Scarface* acquired the status of a cult film (thousands of DVDs are sold every year) and Tony Montana became an icon whose influence over successive generations is still strong. An icon endlessly reprocessed by the cinema (for movies about the mob, there is a "before" and an "after" *Scarface*), merchandising (posters, T-shirts, graphic novels, figurines, and other derived products), and the imagery of gangsta rap, entirely predicated on rehashing the motifs and themes of Palma's film (vulgarity, machismo, an eye for an eye, conspicuous consumption, and dreadful taste). **The magicians of the console too have appropriate *Scarface*'s universe and, in addition to a direct adaptation of the movie (*The World Is Yours*, developed by Radical Entertainment), innumerable video games have fallen into its orbit.** These include the *GTA* (*Grand Theft Auto*) franchise, a colossal market success developed by Rockstar Games in 1997: a pixelated and radical version of the left-field gangster movie (Bellic, the hero of *GTA 4*, is a Euro clone of Tony Montana). The series unfolds in a saga in which capitalist principles are rigorously applied, but in the service of crime. Reworking the political stance of *Scarface*, the game resolves into a wholesale critique of the American model and the American dream. After all, isn't every empire, economic and/or criminal, founded on the same principles?

Scarface, dir. Brian De Palma (1983)

30 FILMMAKERS

VVhy Michael Mann but not Martin Scorsese? Tsui Hark and not VVong Kar-VVai? Bruno Dumont rather than Arnaud Desplechin? VVerner Herzog and not VVim VVenders? As with all art forms, cinema is hard to classify. The following selection of thirty filmmakers, intended to be representative of what might be called "contemporary" film, is based not only on subjective choice (priority is given to creators of visions and forms), but also on the premise that they are still actively making movies. Regrettably absent from this shortlist are Abel Ferrara, Ridley Scott, Alain Resnais, Michael Cimino, Darren Aronofsky, Jean-Claude Brisseau, John McTiernan, James Cameron, Tim Burton, Jim Jarmusch, Brian De Palma, Francis Ford Coppola, Milos Forman, Hou Hsiao-Hsien, John VVoo, Pedro Almodóvar, Gus Van Sant, Steven Soderbergh, Michel Gondry, and Kiyoshi Kurosavva.

PAUL THOMAS ANDERSON (born 1970)

Career

Paul Thomas Anderson began as an assistant TV producer, making a short in 1993 called *Cigarettes and Coffee*. After *Hard Eight*, his first film in 1996, he shot *Boogie Nights* (1998), a orchestral and virtuoso chronicle set in the world of the porn industry. It describes the transition between the euphoria of the 1970s (Dirk Diggler, the central character of the movie, is inspired by porn star John Holmes) and the slumps of the 1980s. Thanks to the immense success of the film, the following year Anderson started work on *Magnolia*, a three-hour saga with Tom Cruise, in which the director further extended his tangled storylines and propensity for converging or intersecting destinies. In 2001, Anderson changed tack and narrative universe, producing a sentimental comedy (*Punch Drunk Love*) that told of the complicated, sometimes plainly deranged relationship between the timorous boss of a small company (Adam Sandler) and a mysterious woman (Emily Watson). With *There Will Be Blood* in 2007, Paul Thomas Anderson once again extended his register with a virulent critique of the myth of the self-made man, showing the inner conflict between dog-eat-dog capitalism and religious obscurantism—that is to say, the two faces of the American success story and of the empire builders who formed the nation.

Style

As putative heir to Robert Altman (*A Wedding*, *Nashville*, and *Shorts Cuts* are models that immediately spring to mind), and to Jonathan Demme (*Something Wild*, *Philadelphia*), Paul Thomas Anderson betrays a taste for polyphonic compositions, for rhyme and counterpoint. Knowing how to alternate long sequence shots (*Boogie Nights*) with frantic hand-held interludes (*Magnolia*), Anderson's operatic style interlards the ordinary and the lyrical, naturalism and the fantastic (the deluge of frogs that closes *Magnolia*), adagio and aria (Tom Cruise's lengthy monologues). The (hard-won) establishment of a community is one of his major subjects: the close-knit world of *Boogie Nights* is centered on a paternal figure (Burt Reynolds), porn mentor and guru; the waltz of characters in *Magnolia* always returns to fathers who find themselves weighed down by errors of the past; Adam Sandler's extended family in *Punch Drunk Love* mollycoddles him to the point of suffocation; while, for the hero of *There Will Be Blood*, a mere hint of kinship is enough to spark murderous intent. Less political than the films of Altman, who deploys his communities as metaphors for an America whose vices his movies dissect, Paul Thomas Anderson organizes his around the solitary, anomic individual of contemporary society, unable to communicate with other people.

Film THERE WILL BE BLOOD (2007)

Three hours of fury and excess, between George Stevens's *Giant* (with Rock Hudson as a paranoid monster) and *Citizen Kane* (if Orson Welles had been an oil tycoon). Beneath a blazing sun in a parched land in the southern United States at the beginning of the last century, a band of pioneers contract a fever for filthy lucre. Among them, Daniel Plainview (Daniel Day Lewis), a worker already fascinated by the mirage of oil and prepared to do whatever it takes to secure its rewards, digs and digs for a gusher. In spite of his companions dropping like flies, their heads smashed to pieces by a nodding donkey, in spite of the gravel and the dust in his windpipe, in spite of the oppressive heat and a crushed leg, the man just keeps on digging. Until one day, oil spurts from the bowels of this inhospitable soil. With lightning speed, Plainview grows rich, leaving with his son for Little Boston, a village in deepest California built on a gigantic oil field. In the midst of this scarred desert, there is nothing but the Church of the Third Revelation, run by an angel-faced priest, Eli Sunday, a starry-eyed charlatan who also dreams of rich pickings from the black gold. He will be the only one to stand up to Plainview—or, rather, the only one to put up the little resistance he can, before ending up with his head crushed to a pulp in a bowling alley in Plainview's mansion. Freely adapted from a novel by Upton Sinclair entitled *Oil!*, *There Will Be Blood* sticks unflinchingly to its central character's terrifying obsession, to his awesome capacity to destroy all around him: Plainview never doubts—not himself (he will make a fortune against Man, God, and the World), not others, and not the humanity he detests and swindles, execrates and crushes beneath hobnailed boots. Nothing will ever shake his determination: not his son, whom he uses as bait to expropriate some local farmers before throwing him aside without the least compassion, nor a man who turns up one day claiming to be his brother, and whom Plainview dispatches with a bullet in his head. For him, the end justifies the means, be it lies, sin, corruption, or murder. Plainview will finish like Kane, wandering like a ghost through his sumptuous residence, a sour multimillionaire, continuing to spew gall and hatred for his fellow man right up to the very last take. One difference: unlike Welles's tycoon, there's no Rosebud, no philanthropic inclinations, and so, for an equivalent of a man so irremediably unsympathetic and hopelessly touching, one thinks more of Kubrick (in the last sequence of the movie). And why touching? Because he is motivated, not by narcissism, but by a pathological obsession for success that becomes almost abstract, and by the certainty that, at the end of a road paved with dollars and pain, it is man himself who is surplus to requirements. Plainview: the last man standing.

Punch Drunk Love, dir. Paul Thomas Anderson (2001)

WES ANDERSON (born 1969)

Career

After studying philosophy, Wes Anderson turned to the cinema, directing his first film in 1996 (*Bottle Rocket*, a short student film developed into a feature), and becoming a director to watch in American independent cinema with *Rushmore* (1998), whose working methods became a credo: a tight group of collaborators and actors; the importance attached to improvisation; a predilection for working on location—as with the boat in *The Life Aquatic*. In 2001, he made *The Royal Tenenbaums*, then *The Life Aquatic* (with Bill Murray in a role parodying Commander Jacques Cousteau). In 2007 he made a movie (*The Darjeeling Limited*) whose storyline (convinced by one of their number, three American brothers go to India to reunite the family) is misleading, since it contains the promise of a journey and thus of an opening out into the world. In fact, conforming to the claustrophilic tendency of all Anderson's films, none of this will come to pass. Like the theatrical release poster for *The Life Aquatic with Steve Zissou*, with its down-in-the-mouth family cooped up in a bathyscaphe, *The Darjeeling Limited* quickly locks itself away into a compartment on a train that resembles a toy. The movies Wes Anderson constructs are essentially autistic—a bubble-cinema entirely turned in on itself, with awkward, ill-at-ease characters. The film stands the eternal Hindu-inspired trip imagined by Westerners on its head. From afar, it's all there (venomous snakes, heady scents, natives in turbans, turquoise interiors) but, as we draw nearer, this satisfying feeling of remoteness recedes: the inhabitants all speak excellent English, our three brave adventurers take part in rituals they make no effort to understand, and the film chugs along to the tune of Joe Dassin's "Aux Champs-Elysées."

Style

The key period in Anderson's cinema is the 1970s, as shown by his choice of actors (Gene Hackman, Angelica Huston) and music (The Stones' "Ruby Tuesday" and Simon and Garfunkel in *Rushmore*), his abundant movie references (the theatrical happenings in *Rushmore* revisit *Serpico*), his favorite directors (the Peter Bogdanovich of *What's Up Doc?* and *They All Laughed*, films to which the comedies of Anderson owe a great deal). Then finally there's the desire felt by Anderson's characters to hide away from the world; this stems directly from Mike Nichols's *The Graduate* (1967), that other aesthetic matrix of the autism that pervades his movies. Anderson's cinema forms part of that venerable tradition of the burlesque (from Keaton to Blake Edwards), constituting the extreme limit of its exploration of melancholy. In accordance with a logic of "overflow," reminiscent as much of the cinema of the Marx Brothers as the later work of Preston Sturges (*Sullivan's Travels*, *Lady Eve*), Anderson's dialog is involved and the screen often saturated with information. At the same time, Anderson's modern-day characters use language rather than action. They talk all the time, but they have nothing to say. In the *Royal Tenenbaums*, Chas (Ben Stiller) is the very embodiment of this propensity, with his pointless chatter and aimless hyperactivity, gesticulating and rushing about to no good purpose. Conversely, or rather at the other end of the spectrum, the Margot/Richie duet is the quintessence of stasis, incapable of any action at all (they spend their time cooped up in a tent or soaking in the bathtub).

Two tendencies inform contemporary American comedy. On one side, the Farrelly brothers, who career down the entropic line of Keystone and Blake Edwards's *The Party* (some banal incident degenerates and triggers the final, collective catastrophe); on the other, the cinema of Wes Anderson, whose melancholy a priori contravenes the laws of the genre as it postulates the impossibility and uselessness of trying to modify the environment, relegating all those who live in it to the margins of events and situations, transforming those supposed to make things happen into impotent witnesses with all the distance, self-awareness, and "*meta-*" of modern individuals—features which, on the face of it, hardly square with the dynamics of spoof comedy. From this point of view, Droopy, the iconic dog in the Tex Avery cartoons (a figure actor Bill Murray might have been born to play), is one of the indisputable sources of Anderson's cinema, which recycles the rhetorical figures of the burlesque (the chases, the absurdity, the frontal shots, the chatter, etc.), but systematically inverts their value. Wes Anderson, a modern burlesque?

The Life Aquatic with Steve Zissou, dir. Wes Anderson (2003)

Film FANTASTIC MR. FOX

If one remembers the animated sequences punctuating *The Life Aquatic with Steve Zissou* or the ill-fitting, skin-deep adulthood on which the immature heroes of *The Royal Tenenbaums* and *Rushmore* were already choking, one should hardly be surprised by this shift to old-school animation (one thinks of Ladislas Starevich, the pioneer of stop-motion). Not really a departure at all then, this exercise in false trompe-l'oeil is, if not its creator's best movie, the most accomplished score in his catalog.

Mr. Fox, a bushy-tailed patriarch still tempted by the demon of youthful high jinks, is a fully paid-up member of the Anderson family—or perhaps he is its true ancestor, so much does he enact the unresolved conflict between the dreary social straitjacket (be a good father, a good husband, a good citizen: the family "road map" that so debilitated *The Royal Tenenbaums*) and the frighteningly titillating desire to send it all to hell.

Having given up stealing chickens, Mr. Fox (George Clooney) has converted to journalism, writing articles nobody reads. He lives a respectable if unsatisfying life, in the company of a loving wife (Meryl Streep), a het-up son, and a little community of disparate rodents—a rather limited weasel, pettifogging opossums and a security guard rat who clicks his paw like George Chakiris in *West Side Story* and envisages the world like a spaghetti western. On the human side are three quarrelsome, sinister-looking farmers, cider-brewers and chicken-breeders, whom the incurable Mr. Fox—still a young scamp at heart—intends to milk for all they are worth. "How can a fox be happy without a chicken wedged between his teeth?" An absurd yet profound question that reveals, as always with Anderson, the impossible dilemma facing his characters: the need (the obligation?) to finally take on one's responsibilities versus the gnawing impulse to escape from them come what may. Hence the strange Indian journey in *The Darjeeling Limited* (with three brothers who want to become one happy family again, but who refuse to let go of their respective dreams), and Steve Zissou (Bill Murray) as an off-the-rails Commander Cousteau, who likes to hide away in a bathyscaphe representing the bubble of childhood (*The Life Aquatic with Steve Zissou*). Adapted from a novel by Roald Dahl (author of *Charlie and the Chocolate Factory*), *Fantastic Mr. Fox* transforms what is a tale of survival into a madcap, melancholic, and sometimes very dark fable on how innocence can be kept alive in a system designed to repress it.

DARIO ARGENTO (born 1940)

Career

Once a film critic on *Paese Sera*, a famous Roman daily, cowriter with Bernardo Bertolucci of Sergio Leone's *Once Upon a Time in the West*, Argento made his first film in 1969. *The Bird with the Crystal Plumage* tells the story of an American author who, one evening, sees a woman being assaulted in a Rome art gallery. With this movie, the first chapter in his "animal trilogy" (followed by *The Cat O'Nine Tails* and *Four Flies on Gray Velvet*), Argento popularizes the *giallo*, a genre of potboiler novel born in 1924, whose cinematographic codes had been established by Mario Bava in *The Girl Who Knew Too Much* and *Blood and Black Lace* in 1964. Inspired by a detective novel by Fredric Brown (*The Screaming Mimi*), *The Bird with the Crystal Plumage* already bears all the hallmarks of the future director of *Suspiria*: the painstaking care taken over its formal beauty, the importance of memory, and a present-day character who feels drawn to inquire into images he cannot understand. But it is in 1975 that Argento acquired his spurs as a cult filmmaker. *Deep Red*, a *giallo* masterpiece, masquerades as a variation on Antonioni's *Blow-Up* (whose lead, David Hemmings, it recasts), to the thumping electronica of The Goblins. Its Italian title, *Profondo Rosso*, reads like an essay on aesthetics in which murder, at the same time savage and elegant, is committed in the manner of a sacred ritual, acquiring in its baroque lunacy a status of a work of art.

The *Suspiria/Inferno* diptych of 1977 marked the director's entry into the field of the fantastic. In 1982, Argento reprised a more raw style in *Tenebre*, a blood-spattered *giallo* set in a modern, paranoid Rome. Then followed in particular *Phenomena* (1984), *Opera* (1987), *The Stendhal Syndrome* (in 1996), and *The Phantom of the Opera* (1999). In 2000, Argento returned to his old stamping ground with *Sleepless*. Seven years later, with *Mother of Tears*, he concluded his famous Mothers' trilogy that had kicked off thirty years earlier with *Suspiria*.

Style

An Argento movie can be recognized at first glance, so total is the coherence of his style and his world. It always opens with a vision (a murder, an aggression, a detail) unwittingly seen by a passer-by. By the finish, one always finds one's way back to the original image, which only then makes sense. Between these two sequences that bookend all his films, one undergoes a lengthy ordeal of deciphering, of tracking, in scenes that are often true tours de force. For Argento, an investigation consists in a succession of aesthetic experiences whose aim is to enlighten. David Hemmings in *Deep Red*, for instance, learns to improve his vision, to sort out his memories, and, by the end of the movie, he returns to the apartment of the first victim and sees finally what he had missed the first time: the reflection of the murderer's face in a mirror. In Argento's pictures, the world is like a labyrinth whose exit one has to find: a sort of kindergarten, which, as scene succeeds scene, is transformed into a trick backdrop (*Four Flies on Gray Velvet*), or a hotel room that opens, via Rembrandt's *Nightwatch*, onto a different space–time continuum (*The Stendhal Syndrome*). One thus understands the importance of the idea of an investigation, for Argento the supreme form of narrative, even if the identity of the assassin in the last analysis matters little, the dénouement devolved for the most part from some banal initial trauma reactivated by a chance event. Argento's cinema is a cinema of sensation that privileges emotion over discourse, affect over reflection, intuition over reasoning. More than just a gifted director of genre movies, Argento is above all an extraordinary inventor of forms for whom the cinema is a laboratory. A modern and popular filmmaker, who, for this reason, occupies an almost unique position in the history of Italian cinema, since he borrows as much from the great Tuscan mannerists as from the movies of Antonioni and Mario Bava.

Suspiria, dir. Dario Argento (1977)

Film INFERNO (1980)

One day, in an old book, Rose Elliot comes across the story of the Three Mothers, three witches, and their three homes in Rome, Freiburg, and New York. Convinced that her block is built on the site of just such a place, Rose asks her brother Mark, who is studying musicology in Rome, to join her, but by the time he disembarks in New York, his sister has disappeared. Opus II in a horror trilogy inaugurated in 1977 with *Suspiria*, *Inferno* is surely the linchpin in Argento's film catalog, an experimental version of the previous chapter, a trippy and alarming movie that opens with a memorable sequence of aquatic terror in which a young woman plunges into a basement in the search of a macabre secret. "The only true mystery is that our lives are governed by dead people," the film's architect once declared. And the dead of *Inferno* skulk everywhere, contaminating places and individuals, and transforming the city into a climatic nightmare controlled by esoteric forces. Here, the chorus of the Hebrews in Verdi's *Nabucco* serves as the soundtrack to gushes of gore, every place is twisted into a maze, and unhinged alchemists scurry down library passageways. A summit of cinematographic mannerism, *Inferno* offers proof of Argento's visual genius, poetic frenzy, and capacity to transform every sequence, every frame into a combination of bedazzlement and fear. Note finally that before he passed away a few months later, some of the movie's special effects (the final appearance of Mater Tenebrarum) were supervised by Mario Bava, godfather of the *giallo* (*Blood and Black Lace*).

KATHRYN BIGELOW (born 1951)

Career

Primarily comprised of muscular action movies and thrillers, Bigelow's filmography could make her into a female equivalent of James Cameron (whose partner she once was) or of John McTiernan: it shows an undeniable taste for the spectacular and for all-male worlds, a palpable sense of action and a predilection for characters tormented by uncertainties of identity. Onetime pupil of Milos Forman and of Susan Sontag at Columbia University, Kathryn Bigelow made her first film in 1987. Near Dark, worthy of the virtuosity and pessimism of Sam Peckinpah, arrived like a thunderclap in the then pallid sky of the vampire movie. With Blue Steel, she cast the ex-scream queen of the 1980s slasher movie, Jamie Lee Curtis (Halloween, Fog) in the role of a female cop tracked by a psychopath, enveloping the story in a dreamy, vapid atmosphere. In 1991, she turned her camera to the world of Californian surfers, infiltrated by an FBI agent whose mission is to dismantle a crew involved in bank heists. Cowritten with Cameron, Point Break is one of the decade's best action movies, much more twisted than it first appears. Apart from an almost "advertising" style that revels in slow-mos and sundowns and the impeccable pecs of Keanu Reeves (cop) and Patrick Swayze (gang guru), the film quietly edges towards a moral conflict that redraws the boundaries between a brotherly pair of enemies. Cyberpunk and futurist, Strange Days follows a cop shorn of his badge as he becomes a trafficker in bootleg recordings through which all forms of deviant pleasures can be experienced virtually, until the day he receives a video of the murder of a friend. Hurt Locker, shot by Bigelow in 2008, earned its director an unusual claim to fame, since with it she became the first woman in the history of cinema to receive an Oscar for Best Picture.

Style

Rough, elegant, and effective, these are words that spring to mind in describing Bigelow's style. With the final sequence of Strange Days that takes place in the overpopulated streets of New York shortly before the year 2000, Bigelow filmed one of the most impressive representations of urban chaos since John Schlesinger's 1975 The Day of the Locust, and proves her ability to introduce a poetic dimension into what are finely honed blockbusters. All her movies explore a specific milieu (surfers in Point Break, the military in K-19, vampires in Near Dark, bomb-disposal units in Hurt Locker) and testify to a tenderness, a nostalgia even, for the oddballs who filled American screens in the 1970s.

Near Dark unfolds on the road among stench-ridden, conservative America, for which a vampire family (redolent of the misfits in Sidney Lumet's Running on Empty or the hippies in Easy Rider) represents a form of marginality that must be eliminated. In the same manner, the surfers in Point Break try to combat consumer society with their alternative, libertarian, mystical lifestyle, exempt from the laws of modern capitalism.

Film THE HURT LOCKER (2008)

Inspired by articles by Mark Boal, a journalist "embedded" with a unit whose mission was to defuse bombs, booby-trapped cars, and roadside devices in Baghdad, The Hurt Locker considers the second Iraq War from the strictly concrete standpoint of three men trapped in a daily routine that is as repetitive as it is extraordinary. Repetitive, since the film moves in concentric circles around the same prototype scene: armed to the teeth, they leave the Alamo camp and venture out into the dangerous streets (the film was actually made in Jordan), like cosmonauts suited-up to confront a lunar landscape ("Saudi Arabia is Mars," a character already observed at the beginning of Peter Berg's The Kingdom). In a zone that is simply impossible to secure since the threat can emerge from anywhere, they spend their time defusing IEDs while the bomb-maker looks on from his hiding place. Extraordinary, since the outcome of each mission depends entirely on the silent duel between team leader Sergeant James and booby traps whose operation and time delay has to be gauged and calculated.

The success of The Hurt Locker relies substantially on the slightly anachronistic nature of this character, a combination of Hawksian hyper-professionalism (at his job, James is the best) and the pathological, pre-Rambo overkill that is already

The Hurt Locker, dir. Kathryn Bigelow (2008)

at a far remove from the post-9/11 modesty inherent in many recent Hollywood war movies. James is in fact so gifted (or hooked) that he craves a daily fix of patrols and homemade bombs, or he will put his team into even greater danger. He will never again be able to return to the fold and to the boring routine of the family home: war has become his addiction, his only love even, as he confesses to his young son in one of the finest sequences in the movie. *Hurt Locker* stands closer to *Objective, Burma!* by Raoul Walsh or Pierre Schoendoerffer's *317th Platoon* than to the antiwar pontificating of *In the Valley of Elah* or *Redacted.* Here the dilemma is not why do we fight, but how? Face down in the sand, among the refuse, in the desert with a handful of miscellaneous misfits whose humdrum hell Bigelow captures perfectly.

BONG JOON-HO (born 1969)

Career

A film that mashes different registers so much (farce, detective film, thriller, comedy, etc.) that it becomes unclassifiable, *Memories of Murder*, Bong Joon-Ho's second feature after *Barking Dogs Never Bite* in 2000, shook the world of Asian cinema to its foundations. The film takes as its starting point a real event (the actions of the first serial killer in Korean history) and follows two demented police inspectors as they undertake their quixotic inquiries. Yet, in spite of an investigation getting nowhere fast, the country's authoritarian regime refuses to call it off and forces the two officers to find a murderer at all costs—even if this means planting clues and fabricating evidence. Bong Joon-Ho then directed *The Host*, the greatest Korean cinema success of 2006 (an audience of more than fifteen million), a monster movie that shows the awakening of a people that had for too long lain dormant and subjected to an external power. Because here, the Beast—a reptilian creature that emerges from the Han River—does not try to reestablish the old, providential order (the inevitable underlying principle of the reactionary disaster movie), but to put a dysfunctional nation to rights, and to shake its population out of chronic apathy. Before the crusade begins, the family in the film vegetates in a middle-class existence on the brink of the abyss. For South Koreans, the plotline of *The Host* asked a simple question: how can they expel the host—a monstrous by-product of American imperialism and Korean cowardice—and so take charge of their own destiny?

With *Mother* (2009), Bong returns to the village of *Memories of Murder* and turns his camera on widowed mother, Kim Hye-ja, and her twenty-seven-year-old son Do-joon, a naive simpleton who is her unique reason to go on living. One evening, a girl is found dead, strangled, her body abandoned on a building rooftop. Skulking in the vicinity at the time of the events, Do-joon is accused and found guilty. After trying unsuccessfully to get a renowned attorney to take on the case, the mother decides to defend her son herself and embarks on a vengeful crusade to prove his innocence.

Style

In four movies, Bong Joon-Ho has imposed himself as one of the key filmmakers of the 2000s, and, by reconfiguring coded genres such as the crime investigation and the monster film, has succeeded in inventing a personal dynamic that blends to perfection popular fiction and political lampoon—the familiar (the little shop-house on the banks of river running through Seoul in *The Host*) and the monstrous thing that lives there, a dragon-like creature spewing out the suppressed emotions of a soporific Korea, caught between an unutterable sense of guilt and impotent rage at Western imperialism. With Bong Joon-Ho, progression means return, resolution depends on rereading: in *Mother*, as in *Memories of Murder*, one has to go back to the scene of the crime and plunge into the little life of a schoolgirl worthy of the name of Laura Palmer, who will reveal the dysfunctional underbelly of an entire community. The audience has to constantly remind itself of what it has already seen, to examine the same image twice (De Palma and Argento are never far away). The great idea behind *Mother*, the narrative ploy that has the plot unraveling like a moral spinning top, consists in making memory loss the driving force behind the movie. The black hole: mentally defective and afflicted with recurrent blackouts, Do-joon possesses, deep in his brain—though he is unable to reach it, the truth of a drama that his mother, convinced in her bones of her offspring's innocence, thinks she already knows, draining her energies as she drags it to the surface. But one doesn't always find what one is looking for. Thus, benighted by the unconditional love she bears for her son, this mollycoddling, suffocating woman (a maternal pendant to the beast in *The Host* which, deep in the bowels of Seoul, broods on human victims) transforms herself, once the truth mutates into a horrific secret, into a murderous harpy. After the exhumation, the burial. And then the question that Bong Joon-Ho's *Mother* asks his Korean audience and his compatriots at large: can the love of a mother, or for the fatherland, justify accepting or suppressing the horror of the world?

Film THE HOST (2006)

It all begins in an American military base in South Korea. A scientist orders a local underling to chuck gallons of toxic waste down the sink. Two years later, some sailors fish a deformed-looking tadpole out of the Han River and throw it back instantly. By 2006, the thing has grown into a cross between *Alien* and McTiernan's *Predator*, clambering out of the water in search of human flesh. In a sequence of total

The Host, dir. Bong Joon-Ho (2006)

panic, it proceeds to swallow up dozens of terrorized Koreans. After the massacre comes the satirical wake (a pastiche of post-September 11 ceremonies viewed through the prism of *manga* overlaid by 1970s Italian comedy) that introduces a weird proletarian family who decide to organize resistance against the foe. After decades spent under the overwhelming and parasitic sway of Uncle Sam, South Korea stands up and takes its destiny into its own hands. At root, *The Host* is a declaration of war on America, and Bong Joon-Ho, author of the splendid *Memories of Murder*, pulls no punches. The end of the film, which sees the survivors and a tramp zapping the beastie with a deluge of Molotov cocktails, makes it clear just how Bong Joon-Ho transforms the classic monster movie (with its mix of carnage and slapstick hijinks) into a serious if far from portentous political critique: serious, when one regards the film as a simple metaphor for the sense of impasse and guilt that clings to Korean society, but light, since Bong Joon-Ho's movie never descends to tub-thumping and remains content to deal in popular yet intelligent entertainment.

LARRY CLARK (born 1943)

Clark appreciates the temptations of escapism (and of the autistic bubble too), but with him reality will out. If Van Sant films from the point of view of the bubble, Clark films from the standpoint of the world around it.

Style

The underlying tension of Clark's oeuvre stems from the constant opposition between the seductive allure of mass culture, its models, imagery, and icons, and an unflinchingly filmed reality that refuses to conform: the horror of the murder concocted by the teenage gang in *Bully* that ruins their lives, or the James Dean-like poses struck by the junkies in *Tulsa*. In *Another Day in Paradise*, James Woods and Melanie Griffith, a couple of aging dopeheads, take under their wing two bereft adolescents whose veins already run with heroin. Together, they hit the road, their heads full of *Bonnie and Clyde*, all shabby, suicidal runaways. But with Clark, one can't hide away for long in fiction—be it in the cinema (Arthur Penn's movie) or in (real and) human life (for an ersatz family never actually coalesces around the young couple). *Ken Park* (2002) plunges us into the lives of four youths, all scarred by parental conflict. Clark's fourth picture highlights the generation gap and, more precisely, that among adolescents who have dissolved the revolutionary ideals of their elders (in this sense, the aspirations of the committed youth of the 1970s were jettisoned long ago) into a depoliticized and almost narcissistic exploration of their own bodies, essentially through sex. In American cinema, a cinema of (always problematic) genealogies, Oedipean tensions between the adolescent world and an elder generation meant to serve as its guide is hardly a recent phenomenon (James Dean for Nicholas Ray, to quote just one). But Larry Clark's kids—and this is the original aspect of his project—have no desire to make their way in, or make their mark on, the adult world, nor even to replace it with a collective project better suited to their desires or utopian ideals. Their only aim is to retreat into the bubble of a lost Eden, indifferent to preexistent pathological models, as well as to the violent irruption of the reality principle. Clark probably best portrays the impermeability of US adolescence, unable to establish the least shadow of an affiliation with preceding generations, in *Bully* (2001). In this way, his cinema, though remaining deeply American, heralds a radical shift, since its portrait of a broken, atomized nation offers no hope of relating to the other, save in apathetic cohabitation—or through slaughter.

Career

A heavily pregnant woman thrusts a syringe into her forearm, three bare-chested teenagers pulling faces inject in the family sitting room beneath a portrait of Jesus, a dead baby lies in its coffin, a young man with a bullet lodged in his leg howls with pain. One could go on describing the photographs in *Tulsa*, the debut album of photographer Larry Clark: a manifesto of sordid Americana which, in 1971 (the year it was published), stirred up a massive hullabaloo—to the point of nausea. Here, Clark already had his material: adolescence, hanging out and taking drugs, poverty, but also the correct distance (a no-holds-barred intimacy often misguidedly construed as voyeurism), and a style that is less theoretical than instinctive, based on an uncompromising realism which—in the wake of models such as Lenny Bruce, Chris Burden, and Bob Dylan—shatters every sexual and moral taboo to smithereens. In *Tulsa* (named for the little city in Oklahoma where Clark was born), in *Teenage Lust*, and in all the movies he has made since 1995 (from *Kids*, his first feature of that year, to *Wassup Rockers*), Larry Clark provides an ongoing X-ray of the soft underbelly of provincial and antiseptic America, which, behind its check tablecloths and apple pies, is in fact a factory for turning out a feral generation prey to violence, squalor, and narcotics. He has become one of the standard-bearers of American independent cinema and—together with Gus Van Sant—the filmmaker of adolescence, whose movies offer a vision that is at once raw and empathic. But Clark's work never shies away from revealing the dark side of the counterculture movement (sex, drugs, and rock 'n' roll), highlighting its excesses and stripping it of its romantic and "revolutionary" trappings. Over time, the comparison between the films of Clark and those of Van Sant, his Portland doppelgänger, seems increasingly to be to the advantage of the former. For the director of *Elephant*, adolescence, ectoplasmic and disengaged as it is, ends up as an subject of poetic celebration—as if the gloriously vacuous dudes of *Paranoid Park* and *Last Days* harbor the secret of a lost relationship with a world about which, deep down, no one much cares.

Wassup Rockers,
dir. Larry Clark
(2004)

Film WASSUP ROCKERS (2004)

A group of young Latinos from the ghetto of South Central travel to—or rather stumble into—the hip district of Beverly Hills. After bumping into two daddy's girls eager for a bit of rough with these Hispanic skaters, Jonathan and his gang are chased out and have to hightail it back home. But the road from the private gardens of the Los Angeles properties with their CCTV and South Central will be long and, for some, fatal.

Wassup Rockers is divided into two distinct parts: an almost documentary section, more narrowly focused on the bodies and daily lives of these teenage fans of punk rock and skateboarding, and then a second part resembling a kind of transposition of Walter Hill's The Warriors. The structure remains identical (the group has to cross hostile territory), the dynamic too (a headlong dash punctuated by exotic or hostile encounters: a party populated by jet-set airheads, a superannuated vigilante who transforms his lawn into a rifle range, etc.), but the nature of the conflict changes: no longer are we faced with running battles between gangs of different colors, but with class war. An hour in, and following a long sequence marking time (a succession of skate tricks and tumbles down a flight of steps in Beverly Hills), Wassup Rockers adopts the traditional movie structure of the chase. But, contrary to the democratic law of the genre, which presupposes that a manhunt reconnects the individuals whatever their ethnic or social origins, the pursuit in Clark's movie demonstrates that it is impossible for people from South Central to build any kind of bridge with those of Beverly Hills. Every encounter results in death or catastrophe, until the murder of one of the group, shot down like a dog in the backyard of a man who sees (and only wishes to see) the other as nothing but a threat.

THE COEN BROTHERS (born 1954 and 1957)

Career

Managing to impose their style in a Hollywood not renowned for welcoming strong personalities with open arms, Joel and Ethan Coen's filmography testifies to an extraordinary knowledge and boundless affection for the kind of genre cinema they revisit in each movie: slapstick (*Raising Arizona*), gangster caper (*Miller's Crossing*), Capra-style comedy (*The Hudsucker Proxy*), good old social farce (*Burn After Reading*; *O, Brother, Where Art Thou?*), western (*True Grit, No Country for Old Men*), and the road movie (*The Big Lebowski*). As for *Blood Simple*, their first feature in 1984, this combines the codes of film noir and an aesthetic inherited from gore. It was here that Frances McDormand, soon to become their favorite actress, earned her spurs. Based on a perfectly classical plotline (the owner of bar employs a private detective to follow a wife he suspects of adultery), the thread tightens around a singularly unsympathetic trio: a dodgy and repugnant detective, a lush vamp, and a lover whose cowardice is equaled only by his stupidity. The Coen brothers' style here is murky and damp, full of nods and winks and dashes of macabre humor. The action takes place in a little village out in the Midwest sticks, the preferred setting for their movies. Without ever lapsing into TV-ad stereotypes, the Coen brothers' treatment of genre tends to the mannerist, in the way of the films of Leone and Sam Raimi. *Raising Arizona* (1986) kicks off in a world close to a Tex Avery cartoon and recounts the mishaps of a dumber-than-dumb couple who will stop at nothing to get a child. In 1991, *Barton Fink*—outtakes from a Kafkaesque nightmare—features the fantastical tribulations of a once-successful writer (John Turturro) searching for inspiration in a dank hotel room. Then came *Miller's Crossing, The Hudsucker Proxy* (in which Tim Robbins as the naive hero born under a lucky star is reminiscent of James Stewart in Frank Capra's *Meet John Doe*), *The Big Lebowski*, and *Fargo*, an ice-cold thriller (in more senses than one). After a something of a lull (*O, Brother, The Barber, Intolerable Cruelty*, the remake of *The Ladykillers*), the Coen brothers produced *No Country for Old Men* (2007), a first-rate film that marked their return.

A goodie, a goon, and a gangster are drawn into a story of biblical simplicity (one lot chase the other lot) that turns out as neither film noir, nor western, nor road movie, but all three at once. A distant and deadbeat cousin to Peckinpah's *Bring Me the Head of Alfredo Garcia*, with a loser hoodwinked by the mirage of easy money (a stack recovered at the blood-soaked scene of a shootout between gringos), an aging, philosophizing sheriff who watches powerless as his world falls apart, and an exterminating angel who sows death and destruction through a slumbering America, *No Country for Old Men* places a declining Far West (set in 1980, the movie deals with a vanished frontier with long-lost values and lost men) in a new but opaque world, shot through with mechanical and unmotivated violence.

Style

The Coen brothers' career splits into two channels: on the one side, dark-hued, sometimes spooky film noirs (*Fargo, No Country for Old Men, A Serious Man*); on the other, left-field comedies, with clueless, confused characters staggering about in an America that's lost its bearings—as in *O, Brother*, a dumb-downed version of *The Odyssey*, and with the gallery of twits that populate *Burn After Reading*. This cross between conspiracy movie and screwball comedy boasts fitness coach Brad Pitt as a kind of lobotomized George Michael, who raises an eyebrow when an idea wanders into his brain; an alcoholic CIA agent; and a pasteboard paranoid Don Juan (George Clooney). In the blue corner, then, short movie treatises on stupidity that juggle speed, black humor, quotation, and wacky details. And, in the red, films that could be termed neoclassical, with *No Country for Old Men* as the acme. Adapted from the novel of the same name by Cormac McCarthy, and infused with melancholy (What have we become? What happened? Why go on?), the first takes of *No Country for Old Men* already set it in the hollow heart of an endless Texan desert peopled by bodies that the Coens film fading from view: alive, they are already dead—or else they have returned from beyond the grave, ghosts in a story blown about by gusts of wind, abstract bodies that flit across the movie, sniffing at one other, but never actually meeting.

*No Country For
Old Men,
dir. Joel
and Ethan Coen
(2007)*

Film TRUE GRIT (2010)

After playing the Dude in *The Big Lebowski*, Jeff Bridges, all gravelly voice and rolling gait, is reborn in the skin of "the Duke," alias John Wayne, the boorish one-eyed U.S. Marshal of *True Grit* (Henry Hathaway, 1969), of which the new *True Grit*, adapted from the eponymous novel by Charles Portis, is less remake than variation. Fourteen-year-old Mattie Ross employs "Rooster" Cogburn to hunt down Tom Chaney, a small-time baddie responsible for the murder of her father. The man-hunters are soon joined by a Texas ranger. There then begins an odyssey through the desert plains of a no man's land not yet called Oklahoma. *True Grit* takes place right in the middle of Indian territory, in a hesitant period of the history of the West, where the law of an eye for an eye was on the wane. Soon, judging and killing will no longer be synonymous, and the movie, which opens with a public hanging at Fort Smith, ends up locked in a courtroom, where the old wolf Cogburn has to answer for his past, in what is the Coens' way of setting out the terms of their dialectic. The whole idea behind *True Grit* lies here: to walk that fuzzy line where the America of yesteryear (barter, theft, revenge, and posse) is constrained to come to terms with the America to come (negotiation, the rule of law, the people). Facing Cogburn, and representing a Far West on the brink of extinction and already a source of legend (the movie ends quite naturally in front of an encampment for a "Wild West Show"), stands Mattie Ross, the embodiment of the America of tomorrow, forced to ride around in a gloomy hinterland searching for a cowardly, scar-faced Liberty Valance, who will soon discover that the writing is on the wall. *True Grit*'s intention is not to play fast and loose with the genre of the western or with its codes, even if sometimes the ghost of *The Searchers* haunts the peregrinations of this strange posse. Choosing instead a partially stylized yet highly allegorical and hyperrealist treatment, it focuses tightly on a handful of characters. Nonetheless, along the road, and without fuss, *True Grit* changes tack and the revenge yarn (to capture the killer) takes a back seat. Among all the corpses, it is the young heroine's journey of initiation (she must slay the dragon, grow up, and perhaps even find a father), with ordeals that even run to an experience of the "pit" (when she falls into a ravine full of poisonous snakes), that ends up at the movie's core.

DAVID CRONENBERG (born 1943)

Career

Not much of a cinemagoer, but with a great love of literature (Burroughs, Ballard, Nabokov, especially), David Cronenberg was born in Toronto and, following the making of two short underground films, became known to the public in 1975 with *Shivers*, a gory, caustic fable describing the devastation caused by a parasite in a spotless apartment building in Montreal. Cronenberg continued to probe the organic body-horror vein in *Rabid* (1977), in which, after a skin graft, a young woman sees emerging from her armpit a kind of sting which she uses to suck people's blood; and then with *Scanners* and *Videodrome* (1982), inspired by Marshall McLuhan's pronouncements on the influence of the media. With *Dead Ringers* (1988) and its twins (Jeremy Irons in both roles) in a strange—not to say pathological—relationship with a patient sporting a trifurcate uterus, and *Naked Lunch*, a Burroughs adaptation, Cronenberg finally attained recognition from mainstream reviewers.

Style

Up to *A History of Violence* (2005), all Cronenberg's films start from a similar initial situation: a cutting-edge scientific or technological experiment degenerates, afflicting the guinea pig with untold organic and physiological transformations. In what is a hallmark obsession of its author, for his characters the frantic search for control becomes the object of a desperate quest (Cronenberg is not a director for chaos), at the same time translating one of the abiding questions of his cinema: Who is really in charge? Deeply Canadian, his oeuvre always seeks to regain the point of equilibrium—like Jeff Goldblum in *The Fly* (1986) who, in an effort to reverse his metamorphosis into an insect, tries, but in vain, to inject human genes back into his body. If, as the director himself concedes, *Crash*, in 1997, constitutes the end product of exploration of the new realities that began twenty years previously, *A History of Violence*, in which he tries his hand at a film noir, signals a fresh turning point (*Eastern Promises* followed in 2006).

The first segment of his work (1975–97) testifies to deliberately disgusting gore excess (see the eye-popping *Chromosome 3*, a blood-drenched version of a family romance, or the ultra-realistic effects in *Scanners* in 1980), somewhere between medical illustration, experimental imagery, and the canvases of Francis Bacon. Cronenberg has never really been interested in the genre movie in and of itself, but in its ability to turn his favorite themes into sometimes monstrous images: genetic engineering, the relationship between the real and the virtual, the mysteries of the flesh, and the schizophrenia arising from the conflict between human fantasy and the normative power of modern society. A man's stomach splits to form a slit into which people put video cassettes (*Videodrome*); a writer rattles away on a typewriter that metamorphoses into a cockroach (*Naked Lunch*); foetuses proliferate in buboes, materializing the hateful thoughts of their genitrix (*Chromosome 3*). His movies abound with such unforgettable (and sometimes frankly repulsive) images. Since *A History of Violence*, featuring a family man with a criminal past that comes back to haunt him, and *Eastern Promises*, a film set among the Russian mafia in England, Cronenberg seems to have toned down his visuals, but the furrow he plows remains essentially the same: conceptual horror, doubt concerning identity, and contamination (through violence or by an alien body).

Film VIDEODROME (1982)

Simultaneously Pandora's Box and lampoon, at once didactic and enigmatic, this is perhaps the alpha and the omega of the Cronenberg oeuvre. The owner of a cable channel that specializes in the erotic one day tunes into a mysterious signal, *Videodrome*, a sordid TV program that sparks uncontrollable hallucinations in viewers. *Videodrome* marks a decisive stage. Decisive because this complex and prophetic movie already articulates the Cronenbergian question par excellence: what has reality become in the age of surgical wars, of television, cloning, reality shows, of the theories of McLuhan ("The medium is the message"), let alone Disneyland? Many sleepless nights have been spent perorating on the meaning of the New Flesh: Max Renn's new flesh, of course—a man-cum-programmable video recorder—but the new flesh of the image too (the snuff show, *Videodrome*, itself), and especially the new flesh of reality. In spite of an unstinting propensity to film every disordered state of the body, Cronenberg's corpus is not so much an encyclopedia of the corporeal guerrilla war waged by the spirit

Crash, dir. David Cronenberg (1997)

against the flesh (an old critical saw), as the unremitting hypothetical questioning ("What would happen if we... ?") of what
we call "reality." From this point of view Crash (1996), his masterpiece, constitutes the ne plus ultra of the thematic: born
in the age of simulation, pale simulacra of humanity, Ballard,
Vaughan, and the other spooks do not seek in the accidents
they provoke some orgasmic shock, but simply an opportunity to experience, via the proximity of death, some fleeting
sense of the concrete.

JOE DANTE (born 1946)

Career

In a career spanning some twenty-five years, Joe Dante has become renowned as one of the most corrosive American filmmakers in Hollywood. Yet, in spite of some genuine hits (*Gremlins*, *Innerspace*, *Small Soldiers*, *The Howling*), Dante remains a movie outsider. Too subtle for the entertainment industry, but to some eyes all too American, the director of *Matinee* long worked in genre movies (science fiction, horror). It all started in 1953, when the young Joe Dante saw a 3D screening of *It Came from Outer Space* (directed by Jack Arnold) and then *Them!* directed by Gordon Douglas. For months, he later avowed, he started in terror every time he heard a cricket chirruping in his backyard. Glutted with comics, with TV series (*The Twilight Zone*, especially, an episode of which he was to make in 1983), and B movies, Joe Dante was just a teenager when 1950s sci-fi was entering its golden age. His entire catalog feeds off these early fascinations when local fleapits screened Roger Corman productions or the even less opulent pictures of William Castle, a director to whom he paid an eloquent tribute in 1993 with *Matinee*.

Indeed it was at New World, Roger Corman's company, that Dante was to begin his career. Initially compiling and editing trailers, he first ventured behind the camera in 1976, in 1978 signing a low-budget horror flick inspired by the success of *Jaws* entitled *Piranha*. Following *The Howling* (1981), in which he pays homage to the werewolf movie, Dante began making a name for himself in the up-and-coming 1980s generation. The predominant subject of his films is without question the power of the image. In *Gremlins 2* (1990), for instance, the sneering beasties from the previous movie have become sufficiently emboldened to have designs on the film medium itself: thus, in one of the more bamboozling sequences in the movie, the gremlins halt the projection of the film and start invading TV channels. Dante's entire filmography (*Innerspace*, *Explorers*, *Looney Tunes: Back in Action*) can thus be boiled down to savage attacks on media propaganda, from wherever it arises.

Style

Like John Carpenter and John Landis, Joe Dante is a pure product of American TV, filling his films with innumerable references (he was also a film critic with *Famous Monsters of Filmland*). If his movies are designed to entertain, the majority can be read on several different levels. In *Gremlins*, his greatest success, made in 1984 under the aegis of Steven Spielberg, Dante disturbs the peace and quiet of a small American town. These cuddly toys that transform into monstrous beasts on coming into contact with water represent the dark side of Capra's America (in subtext, *Gremlins* amounts to a caustic parody of *Life is Beautiful*). The burlesque tone of *The Burbs* inveighs against the average American citizen's sense of property, ready to commit any turpitude to preserve the territory intact. In *Small Soldiers*, Dante offers a negative version of *Toy Story*, and, through the war opposing two armies of toys, denounces the violence inherent in American culture. He describes how he makes a deliberate attempt to resuscitate certain genres and establish links between his movies and those of yesterday, and revels in stirring up emotions and expressing ideas conveyed by the genre movies of the past. Though not strictly necessary (and Dante is no educational crusader), he confesses that his films are appreciated more easily by people who have seen a lot of films and who have a "movie past."

Gremlins, dir. Joe Dante (1985)

Film GREMLINS (1984)

A mildly unhinged inventor gives his son a strange little beast, a *mogwai*, that he unearthed in a shop dealing in Chinese antiques. Keeping this adorable creature means having to respect a series of instructions, chief among them being to keep it away from water and light. In *Gremlins*, the cackling creatures learn all about the American way of life from what they see in films and TV ads, a body of stylistic and ideological information that soon governs their perception of reality. Among the movie models from which the gremlins construct their worldview are the aliens of *Invasion of the Body Snatchers*, the unthinking patriotism of *Rambo*, and the swagger of Clark Gable. In one of the stories, directed by Dante, of *Twilight Zone: The Movie*, a child gifted with the ability to transform his surroundings into anything he wants terrorizes his family with a vast array of cartoon characters.

In the beginning, then, is the Image. This could be the founding principle of Joe Dante's cinema, whose film catalog seems haunted by a twofold question: How can one become oneself when the world forces us to remain mere witnesses to the images with which it assails us? And how, in return, can one make use of these images, these same deceptive fictions, to attain a hidden truth? In this lies the singularity of Dante's initiatory cinema: an insatiable desire to reconcile lucidity and viewing pleasure—in other words, to build an amusing metafilmic oeuvre that a hyperconsciousness of the history of form makes problematic instead of overwhelming.

BRUNO DUMONT (born 1958)

Career

A onetime philosophy teacher, Bruno Dumont made a large number of corporate films and then a short, *Mary et Freddy*, from which he was to draw his first feature, *The Life of Jesus* (1997)–the opening salvo in a trilogy shot in Bailleul, the small city in northern France where he was born. Shot using nonprofessional actors, *The Life of Jesus* heralded the birth of an already finely tuned filmmaker: the everyday life of Freddy, an unemployed teenager who assuages his boredom by riding around on a moped with his buddies, forms the matrix for Dumont's future characters, all overpowered by impulses they cannot control. After *Humanité* (1999), with its depressed cop inquiring into the murder of an eleven-year-old girl, Dumont removed his camera to the American desert: in *Twentynine Palms* (2003), he tracks a couple on the verge of breaking up, whose return to nature and experience of the mineral world ends in a bloodbath. In *Hadewijch* (2009)—the name of a Flemish poet and mystic of the thirteenth century—one follows Céline, a starry-eyed young woman who is expelled from her convent due to her excessive, ecstatic, expressions of faith; almost a caricature, as her Mother Superior puts it. Back in the "real" secular world, Céline tries to live the love she bears Christ by other means, bending to the rhythm of every chance encounter—including Yassine, a young girl of North African origin from the projects, and Nassir, her brother, a convinced Muslim who gives introductory courses on Islam. Reverting to one of the formal principles behind *Flanders* (the brutal shift from the countryside to a theater of war), Dumont describes the trajectory of a figure who just glides from one environment to the next, from bourgeois Paris to the high-rises of the city outskirts, from France to the Middle East, totally unconscious of her transgressive power (social, sexual, and political barriers are blithely ignored). The entire film is coated by this sense of Céline's naivety, by the Christic *punctum* she hunts for in every event (indifferent to what others propose, she watches solely for some concrete sign of Platonic love, unable to see that the flesh she craves must belong, in the end, to a man),

imparting a way of grasping the world that marks a notable turning point in Dumont's cinema.

Style

Bruno Dumont is the author of a demanding, austere body of work, a "no fat" cinema, to use Maurice Pialat's expression. *The Life of Jesus*, *L'Humanité*, *Twentynine Palms*, and then *Flanders* are metaphysical pieces, extraordinarily rigorous from the aesthetic point of view (impeccable cinemascope, an inborn feel for composition and length of scene), which track manifestations of mysticism embedded in ordinary humanity, often silent and opaque (farmers in northern France, the sullen youth of Bailleul). With his nonprofessional actors, his talent for revealing the tragedy behind the everyday, his controversial manner of treating violence as an event no different from any other, and the mental landscapes designed to stand surety for an unarticulated psychology (there is little, mostly functional, dialogue), Dumont's movies have, in a few short years, been hailed as one of the few new and radical phenomena to occur in recent French cinema. His films seem to strain towards the moment that their latent, infinitely differing violence—of varied and confused origin (idleness, social context, cultural level, incommunicability)—at last explodes; his films present characters who all oscillate between debilitating, crippling existential angst and salutary violence.

Film FLANDERS (2006)

Demester tends his farm and, when he's not tilling a field, occasionally finds the time to have his way with a woman, Barbe, with whom he is, apparently, secretly in love. Of easy virtue or perhaps just unhinged, Barbe shares her body (but not her desire) with the few presentable men in the region. Then, together with two other inhabitants of the town, Demester sets off to war. After routine as horror, and horror as routine, then comes the central sequence of the film: a series of rapid, dreadful events (murder, rape, torture, etc.) in an undeclared war against the East that could as well be Iraq or Afghanistan as Algeria. Dumont is not concerned with the place or with the identity of the turban-wearing enemies; neither do history and geopolitical considerations matter, since the film is not dealing with any particular conflict, but with the sense that the war "over there" is simply the continuation by other means of the deathly peace that reigns "back here." There is then no friction between before and after, between Flanders and the East—in other words between daily life

Flanders, dir. Bruno Dumont (2006)

among these peasants and their existence in the military. Moreover, recycling the structure of *Full Metal Jacket* and *The Deer Hunter*, one slips from a take of Flanders to the mountainous deserts of the East, as if the two spaces were connected naturally. Uniformed, shaven-headed, armed to the teeth, Demester and his cohort behave just as they do back in the sticks, just with more intensity and even less regard for law. Such an abrupt juxtaposition of the two parts entails a relation between them: in *The Deer Hunter*, Cimino confronted the self (the American) with its phantasmatic Other (the Vietcong). An opposition that was sometimes specular: the Other as reversed double of the self. In *Flanders*, Dumont tracks the self within the Other, Flanders *in* the Orient. What is the difference, really, between the sex sequences in Flanders (each applicant empties himself in the same heap of inert flesh), and the gang rape the soldiers perpetrate in a foreign land? None, since in both cases, there is no communication. One (Barbe) says nothing and stares at a point in space she will never attain, the other (the raped indigenous girl) cries out, howls even, but in a language her assailants do not understand. Total passivity on one side, useless resistance on the other—the cinema of Bruno Dumont is simply the slow and rigorous grinding down of the possibility that two individuals might come together, and even unite.

CLINT EASTWOOD (born 1930)

Career

He is one of the last of the great and the good of American cinema. In front of as well as behind the camera, he has built up a monumental and eclectic body of work, forging a singular relationship with major traditional filmmakers (Ford, Hawks, and Wellman), whose dilemmas and points of view he continues to explore. In 1963, Sergio Leone discovered a cool, clean-shaven young actor, who was playing the main part in an American TV series (*Rawhide*), casting him in the role of the Man with No Name in *For a Fistful of Dollars*. Becoming famous in the Dollar Trilogy, Eastwood returned to Hollywood, and, after a slew of rather minor efforts, crossed the path of his future mentor, Don Siegel, with whom he would shoot in particular *The Beguiled*, *Escape from Alcatraz*, and, especially, *Dirty Harry* (1971), a box-office success and the cause of some enduring misconceptions. The same year he went over to directing, making his debut feature (*Play Misty for Me*), the onset of an idiosyncratic career that has passed through several phases and every genre: the period of rectification (*Magnum Force* was a response to the supposed fascism of *Dirty Harry*; *The Gauntlet*, a denial of his supposed misogyny; *The Outlaw Josey Wales*, evidence of his altruism), the period of development (*Bronco Billy*, *Honkytonk Man*, *Bird*, and *White Hunter, Black Heart* widened his filmmaking spectrum), then the era of critical recognition and artistic maturity that began with *Unforgiven* in 1992.

Style

Today Clint Eastwood is one of a handful of American directors able to connect in one fell swoop perfect classicism and hard-bitten B movie, John Ford and Don Siegel, an elegy to America (glorifying its scenery and communities) and its critique (*A Perfect World*, a jet-black description of the 1950s, or *Mystic River*, with its ruined childhoods in small-town America). In *Unforgiven*, Eastwood reactivates the codes of the traditional western (Anthony Mann's *Man of the West* and an old-timer forced to pick up his gun one last time) and inverts the famous diktat from *The Man Who Killed Liberty Valance* ("When the legend becomes fact, print the legend.")

Kinship, justice, belief, openness to the Other, and the constitution of the American people form a vast corpus of Eastwood themes that recur in *Breezy*, *Honkytonk Man*, *The Bridges of Madison County*, *Absolute Power*, *Mystic River*, and *Changeling*. For Eastwood, affiliation does not present a means of retrospectively verifying one's origin (Where do we come from? To whom or to what must we render account?), but a way of looking back into the past, to see the persistence of what recurs and of what lasts (a trauma, a child, a film).

At almost eighty, Eastwood is like Frankie Dunn, the coach in *Million Dollar Baby*, always in training. If the conflict between classicism and modernity haunts his films, the point is neither to turn his back on the latter, nor to reject, or even resurrect the past, but to go beyond it. *Million Dollar Baby* could just have been a realistic film about boxing, in the footsteps of Robert Wise's *The Set-Up*, but it actually sneaks through the gaps in the genre, counter-punching against the way a knockout is normally administered: either the fight is won with a single uppercut (so no suspense), or it is lost forever (so no "success story"). In an Eastwood film, a relationship is not a given, it has to be forged; and this, coincidentally, circumscribes something often loosely called classicism, which, rather than a fixed state, in fact a dynamic, a limit that is also a horizon.

Million Dollar Baby, dir. Clint Eastwood (2004)

Film GRAN TORINO (2008)

A Korean War veteran, a bitter, hardened widower, full of xenophobic prejudices, feels a growing affection for one of his young Korean neighbors struggling to go straight. With *Gran Torino*, Eastwood returns to the roots of his own mythology, both by reverting to a series of images (the script borrows the basic structure of the revenge movie), and by playing ironic games with his status as an icon (he wags his finger in the direction of a gang of Korean hoodlums, but Dirty Harry's clenched teeth have degenerated into an overplayed snarl). For its wrinkly hero, *Gran Torino* is a story that teaches an old dog new tricks (how can one open up to the other, how can one exorcise the phantoms of the past?—the John Ford line), while, for the young man he takes under his wing, it becomes a tale of initiation (learning a trade, becoming a man). This twofold narrative is soon undermined, though, by a boomerang effect that comes from a very different world of fiction, from the genre movie itself (revenge): thus, for one last time, Kowalski will have to have a showdown with an Asian gang. The hero of Eastwood's twenty-ninth film thus comes from far away, from the extreme end of a gallery of charac-

ters whose stories both explore an archaeology and film what is to come. What would the retired San Francisco cop have made of a multiethnic quarter of Detroit with its marauding hoodlums? What kinds of recruits would Sergeant Highway from *Heartbreak Ridge* or the grizzled trainer of *Million Dollar Baby* knock into shape here? Would the gunfighter from *Unforgiven* have endured his last shootout on these streets? Thus, the moral trajectory of Kowalski, onetime worker in a long-gone Ford factory, overlays exactly that of Eastwood the actor: from the boorish old loner who hurls racist insults at his Korean neighbors, to martyr, via the figures of vigilante, father, and ghost. With formal audacity and a splendid freedom in tone, Eastwood's film shifts seamlessly from tragedy (a dead man walking) to silliness (as in the sequence where old Walt greedily devours the food served to him by a group of Korean grandmothers) with the same elegance. In 2009 *Gran Torino* certainly captured the mood of an America which, on the brink of electing Barak Obama to the White House, seemed ready to look at least some of its demons square in the eye.

DAVID FINCHER (born 1962)

Career

His movie debut could have proved fatal: in tackling, after Ridley Scott and James Cameron, the third episode in the *Alien* series in 1992, David Fincher was taking quite a risk. But his dark vision of the myth (even if it was cut by the producers, spawning a later obsession with control over his output) convinced the critics and the erstwhile guardians of the temple alike. With *Seven* (1995), in which two detectives pursue a serial killer whose murders are based on the seven deadly sins, Fincher imposed himself as one of the blue-chip stocks in American cinema. Five years after *The Silence of the Lambs*, *Seven* renews and stylizes the serial killer movie. After *The Game*, he made his cult movie, *Fight Club*, an anarchistic fable adapted from the eponymous novel by Chuck Palahniuk (the film explodes the consumer society and extols bodily self destruction as the ultimate act of resistance). *Zodiac*, his best film, recounts one of the most spectacular investigations in all American criminal history, the hunt for the serial killer of that name who, from 1968 to 1978, terrorized California. Fincher used its effect in the collective imagination as a metaphor for American film in the 1970s, following its trajectory with painstaking accuracy: starting out supercharged and energetic, the movies of the New Hollywood were soon gripped by exhaustion and depression, before entering the ghostly world that still obsesses us. *The Curious Case of Benjamin Button*, made in 2008, takes as its starting point a short story by F. Scott Fitzgerald that describes the tragic destiny of a wrinkled old man who grows up backwards—that is, from advanced age to youth, offering a thousand morphological and technological excuses for Brad Pitt to successively embody some of the great icons of Hollywood masculinity: leather-period Brando from *The Wild Bunch*, Redford in *This Property Is Condemned* and *Gatsby*, and, finally, Brad Pitt, in an overlap between character and actor that rapidly evolves into the conceit of the movie. With *The Social Network*, Fincher records at breakneck pace the meteoric rise of Mark Zuckerberg, at the time just twenty-six, an exceptionally gifted and unsympathetic, obsessional, almost autistic teenager, who at an early stage in the movie seems to have kissed goodbye to all hope of relating to the other—in other words, to the female sex (symbolically, it all begins the day he is jilted by his girlfriend), as he stuffs reality, emotion, the unexpected, and his entire environment into a churning mix of algorithms, codes, and programs. From this comes the brilliant irony of a character, neither attractive nor particularly interesting (nothing excites him more than tapping away on his PC), who produces a global social network out of his frustration and inability to communicate with others.

Style

Coming from the world of advertising and music video (Sting, Michael Jackson, and Madonna), David Fincher quickly acquired a reputation as a maniacal control-freak filmmaker in the Kubrick vein. His manner is initially arresting for its virtuosity (sometimes overplayed: see the innumerable camera effects in *Panic Room* in which the apartment, the unique setting for the plot, is filmed from every possible angle), visual bulimia, and a taste for a creative challenge. With Michael Mann, he is a filmmaker amply abreast of new technologies. To date, his anarchistic tendencies—The system's there. Why not destroy it?—have attained their zenith in *Fight Club*, with the symbolic explosion of the buildings with which the narrative ends expressing the guiding principle stated by Brad Pitt (his pet actor) towards the midpoint of the movie: "Reject the basic assumptions of civilization and especially the importance of material possessions."

Film ZODIAC (2007)

Tracking every move made by the three men appointed to investigate the crimes in *Zodiac*, Fincher's movie joins a long line of exposé films of the period in which it is set—more precisely, Pakula's *All the President's Men* (1976), whose factual and documentary obsessions it reworks. Except for the few sequences of the murders, sober and of singular visual beauty, the treatment in *Zodiac* is muted, almost understated. Fincher takes time detailing each fact step by step, the minute advances, the many setbacks, sparing us none of the various phases of the investigation, with its innumerable dead-ends and false dawns.

The months and the years shuffle on, while a film, *Dirty Harry* (1971), with the psychopath Scorpio tortured and shot down by Clint, shows the solving of a case that, back in reality, our officers are no closer to filing. Then people become worried

Zodiac, dir. David Fincher (2007)

about other news, Watergate's on the horizon, the US is gradually changing, another decade begins, *Star Trek* hits the screen. But for these three men, the obsession remains. Little by little, the film sinks into a melancholy, saturnine stasis—like the killer, who seems to have vanished into thin air leaving just a dark, almost abstract, shadow, a fantastic projection of the minds he has ended up by warping, destroying. For the cops, nothing counts anymore: not their family, their private lives, nor current events. The characters droop, the 1970s recede into the distance, and Fincher reaches the horizon that really interests him. For all three characters, the time has come to make a choice: to rejoin the march of history, to forget Zodiac, and to climb into an autistic and neurotic bubble, safe from a changing world, or to go back to the beginning (Graysmith, played by a moonstruck Jake Gyllenhaal), like a criminophile (a cinephile?), armed with fictional models (*The Most Dangerous Game*) and with an energy his elders palpably lack. Once the initial euphoria dies down, it's best to throw in the towel (Zodiac now melts into the background) – an option gloriously embodied by Inspector Toschi, who, if he continues to ply his trade in the present, remains haunted by an unresolved past, a face imprinted with the opaque veil of a ghost, Zodiac, whose disappearance brings with it his own partial eclipse.

WILLIAM FRIEDKIN (born 1935)

Career

Training in Chicago as a maker of TV live broadcasts and documentaries (*The People vs. Paul Crump* focused on the case
of a man condemned to death, who subsequently had his
sentence commuted due to the film), Friedkin was, with
Francis Ford Coppola and Martin Scorsese, one of the boy
wonders of New Hollywood. Beginning his career in 1967
with *Good Times*, a hippie musical with Sonny and Cher, he
is the author of some of the groundbreaking films of 1970s
American cinema, including *The French Connection* (1971),
which, with *Bullitt* and *Dirty Harry*, laid the foundations of the
realistic urban thriller, *The Exorcist* (1973), the first horror
movie to be produced by a major (Warner), and which sparked
a wave of films about the phenomena of possession, and
Sorcerer (1978), an eye-popping remake of Clouzot's *The
Wages of Fear*. The 1980s opened with a much-discussed
film, *Cruising*, with Al Pacino in the role of an undercover cop
infiltrating New York's gay scene. Inspired by a series of savage murders perpetrated in the gay community between
1969 and 1979, the movie was shot for the most part in real
gay clubs in Greenwich Village and in the Ramble, a wooded
part of Central Park much used at the time for "cruising." This
was followed by *The Deal of the Century* (1983), a ferocious
satire on arms dealing and on America's policy of interfer-
ence; by *To Live and Die in L.A.*, one of the great crime movies
of the Reagan era; and then by *Rampage*. After a less reward-
ing interlude (*The Guardian*, *Jade*, *Blue Chips*), Friedkin's career
enjoyed a second wind at the beginning of the 2000s with
Rules of Engagement, *The Hunted*, and *Bug*.

Style

Filmed with a handheld camera like in a war report (he is
reported wanting to give the impression that the camera just
dropped from the sky and started filming), among onlookers
who were really frightened and vehicles that were really
smashed, the car-chase sequence in *The French Connection*
interweaves the codes of the genre with techniques inherited from documentary. The movie also provides an eloquent
record of a certain state of the urban realities (here,
Manhattan and Brooklyn) at a given time, showing its architecture, politics, and inhabitants (see in particular the clear-cut
opposition between the well-off districts and the poor quar-
ters that carve the territory up between themselves, gradually
excluding the middle classes). Three years after *Bullitt*, from
the point of view both of direction and editing (rapid-fire cuts
create a breathless rhythm), Friedkin, a virtuoso of the realistic action movie, invented the modern form of the chase, a
form he perfected in *To Live and Die in L.A.*, to which the best
American action movies, even if they indulge in more explosive pyrotechnics and deploy greater means (more vehicles
equal bigger crashes), still adhere. Fascinated by moral ambiguity and by evil in all its guises (one of his models is Fritz Lang),
Friedkin's cinema consists in a brutal slide into formlessness,
into a magma—the dark side of humankind (its impulses,
instincts, and animality), and of its cities (wasteground, mud-
clogged quarries, porches stinking of urine, alleyways choking
with trashcans). The overriding theme of his movies is slip-
ping, falling: it is always the specific angle of the slippery slope
that predetermines the story. An entire milieu can slide (that
of drug trafficking in *The French Connection*, S and M-tinged
homosexuality in *Cruising*, counterfeiting in *To Live and Die in
L.A.*, the interface between politics and law in *Jade*); someone can fall into the void (William Peterson's premonitory
bungee jump in *To Live*); or, more simply, into oneself—that is,
in accordance with Friedkin's theorem number one: the Other
is never anything else than that part of ourselves that we
dare not face up to.

The Hunted, dir.
William Friedkin
(2002)

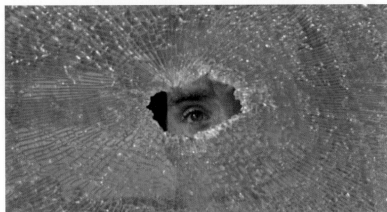

To Live and Die
in L. A.,
dir. William
Friedkin (1985)

Film BUG (2006)

The first shot of Bug: from far above in the sky, the camera slowly descends on a dilapidated motel, narrowing the field of vision to a room that it will then almost never leave. Here lives Aggie, whose husband is in prison, who cannot come to terms with the fact her son has gone missing, who drinks forlornly in the evening, and who is about to receive a visit from a strange vagrant. Initially wary, the woman gives herself to the man and contracts a virus. As with any process of parasitism, to succeed it takes a parasite and a host body, a fanatic and a fragile mind–the devil and a little girl of long ago (The Exorcist). Here it is a paid-up paranoiac and a feckless young female.

Bug, a chamber piece made on a modest budget, is essentially a story about insects, and more narrowly about parasites, but, though one would not think it from the title, the insects in question are invisible, probably nonexistent, yet sufficiently powerful to transform a shack out in the sticks occupied by two oddballs (Ashley Judd and Michael Shannon) into the venue for a supranational plot that soon involves the army, the CIA, the FBI, and the US government. "Bug" of course means something quite different in espionage terms, and Friedkin has in his sights the state of mind of post-9/11 America, convinced it is besieged by an omnipresent, protean, and invisible threat, and which lives hunkered down between four high walls. In Michael Shannon, the nation's obsession with security is symbolized by a mind that imagines that its body has been "bugged" by the Other. Like weapons of mass destruction, but strictly in the mind, the insects he sees everywhere lead to the worst-case scenario—a scenario that Friedkin, a filmmaker who pushes things to the limit, never balks at filming (see the disturbing scene where, like Jeff Brundle in Cronenberg's The Fly, the man tears at his own face to get at the microscopic animals burrowing beneath his skin).

JAMES GRAY (born 1969)

Career

A native of New York, James Gray studied film at USC (University of South California), shooting his debut feature, *Little Odessa*, in 1994. In this he describes the problematic return of a killer to Brighton Beach (Brooklyn), the Russian neighborhood where he grew up. In *The Yards* (2000), Gray films another difficult homecoming, that of a man who has just come out of prison (Mark Wahlberg), and who is drawn into the dubious activities of his uncle, the head of the rail yard in Queens. The movie was a flop at the box office, which meant a wait of some seven years for Gray's third feature, *We Own the Night*, a very dark crime thriller spliced with a Greek tragedy, again set in New York, showing the clash between two brothers, an exemplary cop (Wahlberg again) and a hustler nightclub manager (Joaquin Phoenix), who is in the pay of the local mob. With *Two Lovers*, James Gray blends Dostoevsky and Visconti's *White Nights* into a melodrama that analyzes the ebb and flow of desire between three individuals.

Style

If James Gray has taken up a torch at all, it is that of Francis Ford Coppola (whose *Godfather* trilogy hovers over his movies), even to the point of him casting actors like James Caan and Robert Duvall who—in *The Yards* and *We Own the Night*—play patriarchs shorn of the authority once wielded by Marlon Brando. All Gray's movies are about the family, complete with emotional upsets and moral dilemmas, with prodigal or disavowed sons, with the social context constituting the determining factor. Stylistically, the cinema of James Gray is characterized first and foremost by a marked rejection of formalism, of visual experimentation, and of all that anchors a film in the aesthetic codes of its period. His intensity as a director who privileges long sequences explored to the point of maximum emotional intensity, as well as the care taken over photography (with, in the background, artists like Georges de La Tour for *We Own the Night* or Caravaggio for *The Yards*), make him a filmmaker more concerned with touching the audience's heart than its eyes. For Gray, experimentation

remains on the surface, it lacks content. For him, it has shown itself up as a dead-end (he references Lucio Fontana and mentions Derek Jarman's film *Blue*—with its single, color-saturated take lasting an hour and a half—as the ne plus ultra), and quotes Jean-Pierre Melville as saying that it takes more guts and talent to make a classic film than a modern film.

James Gray is the great classic director of the generation of American filmmakers who appeared during the 1990s (P. T. Anderson, David Fincher, Darren Aronofsky).

Film WE OWN THE NIGHT (2007)

Exuding the same fumes as Abraham Polonsky's *Force of Evil* and Elia Kazan's *East of Eden*, two films noir haunted by treason and moral choices, this modern-dress Cain and Abel delves into the heart of a family of Russian-American police officers in Brooklyn in the late 1980s. Mark Wahlberg and Joaquin Phoenix play two brothers on opposite sides of the law, the model son and the black sheep: Joseph follows in the footsteps of his god, his father (Robert Duvall), and proudly wears the uniform of the NYPD; while Bobby has jumped ship (and changed his surname) and now runs a joint for a member of the Russian mafia. At some point, his father tells him, you'll have to choose between them and us.

We Own the Night goes on to recount the story of that "point." A family tragedy, then, but more specifically a biblical one, haunted by themes of redemption, salvation, and moral dilemma, Gray's movie is filmed essentially from the point of view of the "bad" son, tracking the twists and turns of his arduous conversion. How can one return to the bosom of the Good? How can Bobby find a place in his rigid, suffocating family setup? How can one graduate from avenging passion (see the brilliant sequence of the father's murder beneath torrential, purifying rain) to brotherly love? Not for a second does *We Own the Night* doubt the existence of an objective, or rather religious red line that separates the world of the fallen from the realm of sacrifice. Here, the moral compass, in accordance with classic law, always points in the same direction. Only the men panic, change sides, lose their bearings, before eventually regaining them. Taking up where his two previous movies left off, James Gray here reaffirms a rigorously classic idiom typical of the mood of a certain contemporary American cinema (*Zodiac* and *The Assassination of Jessie James*). Eschewing baroque extravagance, visual high-wire acts, and a thirst for power, he chooses instead to return to the basics of the genre (here film noir and its tragic dimension) and to a text (the Bible)—that inexhaustible wellspring of Hollywood scripts and films.

We Own the Night, dir. James Gray (2007)

WERNER HERZOG (born 1942)

Career

Werner Herzog made his entrance in 1967 with *Signs of Life*, a film centered on the troubled existence of a German soldier during World War II who topples into madness. The movie carries the germ of Herzog's entire oeuvre: a fascination for people on the margins, a taste for formal extremes and for characters haunted by madness, often gloriously embodied by his alter ego, Klaus Kinski (*Aguirre*, *Fitzcarraldo*, *Nosferatu*), and especially his trademark interweave of documentary and fiction ("disguised fictions," as he calls them). *Even Dwarfs Started Small* (1970) describes the revolt of a group of midgets ensconced on an island; *Land of Silence and Darkness* (1971) filmed the daily life of a deaf woman and a blind man; *Stroszek* (1977) tells the absurd saga of a simple-minded European in America (played by Bruno S., a man with mental health issues himself). In *Heart of Glass*, using actors playing under hypnosis, Herzog recalls how an eighteenth-century Bavarian village gradually sank into insanity.

Though one of the new generation that rebuilt German cinema in the 1960s (along with Rainer W. Fassbinder, Wim Wenders, and Volker Schlöndorff), Herzog plows a different furrow, since his work does not refer to contemporary German society. In 1972 he crafted his best-known movie deep in the Amazonian jungle, *Aguirre*, about an unhinged conquistador who stopped at nothing in his quest for El Dorado. Herzog, in his search for larger-than-life experiences, continued in the 1980s and 1990s to make films and documentaries: in Australia (*Where the Green Ants Dream*) and in Africa (*Cobra Verde*, about the life of a slave trader). In 2001, he made *Invincible*, and then the documentary *Grizzly Man* (2006), composing a phony remake of Abel Ferrara's classic, called *Bad Lieutenant: Port of Call New Orleans*, in which a dazed, tortoise-like Nicolas Cage creeps about a gooey post-Katrina America populated by alligators that, out of the corner of their beady eyes, quietly contemplate humanity in free fall.

Style

Romantic, extreme, visionary—Herzog's style is predicated on power, hyperbole, excess, sometimes even on out-and-out lunacy: in the Homeric shooting conditions of *Aguirre*, in the paddle steamer literally dragged to the top of a mountain in *Fitzcarraldo*, in the journey he undertook on foot in 1974 from Munich to Paris to see the then dying historian of German cinema, Lotte Eisner (an experience recorded in the book *Of Walking on Ice*), Herzog's trajectory betrays an insatiable desire to empathize with all the forms of life (and survival), and to explore uncharted territory. This search for physical, ecstatic experiences of course brings his style closer to the sublime in painting (the pictures of Caspar David Friedrich immediately come to mind) or in opera (he has directed several, including a production of Wagner's *The Flying Dutchman* in 1993), and left-leaning criticism has long suspected Herzog of being fascinated by the superman and a thirst for power. A closer examination of his work, with its extraordinary diversity of approaches and subjects, shows such objections to be wrong-headed. "Don't you hear that terrible screaming all around you, conventionally called silence?" runs the epigraph Werner Herzog placed at the beginning of *The Enigma of Kaspar Hauser* (1975), over the image of a wheat field lashed by the wind. For Herzog, directing means remaining receptive to an often impressive, always melancholy, nature (witness the shots of the shoreline in *Nosferatu*), infused with signs that have to be gleaned, and then interpreted. Herzog's gnostic output is haunted by the notion of the secret and, for him, making films, like writing books or more simply living his life, consists in scraping away, through catharsis or trance, at the hidden truth behind a reality that escapes us.

Film GRIZZLY MAN (2006)

Between 1997 and 2003, Timothy Treadwell, the "grizzly man" of the title, shot hundreds of hours of film high in the Alaska tundra. Closely involved in bear conservation, at once militant ecologist, animal poet, documentary maker, and actor *manqué*, he ended up torn to pieces by the razor-sharp claws of one of the animals to which he had dedicated his life. Using video footage made by Treadwell, Herzog builds a composite, tragic yet irredeemably modest film that deals in various registers: private diary, nature documentary, self-portrait (of a man who seems unable to tell the difference between his childhood teddy bears and the frightening predators with which he dreams of cohabiting in harmony), and an investigation into the quest and ultimate disappearance of an

Grizzly Man,
dir. Werner
Herzog (2006)

infantile individual whom we can't be sure was a visionary, a showoff, or just a nutcase. The uncertainty also affects a piece that bears many of the hallmarks of a hoax—like those phony documentaries that weave a fiction from a cache of lost film (certain scenes in *Grizzly Man* remind one of *The Blair Witch Project*, *Cannibal Holocaust* or Jean-Teddy Filippe's *Les Documents Interdits*). With *Grizzly Man*, though, Herzog gets down to the theoretical bare bones of his cinema, since here fiction and documentary interlock to the point of fusion: reshooting some of his own footage some fifteen times, Treadwell himself appears as a grotesque version of all the megalomaniacs that people Herzog's movies (from Aguirre to Hanussen), developing a vision of the world and of nature radically opposed to Herzog's own, who, off camera and in a voice-over, has no hesitation in taking his subject's ideas to

task. Herzog sees the public's view of nature in technologically advanced cultures as sentimental and anthropomorphic, referring to *March of the Penguins* in France, and Walt Disney in America. It is not so much the industry that he criticizes, though, as the Disney-ization of the whole civilized world. In spite of a measure of respect for Treadwell, he sees his enterprise as an aspect of this process.

JIA ZHANG-KE (born 1970)

Career

Since the end of the 1990s, Jia Zhang-Ke has consolidated his place as a leading figure in the Sixth Generation of Chinese filmmakers (Wang Chao, Wang Xiaoshuai, Yu Lik-Wai) who emerged after the massacre in Tiananmen Square in 1989. Unlike predecessors such as Chen Kaige and Zhang Yimou, Jia Zhang-Ke does not try to cast light on contemporary China by exploring its past, but films the flip side of its economic miracle (poverty, corruption, criminality) directly. After studying in the Taiyuan School of Art and then at the Academy of Film in Beijing, Jia Zhang-Ke founded the "group of experimental film," China's first independent production structure. After two shorts, he shot *Pickpocket* (1998), which already contains the majority of the themes developed in his future output: an apathetic youth that finds it increasingly difficult to construct or even imagine a future (*Unknown Pleasures*, in which a character exclaims "There is no damn future!"); the disintegration of the Chinese working classes in the face of the rise of a caste growing ever richer (*Dong*, a documentary about the famous Three Gorges Dam, and *Still Life*); the superficial models of consumerism (*The World*, and its gigantic amusement park with reduced-scale monuments from around the globe; or *I Wish I Knew*, which added a discordant note to the celebrations for the World's Fair), which simply amplify the ambient loneliness and dejection. Although his films have been met with considerable acclaim in Europe (*Still Life* received a Golden Lion at the Venice Film Festival in 2006), they are practically unknown to the Chinese public, as they tend not to be widely distributed through official channels (except for *The World*, which in 2004 was passed by the regime's board of censorship).

Style

A finely tuned realism (a witness, rather than militant, since he never films "against" anything); a nose for an inert modern youth for whom solidarity and community are a foreign language; a quasi-documentary feel with a direction that strives to draw—in as much detail as possible—real life in a nation undergoing root-and-branch economic and social metamorphosis; a total rejection of miserabilism: these are the chief characteristics of the highly contemporary style of Jia Zhang-Ke, who regularly alternates documentary and fiction. Referring to the high definition he deploys in *The World*, the director emphasizes how its texture feels in step with the modern world, and its color is perfectly adapted to depicting contemporary reality, like "the packaging one can see all over Asia."

Film STILL LIFE (2006)

Planting his camera on the banks of the Yangtze, Jia Zhang-Ke shows the effect of the building of a gigantic dam on a country that, in June 2003, chose to throw open its doors to a breathtakingly rampant capitalism. This vast architectural declaration of intent resulted in the exile of hundreds of thousands of people, in the destruction of ageless cities, and in a transformation in human relations, poisoned by an omnipresent and pathetic venality, ready (as shown in the famous shot of gangster Chow Yun Fat lighting his cigar with a dollar bill in John Woo's *A Better Tomorrow*) to trade in anything: a room, a magic trick, or a woman, for a few yuans more. Like its very last shot (a tightrope-walker is shown edging along between two ruined buildings), *Still Life* constantly hovers in this in-between zone, both temporal (the first part of film takes place as the dam is being constructed, the second a few years afterward) and spatial: Sanming, a miner from northern China, returns after an absence of sixteen years to Fengjie, a two thousand-year-old city flattened by works on the dam, in search of his wife and the little daughter he does not know. Like a character in an American road movie, the exhausted hero of *Still Life* wants to go back home, but finds his origins have been washed away. There, on starvation wages, he is employed on the building site, thus taking part in spite of himself (a man has to earn his keep) in the gradual obliteration of his past. A single panoramic shot, and we jump forward in time. Fengjie is no more than a distant memory. In its place stands a huge, shimmering dam that serves as the backdrop to the story of Shen Hong, a young woman who has also come back to the city, hoping to find her husband,

Still Life, dir. Jia
Zhang-Ke (2006)

whom she wants to sue for divorce. *Still Life* could just have been one more film deploring the horrors of a brutal and homogenizing capitalism (something Jia Zhang-Ke also addresses), but it is less crude than that. In framing the basic aesthetic paradox behind showing a catastrophe in slow-motion, it delineates the permanent upheaval brought about by the hysterical efforts of a nation to convert to progress—in contrast to the relative immobility of the human figures, who drag themselves around, little more than witnesses to an overwhelming and destructive force to which they themselves contribute but from which they will ultimately be excluded.

Beneath the waters, a city wiped off the map of living history; in the air, a building erected by the site's tycoons that shoots up like a rocket; in the middle, thousands of stupefied, dazed men, standing about wondering how they are going to live in this new world, how they can eke out their few paltry possessions (a tea bag, a cigarette, a pack of candy), and stem with their memories the flow of time. Some find what passes for salvation in a radical break (divorce), others in starting a new family and beginning anew.

ABDELLATIF KECHICHE (born 1960)

Career

An actor in the 1980s (in André Téchiné's *Les Innocents* and Nouri Bouzid's *Bezness*), Abdellatif Kechiche moved to directing in 2000, with *La Faute à Voltaire*, a portrait of an illegal immigrant played by a young Sami Bouajila. *L'Esquive* (2003) follows high-school pupils in a deprived Parisian suburb rehearsing a play by eighteenth-century playwright Marivaux that provides the English-language release title, *Games of Love and Chance*. At once romantic and socially aware (quite at odds with the common stereotype of city youth), the approach bore further fruit in a public and critical triumph in 2006, *The Secret of the Grain*. Stooped and taciturn, Slimane has been working in the shipyards of southern France for thirty-five years. Now sixty and worn out, he has a boss gently shepherding him toward the door, and a personal life split between his ex-wife with her vast family and the woman who runs the Orient Hotel and her daughter, Rym (Hafsia Herzi, the revelation of the film). Slimane decides to do something before it's too late, purchasing an rickety old tub in the port of Sète in the hope of converting it into a restaurant specializing in fish couscous—in, that is to say, "grain" and "mullet" (as in the original French title, *La Graine et le Mulet*). The project galvanizes the energies of an entire close-knit, food-loving, loquacious North African community, ravaged by private conflict (rivalry, jealousy, adultery) and collective grievances (the wounds of history gnawing away in the souls of the old, the understated hostility of the "real" French) that the film does not skate over. His subsequent feature was the much-vaunted *Black Venus* (2010).

Style

One example: *The Secret of the Grain* kicks off in minor mode, with lengthy scenes that deceptively remind one of a big-screen version of a through-the-keyhole TV series. It all feels true-to-life (unedifying chat on a building site)—a little too much, even (a little girl refuses to use the potty, preferring to urinate in her diapers). Consisting in extending each sequence to breaking point, in the end Abdellatif Kechiches's idea bears fruit: beyond all the (remarkable) acting skills on show and the (false) impression of a transparent, underwritten narrative for which two and a half hours of chunks of cinéma vérité (a family meal, a showdown between mother and daughter, a woman pushed into a nervous breakdown by her husband's infidelity) would have been sufficient, the power of *The Secret of the Grain* (as with the movies of Dumont) derives primarily from its treatment of time—in the feeling that what is occurring on screen is happening here and now, like in a live broadcast. With these torrents of words that nothing (except perhaps exhaustion on the part of the actors) seems able to stem, one is of course reminded of the cinema of Pialat or the voluble, earthy Italian comedy of the 1970s, but also of the movies of Cassavetes and of the great scene of the meal in *A Woman Under the Influence* that Kechiche recalls as he focuses on that fragile point of balance between conviviality and underlying tension—as in the glorious sequence of the family get-together when, like in a leaking boat, the mother-captain is the only one to man the pumps. A dry-eyed melodrama that delves deep into the private lives of ordinary people; or rather a chamber tragedy, since the film possesses the rare ability (and scope) to endow what is an unassuming story with grandeur.

Film BLACK VENUS (2010)

Black Venus describes the suffering endured by Saartje Baartman in the early nineteenth century: a callipygian serving girl, she was exhibited as a curiosity first in England, then in France, under the moniker of the "Hottentot Venus." Taking up where the final sequence of *The Secret of the Grain* left off (an interminable belly dance that parallels the efforts of an exhausted old man as he wanders around looking for his moped), the movie explores its every ramification. The setup is also the same (a stage with spectators): relayed for two and a half hours, from the Royal Academy of Medicine, whose members expound (via the anatomist Georges Cuvier) on the links between the cast of this "female specimen" fresh from Africa and the other primates, to the brothels of the capital, where the mere sight of the atypical physique of Saartje, now forced into prostitution, sends customers into raptures. From London to Paris, from sordid streets where "monsters" of all kinds are paraded, to the libertine salons of the Restoration, a practically naked Saartje dances and dances, her face impassive, delivered up to the uneasy yet fascinated gaze of a Europe in the grip of a curiosity at once

The Secret of the Grain, dir. Abdellatif Kechiche (2006)

instinctual and morbid. A powerful and necessarily uncomfortable film, radical and theoretical, though never degenerating into sterile, navel-gazing auteurism, the path carved out by *Black Venus* is necessarily a risky one, as it puts our eyes through an exhausting ordeal in an unusual, disturbing manner. Far from the benevolent pathos chosen by David Lynch for *The Elephant Man*, or the bestiary in *Santa Sangre*, and further still from the right-thinking documentaries made by Gualtiero Jacopetti and Paolo Cavara in the 1960s (the *Mondo Cane* series), Kechiche's camera aims at (and attains) that nerve where—as again and again we are confronted with sequences of exhibition; as the characters dissect the body with first their eyes, then rulers, dividers, and eventually scalpels—our gaze gradually liberates itself from its reflexes (voyeurism, unease, lassitude, etc.) to become the subject itself. From this point of view, while *Black Venus* harks back to a distant past and to ways of thinking that at first seem alien, the movie addresses a raft of issues that are still relevant in the modern world. One can compare Saartje's fate to that of the Roman slaves in the amphitheater, abandoned to the tender mercies of a bloodthirsty, jeering crowd. One can also admire the way in which Kechiche, this time from a resolutely contemporary perspective, extrapolates the "madness of seeing" characteristic of present-day society (the expression is borrowed from a title by Christine Buci-Glucksmann, *La folie du voir*), and the consequences of exploiting the image of an Other (TV reality shows?) which, once consumed, even sexually (the ultimate frontier of total exposure foreshadowed by the horrors perpetrated on Saartje), is seen as no more than detritus to be disposed of without a second thought.

TAKESHI KITANO (born 1947)

Career

For the Western public, the name of Takeshi Kitano is syn-onymous with *yakuza* movies, a gangster genre (*Sonatine*, 1993, and *Hana-Bi*, 1997) through which he has earned an international reputation. But in a previous life, in 1970s Japan, Kitano was known as "Beat Takeshi," an underwear-sporting TV firebrand ninja, whose weekly shows (*manzais*, satirical sketches), dealing in an explosive brand of lowbrow comedy with saké sauce, enjoyed a cult following.

A native of Tokyo, in the 1980s Takeshi Kitano changed tack, starring in Nagisa Oshima's 1983 film *Furyo*, where he played the role of a sadistic sergeant opposite David Bowie, and in *Violent Cop* (1989), where he was the lead as a psychopathic detective. During the shoot of the latter movie, director Kinji Fukasaku fell ill and proposed that Kitano replace him. Altering the script, Kitano transformed his character into a tight-lipped, solitary anti-hero.

An immense success in Japan, the movie marks Kitano's beginnings as a filmmaker and fixes the prototype for the characters portrayed by Kitano the actor, up to *Outrage* (2010). Still, in between his *yakuza* films, Kitano explores different routes: *Kikujiro* and *A Scene at the Sea*, in which he looks at the world from the standpoint of a young deaf and dumb surfer who is prey to an unlikely obsession—to conquer the ocean with a piece of wood unearthed in a dumpster. In 2008, he revisits the legend of *Zatoichi* (which are to popular Japanese culture what the Nibelungen are to the Germans), a tale centering on the peregrinations of a blind, sword-wield-ing masseur who plies the land in search of odd jobs. With its spurts of blood and whirling limbs, *Zatoichi* joins the long line of movies in the great tradition of *chambara* (samurai films drenched in gore) that Kitano, a screenwriter of dazzling and elliptic violence, here elevates to an acme of perfection.

Style

Kitano's cinema is predicated on contrast. An author of a con-jointly contemplative and explosive body of work, in which long sequence shots alternate with outbursts of violence (as shown in his masterpiece *Hana-Bi*, where the crime yarn is constantly being waylaid by a more private drama—a woman is dying—and a near animist sense for nature. His direction constantly oscillates between grace and baseness, between poetic pessimism and a form of irony that simultaneously evokes the crime fiction of Seijun Suzuki, the westerns of Sergio Leone, and a nose for visual jokes worthy of Tati. One of the avant-garde talents of 1990s Asian cinema (with Wong Kar-Wai, Hou Hsiao-Hsien, Tsui Hark, and John Woo), Kitano shows an incredible ability to blend a taste for the burlesque and a latent sadness that verges on poetic melodrama—as in a reference to Cocteau in *Kikujiro*, he paints eyes on closed eyelids, or in the image of a broken kite that ends *Hana-Bi*. In *Zaitoichi*, he seeks less to affirm his mastery of the genre and its rhetoric (from *The Matrix* to *Kill Bill*, every choreographed combat sequence since the end of the 1990s is practically a Japanese byproduct), than to revitalize it with playfulness and buoyancy. The blood, fake and digitized, the omnipres-ence of masks and the final tap-dance sequence amount to a rejection of the violence inherent in the genre that Kitano here distills into a life-enhancing spectacle.

Film OUTRAGE (2010)

In *Outrage*, the world closes back once more onto rival gangs of *yakuzas* who, for some two hours, will kill, humil-iate, and maim each other with the unique purpose of entitling themselves to wear the cream-colored sports-wear of the clan leader. The story, at the same time minimalist and impenetrable (the audience ends up losing track of the protagonists' endless volte-faces), can be sum-marized as a series of thorough beatings; as if Kitano's cinema, since the accident he suffered in 1994, has nar-rowed its focus to the face, become the theater for every kind of disfiguration. A film of convalescence, where the longed-for second wind depends on fists and box-cutters, *Outrage* prolongs (but solely to bring to end), the three main lines of Kitano's movie-making: from the buffoon "Beat Takeshi," via the instant of grace (Kitano as cool-hand nihilist remodeling the *yakuza* movie in the 1990s), to Kitano the actor, remembered especially for *Blood and Bones*, a film by Yoichi Sai in which he plays a tireless thug carving him-self a path to social success through violence and abuse.

Brother, dir. Takeshi Kitano (2000)

It is difficult, therefore, to know if this is fish or fowl—whether we are watching the ultimate in hardboiled cinema or a blood-soaked farce-cum-fable about the absurdity of capitalist society, of which the *yakuza* are simply a hyperbolic and grotesque extrapolation.

It is soon clear that Kitano is far less interested in the development of a (deliberately) repetitive narrative that he gleefully perceives as leading to a dead-end (for there will always be *yakuza* no. 2 to splatter the brains of *yakuza* no. 1), or in yet another depressing variation of the old timer who has to give it one last shot, than in the peculiar process of social climbing that it describes. Kitano here plays a "middle class" *yakuza*, aging but far from busted, both witness to and actor in an inarticulate existence (no external reality filters through into the *yakuza* bubble), prey to an inextinguishable and pathological lust for power fueled by self-destructive impulses. The splendor of *Outrage*, and its sarcastic side, stems from how it pares down the functioning of this mafia universe to its absolute bare bones (mechanical rituals, fingers sliced off including for

no reason, a series of double-crossings and compromises that they are no longer even especially eventful), so that it becomes light and superficial, but without obscuring the seriousness behind the film.

DAVID LYNCH (born 1946)

Career

The story isn't really the point for David Lynch. What can one say, for example, about his debut feature *Eraserhead*, made between 1975 and 1980? Is it the tale of a man (Jack Nance) with nightmares about becoming a dad? Or is it about a child monster looking like a chicken born into a strange family inhabiting an airless, postapocalyptic world? Or are they all the weird and wonderful, Kafkaesque visions of a filmmaker exploring the dark side of the human psyche? *Eraserhead* is, in fact, all this and much more—like all David Lynch's movies, indeed, with the exception perhaps of *Elephant Man* and *Dune*, both more traditional in form and narrative.

Born in Missoula, Montana, in 1946, Lynch's early contacts were with painting and drawing: "I learned that, just beneath the surface, there was another world, and, if one dug deeper still, other worlds besides." After a mildly turgid adaptation of Frank Herbert's saga (*Dune* in 1984), with *Blue Velvet* (1986) he laid out the building blocks for an interiorized, angst-inducing cinema, dealing in large doses of atmospheric imagery and involving narratives (*Lost Highway* and *Mulholland Drive*) practically without parallel in contemporary cinema. An artistic all-rounder (filmmaker, painter, musician), in 1990 Lynch made *Wild at Heart* (Palme d'Or at the Cannes Film Festival), plunging the couple of Nicolas Cage and Laura Dern into a nightmarish road movie, populated with weird characters and featuring a fairy straight out of *The Wizard of Oz*, one of the director's favorite movies.

Dovetailed from two at the same time distinct and symmetrical parts, *Lost Highway* (1997) is one in a category of unclassifiable films. "I don't like pictures that are one genre only, so this is a combination of things. It is a kind of a horror film, it is a kind of a thriller. But basically it's a mystery. For me, a mystery is like a magnet. As soon as a thing is unknown, it has a pull to it." There then followed *The Straight Story* (1999), in which an old grouch drives his lawnmower several hundred miles to visit his long-lost brother. In 2001, Lynch made one of the most outstanding and influential films of the decade: *Mulholland Drive*, the Hollywood dream as lived by a fledgling actress, with *Vertigo* in the director's rearview mirror.

Style

Beneath the ostensibly unremarkable, inoffensive surface, lurks a chaotic world riven by unseen, sinister powers: this would be a fair description of the average Lynch picture, from *Blue Velvet* to *Mulholland Drive*. The former kicks off by delineating life in an American small town where not much happens. The houses, the inhabitants, the flowerpots, the pets—it's a triumph of the American way of life; it's all there, like in a postcard. Then, suddenly, the veneer cracks, and the camera stumbles across a severed ear decomposing on a manicured lawn and plunges down its auditory canal, as in a prelude to the descent into hell. The film can then begin in earnest, revealing beneath the antiseptic surface a universe throbbing with perversions and murderous impulses. In *Twin Peaks: Fire Walk with Me*, a movie he made in 1992, after the TV series, Lynch again subverts the Norman Rockwell picture of life in an American residential suburb: goodie-two-shoes coeds morph into sex-crazed nymphettes; a fine family man seems guilty of incest with his daughter; a paragon of youthful womanhood (Laura Palmer) is found dead. Quite apart from a talent for summoning up strange visions (a charred ghost emerging from behind a diner, a be-suited dwarf plugged into the AC current, a cadaverous Man from Another Place who haunts the thoughts of a saxophonist convinced that his wife is having an affair), Lynch's cinema is characterized by the progressive unsettling of reality and of the laws of space–time, resulting in a disturbing yet half-familiar world, where everything is at once similar and dissimilar. As with Argento, Lynch's images appear indefinable, caught between two contradictory but compatible states, between illusion and reality, past and future, outside and inside, evincing the feeling of an esoteric world overlaid by its mysterious double.

Mulholland Drive, dir. David Lynch (2001)

Film MULHOLLAND DRIVE (2001)

After the motorized lawnmower of *The Straight Story*, David Lynch returns to the tortuous side-roads of *Lost Highway*. A testimony to its creator's inexhaustible playfulness: he is a great purveyor of optical illusions and puzzles, tracks that snake into labyrinths, details that open up into bottomless pits, and mental spaces that should not perhaps taken too seriously. The curtain rises on Mulholland Drive. Rita, a mysterious femme fatale (Laura Elena Harring), survives a car accident but emerges with amnesia. She then crosses the path of Betty Elms (Naomi Watts), a Canadian actress who has just touched down in L.A., hoping to make a career in Hollywood. Like *Lost Highway*, its movie twin, *Mulholland Drive* leaves the door ajar to a vast range of interpretations. At the time it came out, conscious of the hermeneutic fever the film was about to propagate, Lynch provided "ten keys" to guide (in other words, to further confuse) the audience through his Pandora's box. In one putative reading, the first half of *Mulholland Drive* presents Diane's dream—or, rather, the idealized version of her arrival in Los Angeles and her meteoric success, while the second marks the violent irruption of the reality principle: murder, the mafia, treason, rotting corpses; i.e., the real, sordid story of the young woman, and, in passing, a poisonous if sensual critique of Hollywood as nightmare factory. Imagine a psychotropic version of Billy Wilder's *Sunset Boulevard*. Perhaps that will give you an idea.

TERRENCE MALICK (born 1943)

Career

He resembles something like the Thomas Pynchon of contemporary cinema—an enigmatic and invisible man (not expected to provide photographs, interviews, or indeed any physical effort to promote his movies), a living legend about whom little is known and who has made five films since 1974. Born in Illinois, Terrence Malick began behind the camera aged thirty with *Badlands*, after studies at Harvard and the American Film Institute. This murderous rampage of a teenager couple in the 1950s Midwest clashed with the road movies of the time (whose model was essentially *Bonnie and Clyde*) by its sense of distance and its constant emphasis on nature as a purifying medium, which, however, can do nothing to forestall the final (and long-expected) scene of carnage. Four years later Malick made *Days of Heaven* headlining (after Martin Sheen) another young actor, Richard Gere. Shot in daylight on the plains of Alberta, *Days of Heaven* follows the path of a workman from Chicago as he discovers the life of a farmer. The movie offers confirmation of Malick's animist style, to which is added a mystical (Christian?) quest, illustrated here by a plague of locusts lifted straight from the Bible. A lengthy period of silence followed, ending with *The Thin Red Line* in 1999, a three-hour movie recalling one of the bloodiest episodes in the war for the Pacific, the Battle of Guadalcanal. *The Thin Red Line*, however, was not what was expected of a war movie (the more traditional *Saving Private Ryan* came out at the same time), and confronts instead human cruelty with the spectacle of nature at her most grandiose and indifferent. This was followed in 2005 by *The New World*, whose title is a direct reference to Walt Whitman ("I heard that you ask'd for something to prove this puzzle, the New World"), and *The Tree of Life* (2011), where the tumultuous youth of a boy growing up in the 1950s intersects with an analysis of the genesis of humankind sparked by the Book of Job.

Style

At first sight, Terrence Malick's cinema lies outside the traditional scope of Hollywood cinema, and the genres he feigns to adopt. The works he composes are lyrical, melancholic, and of course (the adjective commonly employed by writers trying to describe his style), pantheistic. What does this actually mean? A way of shifting the view of history of particular men onto that of humanity generally, of reconnecting (like Vidor, Flaherty, or the Murnau of *Sunrise* before him) with a Nature that harbors a thousand secrets, and of returning to the ideas of the American transcendentalism of Whitman or Emerson, with its essentialist relation to the world. The rugged prairie and the grasshoppers falling from the sky that close *Days of Heaven*, or the first scene in *The Thin Red Line*, with an alligator waddling in a backwater—the image of a lost paradise, here a Melanesian Garden of Eden soon to be flattened by bombing. In *Badlands*, Kit (Martin Sheen) models his cavalcade on the rebellious James Dean, and, blissfully unconscious of reality, probably believes he can escape from its guiding principle by enacting his own death. Holly (Sissy Spacek), the girl who imagines herself as Kit's Bonnie Parker, occupies a more ambivalent position, at once inside the situation but outside herself (her voice-over comments on their adventure as it unfolds), with one foot in the real and the other in her unsophisticated representation of it. And when Holly builds her own small world with Kit in a clearing, it resembles a makeshift camp modeled on pictures from the stories they knew as children, halfway between Tom Sawyer and Tarzan. Not a return to the sources of hippiedom, but to those of preindustrial innocence. Malick's movies resemble daydreams, while the story, however violent it may prove to be, comes over as muted, hushed. It is Holly, the lunar Lolita of *Badlands*, her voice-over a means of excluding herself from a world whose origins are to be sought only in the imagination; or the final segment of *The New World*, which attains a peak of intelligence and poetry when, having been received at the English royal court, the young Indian girl experiences the magic of the Old World in a garden in London.

The New World, dir. Terrence Malick (2006)

Film THE NEVV VVORLD (2006)

The year is 1607. Three English ships in search of the treasure they think they will find in the still unexplored territories of America hove into view and make land in Virginia. There, this first community of colonists to settle in the New World founds Jamestown. A British officer, John Smith (Colin Farrell), is dispatched to make first contact with the tribe of the Powhatans and is bewitched by one of the chief's daughters, the young Pocahontas (never named as such in the film). As war spreads (the only law the English observe is that of the gun), the contemplative exploration of this earthly paradise gains pace (Malick's pantheism has finally found its true home, as America at that time was nature, fantasy, and a history about to start again all rolled into one). *The New World* tells at the same time of a love idyll that ends in the knot-gardens of London, of the nightmare lived by a handful of colonists who, nibbling at the fringes of the great continent, owe their salvation to a single young Indian girl, and finally, and especially, nothing less than of the foundation of the American nation. From the (extraordinary) opening sequence, Malick turns the myth inside out like a glove: the arrival of the ships is filmed from the coast, not then from the time-honored viewpoint of the colonists, but from that of the Indians, who see the ships weighing anchor as offering a potential New World for them. Consequently, the film rehearses the history of America backwards, throwing the epic of conquest out of the window (the mythology of the Frontier no longer exists), and focuses instead on the trajectory of the young Indian girl (Q'Orianka Kilcher), whose every appearance amounts to a séance of possession. From the shimmering forests of Virginia to the corseted world of England, it is the young woman who lives the dream, not the soon dejected colonists. Because the New World described in Malick's movie is not that Promised Land vaingloriously trumpeted by the western, nor that of a space over which the Old World will proclaim itself master, but Old Europe, in which a Native American girl disembarks and, totally unexpectedly, finds her place.

MICHAEL MANN (born 1943)

Career

Michael Mann belongs to the generation of the New Hollywood mavericks, and continues down the paths they trod. But, while his colleagues of the 1970s were making their debuts, Mann was making socially committed documentaries, including *17 Days Down the Line* (1972), telling of the trials and tribulations of an American reporter in Biafra and Northern Ireland, and a TV film, *The Jericho Mile* (1979), which already offered proof of painstaking attention to realism (the movie was made in a genuine prison with genuine inmates). In 1981, Mann shot his first feature, *Thief*, a melancholic crime thriller about a burglar eager to go straight and have a family. Mann then made *The Keep*, a cross between a war movie and Gothic horror, and in 1986 adapted the novel *Red Dragon* by Thomas Harris (*Manhunter*, the first appearance of the Hannibal Lecter character on film), before turning to television. There, he created and produced the cult series *Miami Vice* (1984 to 1990), whose cops in Cerruti suits, slow-mos of pink flamingoes taking off, voluptuous girls sporting G-strings, and glass-and-steel urban settings distill a portrait of 1980s America—that of individualism and Wall Street, of conspicuous success and phoniness that will serve as a laboratory for Mann's future movie career (the formal bases for *Heat* and *Collateral* appear in it). In 1992, Mann made *The Last of the Mohicans*, after the novel of the same name by James Fennimore Cooper, and then the impressive *Heat* (1995), a three-hour long crime thriller with Al Pacino and Robert De Niro, the ne plus ultra of the American cinema of the 1990s in which he reached artistic maturity. This was followed in particular by *The Insider* (2001), *Collateral* (2004), *Miami Vice* (2006), and *Public Enemies* (2008).

Style

Mann is surely the greatest stylist and inventor of forms in contemporary American cinema (can it be a coincidence that he was the first to try out HD?), a "super auteur" within the Hollywood machine who, beneath the veil of genre and his characters obsessed with professionalism, has developed an aesthetic identifiable from a single take: a mix of fascination and angst with respect to the modern world, a melancholic relationship with passing time, and the utilization of metallic, geometric forms tinged in blue (*Heat*), which dissolves individuals into apparitions, into disembodied beings, almost into living dead.

Mann's formal system is designed to generate encounters, collisions, intersections that immediately acquire a metaphysical dimension. Thus, his movies proceed not only from a perfect understanding of the modern city (Los Angeles, especially), affiliating them 100 percent with the urban action movie, but also from the concrete geometry of their relationships. Here, inside an anonymous environment that emphasizes transparency (void of the contemporary world?) and existential angst, a man's fate is inextricably caught up in the formal and topographic dynamics that reformulate his life.

For instance, *Miami Vice*, a dazzling synthesis of impressionism and hyperrealism shot in HD (a technique that Mann and head of cinematography Dion Beebe had inaugurated in *Collateral*), coalesces into an unusual sensory experience. The palpable graininess of the image, the increased sensitivity to light of this medium, the dilution of the hues; all confer a density never before seen on a movie screen. A flash streaks through the sky, a palm tree flexes in the wind, and the incandescent night tracked by Mann's camera spawns a hypnotic film where man and nature dissolve one into the other, palpitating together in the same tragic breath.

Film MIAMI VICE (2006)

Miami Vice, one of key films of the 2000s, follows a path halfway between crime movie and spy film. Before shattering into a thousand fragments, the fiction opens with the murder of an FBI agent who has infiltrated the drug world. On a mission to clear up the affair, two police inspectors from Miami, Sonny Crocket and Ricardo Tubbs, go undercover as hardened traffickers and reach the financial brain of the cartel, a vast organization with awesome means at its disposal. In a few short minutes, Mann evacuates the picturesque typical of the genre (colorful gangsters, henchmen from the wrong side of the tracks, smooth operators boasting infallibly dreadful taste—that is to say, the entire *Scarface* scrapbook of 1983—to weave a mafia fabric with vaguer contours, a state within a state, as at ease arranging to wire massive amounts of dirty money as at clinically topping those who fail to pay up. On the face of it, Michael Mann seems to revert to the vein of a 1970s exposé film (*Three Days of the Condor* or *The Parallax View*, as already in *The Insider*), redeploying its shifting identities, its obsession with plots, and its all-encompassing paranoia. But, deep down, Mann films this high-flying, drug-trafficking caper in the style of a war movie, where the question is essentially one of logistics, monitoring, information pooling, and technological supremacy. The world of *Miami Vice* is without borders; exploded and fragmentary, it is held together solely due to the financial river that runs through it, possessing no logic other than that of supply and demand imposed by the various vested interests. It does not even matter whether what is bought is legal or not; nor does the nature of the market matter, since the film treats capitalism as a war (the drug godfather watches Bloomberg TV), exploiting the resources of the Third World (here, the Dominican Republic, Paraguay, and Uruguay), remorselessly eliminating every competitor with sure-footed violence. As a counterpoint to the chaos and opacity of human relationships, the film indulges in countless effects of surface (picture windows, beachfront villas) and slippage (offshore, in planes, in supercharged automobiles). This is indeed the great subject of the cinema of Michael Mann: How can man keep hold of a disembodied world, so transparent and yet, at root, so opaque? How can he keep from disappearing? Like all Mann's movies, *Miami Vice* is recounted from the point of view of the sliver of time remaining to us. "Time is luck," Gong Li is constantly telling Colin Farrell, echoing the melancholy crook played by Robert De Niro in *Heat*.

Miami Vice, dir. Michael Mann (2006)

NANNI MORETTI (born 1953)

Career

Where he lives, in Rome, Nanni Moretti is known for two passions: the cinema and water polo, a sport he long played professionally. His movies often depict the marriage between sport and the mind, like the bereft character he plays in *The Son's Room*, who tries to straighten himself out by playing tennis. The films of the self-taught Moretti, whose parents were both teachers, are rooted in the history of contemporary Italy, on which they provide a pitiless commentary. With *Ecce Bombo* (1978), his second movie, he paints a caustic portrait of his own 1970s generation through the doubts of a lefty student. After *Sweet Dreams* and *Bianca*, Moretti made *The Mass is Ended* (1985), in which he plays a priest worried about the meaning of his life and the nature of his faith. In *Palombella Rossa*, his role is that of an Italian Communist Party apparatchik and water-polo player who, following a car accident, loses his memory and finds himself competing in a match with some bizarre individuals. *Caro Diario*, made in 1994, is divided into three parts, connected by the wanderings of its main character (again, Moretti himself). The film opens with a long ride on a Vespa through the streets of Rome to the beach at Ostia where Pier Paolo Pasolini was killed in 1975. Buoyed along by Keith Jarrett's *Köln Concert*, the sequence is surely one of the great moments in Moretti's cinema. In 2001, he was awarded the Golden Palm at the Cannes Film Festival for *The Son's Room*.

Style

As the title of his debut film (*I Am Self-Sufficient*) announces, Nanni Moretti's cinema favors the autobiographical form: acting in the majority of his own movies, Moretti, somewhat in the manner of a politicized Woody Allen, addresses the world around him as much as his private life, dissecting Berlusconi's Italy, X-raying all its "monsters" and its fault-lines (politics as spectacle; the TV industry; political militancy), but also expressing his joy at becoming a father (*Aprile*). His detractors have reproached him for narcissism and ideological rigidity. A savage adversary of American cinema (in *Caro Diario*, he lays into

a journalist who had the temerity to praise John McNaughton's *Henry, Portrait of a Serial Killer*), he also runs a small movie theater in the heart of Rome that shows his favorite films. Moretti is one of the few Italian filmmakers to have emerged in the 1980s, reactivating the dual heritage of neorealism and the cruel—carnivorous even—irony of the Italian comedy of Risi, Monicelli, and Scola. Restrained and neurotic, burlesque and caustic, the style of Moretti's oeuvre is fundamentally informed by few questions: How can Italians get beyond the endemic stalemate of their political life? How does one create a new way of writing and making films? How can one fight cancer?

Film THE CAIMAN (2006)

The Caiman is the title of a script (in the film) handed one day by an unknown young female director to Bruno Bonomo, a producer of B movies in the 1970s, who, by the time the movie takes place, is teetering on the brink of bankruptcy. *The Caiman* recounts the life of an unscrupulous businessman, who, thanks to a suitcase crammed with banknotes that (literally) falls from the sky, sets out to gain power. Bonomo initially spots an opportunity to make a fortune by making a traditional mafia movie, but, as he reads on, it dawns on him that the Caiman in question is in fact none other than Silvio Berlusconi. In spite of the withdrawal of Italian state TV, droves of actors discovering they have subsequent engagements, and the collapse of his marriage (an issue he refuses to confront; probably the finest aspect of the movie), Bonomo stands firm, and, on a shoestring budget, produces a film showing the last days of the "Caiman," his (real) trial, and his (imaginary) condemnation. The portrait of the Italy of the last thirty years that Moretti presents here amounts to a damning caricature, and resembles the comedies of the glory years of the 1970s, concurrently tragic and comic: comic, if one considers the rise and rise of the entrepreneur to the Presidency as a sorry succession of financial swindles and political dirty-dealing, of photo-ops and sound bites.

The point though is that, after three decades of satire and caricature, Berlusconi continues to tighten his grip on the structures of power and on public opinion alike. Laughed at, openly sneered at, the man has gradually become likeable, omnipresent, like an inoffensive buffoon who forms part of the furniture. "In any event, Berlusconi has already won because he has changed people's heads," as Moretti the actor declares when Bruno offers him the part of Il Cavaliere. How can one hope to fight when comedies are made and yet all

The Caiman, dir. Nanni Moretti (2006)

the laughter ends up serving the person being denounced? How can one's opposition be effective when, as the Caiman says, "The Left can only do one thing: hate me"? The hour had come to take Berlusconi seriously and to revert to the style of the great left-leaning fictions of Elio Petri and Francesco Rosi. Just like the caiman—a snarling, cold-hearted beast. Little by little, the film within the film shifts from B movie to Shakespearean drama, and, when Moretti returns at the end with the drawn features of his political adversary, the tone is serious, almost tragic. Alone in a car resembling a tomb, the Caiman spouts snatches of his known speeches (a UN diplomat is called a "Kapo"), but, in Moretti's mouth, they resonate differently, sounding at once newly minted and spine-chilling.

GASPAR NOÉ (born 1963)

Career

Born in Argentina to a father who was a painter and a militant mother, Gaspar Noé arrived in France at the age of twelve. After studying philosophy and cinema (at the École Louis-Lumière), in 1985 he assisted filmmaker Fernando Solanas in *Tangos, the Exile of Gardel*. *Carne*, a short he made in 1991, describes the sordid daily existence of a butcher (Philippe Nahon) bringing up a daughter afflicted with psychosis. *I Stand Alone*, his debut feature, continues in the wake of *Carne*, and Nahon once more plays the character of the solitary, nihilistic butcher (the film is rather awkwardly punctuated by title cards in the misanthropic vein of Louis Ferdinand Céline), who, since he has nothing to lose, slips into the unknown and into violence. The release in 2001 of *Irreversible* raised horrified highbrows among the more shockable critics. This exceptionally violent and squalid revenge yarn, in which two men (Vincent Cassel and Albert Dupontel) supposedly hunt down the rapist of the partner of one of them (Monica Bellucci), constitutes the most radical film by its director, and in the cinema of the 2000s generally. In *Enter the Void* (2010), brother (Oscar) and sister (Linda) eke out a living in Tokyo, setting up little dope deals and hanging around strip joints. One evening, Oscar, denounced by one of his customers, is killed by the police in a nightclub. His spirit leaves its physical husk and wanders through the streets of the Japanese capital. "The pleasure of making cinema," Gaspar Noé declared when the film came out, "is to impose technical challenges on oneself that one then tries to overcome. Nothing satisfies me more than creating images that have never been seen before. In *Enter the Void*, I tried to place audiences in an hypnotic state, a shamanic trance even, like in a drug trip."

Style

Kubrick's *2001* (explicitly quoted in the last take of *Irreversible*) is his filmic starting point, and his cinema is imprinted by a pessimistic metaphysics of violence. With visual experimentation as his credo, for Noé, genius, native guile, and naivety overlap seamlessly.

In *Enter the Void*, the spirit of the deceased flits from building to building, disappears down a hole and reemerges from another, crisscrossing the borders of space–time. Fascinated by the subjective experience in *The Lady of the Lake* (1945), Noé's film is extreme in form, unstinting in its quest for technical brio, and, thus, for new images. The vaporous atmosphere of what is an artificial yet fascinating Tokyo, both kitsch and down-at-heel, the poetic deployment of digital effects, and, especially, the originality of certain takes confer an undeniable beauty on the film. Noé's style presupposes a pact that the audience must decide to enter into, or not: in *Irreversible*, the back-to-front narrative structure means that a banal story of vengeance is transcended; in *Enter the Void*, the idea is to show us what it is to be immersed in a dead man's soul, to float above the world, to penetrate through every available aperture (some are very strange indeed), with an omnipotent camera that glides fluidly and generates a sensation of weightlessness. If *Enter the Void* and *Irreversible* can seem interminable (repulsive even in the second case) to those left cold by the experiment, they nonetheless make a novel and sometimes breathtaking impact in comparison with the restricted formal parameters characteristic of much contemporary French cinema.

Film IRREVERSIBLE (2001)

You need a strong stomach. And unflinching eyes, too, if you are going to able to bear this almost uninterrupted vision of wet, red tunnels. Released in 2001, to a sulfurous whiff of scandal, *Irreversible* is surely one of the most radical films of the 2000s, with a cerebral if grimy rawness, halfway between Leonard Kastle's *Honeymoon Killers* and the experimental films of Kenneth Anger (the sequence showing gay backrooms recalls the deliriously scarlet S&M of *Scorpio Rising*). Through this undeniably brilliant stylistic exercise (composed in thirteen sections and six "takes," the story is told in reverse, from end to beginning), with its terrible rape scene filmed uninterrupted, Noé investigates a form of violence that has less to do with the law, with morality, or with social context than with the strictly negative impulses that the film

Irreversible, dir. Gaspar Noé (2001)

exalts. The sexual aggression and the terrible disfigurement inflicted on Monica Bellucci do not have their source in a pathology, but in the simple pleasure of assuaging, here and now, an impulse to transgress (to possess the other and then annihilate its beauty). The vengeance of Dupontel and Cassel forfeits the cathartic function it enjoyed in the genre (see the *Death Wish* series, with Charles Bronson), not only because the effect precedes the cause in the narrative, but also, as we will subsequently learn, because the man butchered at the beginning of the film is not the rapist. Like the image in the movie's first take, where the camera circles above two men flopped in a seedy hotel room, *Irreversible* consists in a powerful sensory experience that betrays its creator's passion for images on the edge. For instance, the soundtrack includes frequencies as low as 27 hertz, liable to induce physical nausea in the hearer.

PARK CHAN-WOOK (born 1963)

Career

Born in Seoul, a onetime film critic, Park Chan-Wook made his debut movie in 1992 (*Moon Is the Sun's Dream*), but finds his true voice eight years later with *Joint Security Area*, which tackles the conflict opposing the two Koreas. In 2002 he signed *Sympathy for Mister Vengeance*, the first opus in a trilogy on revenge that was followed by *Oldboy*, which earned him an international reputation. How can one describe this insane film, so characteristic of its author? Quite simply, revenge is an octopus best eaten … alive. For no discernible reason, a rather strange father is kidnapped by persons unknown, and locked up in a room with a television as his only link with the outside world. Through it, he learns of the return of Hong Kong to China, the attacks of September 11, and the slaughter of his wife, for which he is named as the number one suspect. Finally released, Oh Dae-soo starts his manhunt, tracking down his assailant like a bulldozer, with only one thing on his mind: vengeance. With hammer blows, with dentist's pincers, and with supercharged fists, Oh Dae-Soo imprints on the film an energy that veers violently between breathlessness and suffocation, between sublimity and overkill. The finest sequence: the camera tracks along with Oh Dae-Soo, caught like a rat in a corridor filled with goons out for blood, in which he resembles a dark superhero (*Oldboy* was adapted from a *manga*), indestructible, constantly in overdrive—just like the film, often dazzling, occasionally stifling.

With *I'm a Cyborg, But That's OK* (2006), Park Chan-Wook plunges us between the four spotless walls of an asylum for the (largely inoffensive) insane. Here, rage that has been bottled up all too long (*Oldboy*) is replaced by the prolonged, poetic rehumanization of a young woman convinced she is an automaton. It all begins on the assembly line in an electronics factory, a chilly and eminently Korean vision of Chaplin's *Modern Times*, where one discovers armies of docile female workers dressed as little red riding hoods. Suddenly, one of them, Young-Goon, slices open a vein, inserts two wires, and, following instructions from a disembodied electronic voice, plugs herself into a socket. A mental and real short-circuit,

Young-Goon henceforth thinks she's a cyborg, refuses to eat, only talks to coffee machines and radio sets, and ends up being packed off to a psychiatric unit filled with oddballs whose minor pathologies the movie delineates. There, she meets a young man sporting a rabbit mask who will try to bring her round to a semblance of humanity. Unlike in an "asylum film," often an occasion to tell the story from the point of view of a "normal" person who has infiltrated a clinic (see the voluntarily interned journalists of *Shock Corridor*, as well as *One Flew over the Cuckoo's Nest*), from the start *I Am a Cyborg* sees things from the objectively madcap standpoint of its heroine—a metaphor for a world of consumerism that has mutated into a programmable society. In the end, the film seems to say, we all are cyborgs, with ersatz imaginations, automated behavior patterns, and mechanical reflexes. A *kawaii* ("cute," in Japanese), yet poetically subversive movie, in which one can flick through an album of drawings by a psychopath, or walk about wearing grandma's dentures, *I Am a Cyborg* is a great film about love between people whom the "society of spectacle" has made ill.

Style

With their unadulterated power of proliferation, their breakneck speed and exhaustiveness, the movies of Park Chan-Wook—emblematic of contemporary Korean cinema—seem afflicted by an insane archival addiction, violent yet lyrical, at once mannerist and experimental, a combination between collector and fetishist. Hyperinventive aesthetically, his films sample various worlds—like *I Am a Cyborg*, which mashes dream sequences from the films of Michael Gondry, with the cartoonesque left-field of Tarantino/Rodriguez's grindhouse, and the syrupy universe of *Charlie and the Chocolate Factory*. If rooted in this formal and narrative superabundance, each film nonetheless ends up speaking with a voice of its own, with its own unique and majestic manner. One needs courage to embark on the adventure that is watching the films of Park Chan-Wook: one must not be afraid of brutal changes in register, one has to enjoy the switch from burlesque tragedy to private melodrama, from the crudest gore to the most over-the-top fantastic. But what one discovers at the end of this often exhausting journey dispels one's misgivings.

Film THIRST (2009)

A Catholic priest undergoes a transfusion with blood from an unknown source and is transformed into a vampire, meeting a friend with whom he had lost contact and embarking on a destructive love story with his young wife. A vampire movie with layers like a palimpsest, a gore melodrama flicking between Douglas Sirk and the burlesque blood-fests of Peter Jackson, a morbid film of the family, in Polanski mode, where normal surfaces conceal the deep-rooted horror beneath, *Thirst*, like all Park Chan-Wook's films, flows from a wellspring of forms and films: the rather simple-minded if humanist priest played by Shin Ha-Ky (the director's favorite actor) does not manage to reconcile his profound humanism with the mad love that binds him to Tae-Joo (the captivating Kim Ok-Vin), a poor little Korean match girl, hamstrung by a deadweight of a family and an impotent husband, who, once bitten, morphs into a carnivorous ingénue. Now without any scruples, monstrous yet moving, angel *fatale*, Tae-Joo (like a remote cousin of Argento's Jenifer) feels she has to make up for lost time, for a stolen youth. But she will never be able to rid herself of the dreariness of Korea (what occurs to her ghastly mother has to be seen to be believed). This is a concentrate of the vital energy characteristic of the cinema of Park Chan-Wook, which always revolves round an obsession with revenge. Detractors may argue that the film lacks rigor and tension—that it's overwritten, overflowing, overlong. Perhaps. But the tireless inventiveness of Park Chan-Wook, his capacity to reorganize melodrama and vampire movie (Kill for love? Or be a coward, and keep going by sucking up the blood of dying patients off a drip?), sweeps all before it. One glorious idea among many others: in *Thirst*, there's no need for a modern Van Helsing since the pious, the chaste, the virtuous—in other words, the ghoul hunter—is ensconced within the vampire's own split personality: unbridled impulse and its opposite in the same body.

Thirst, dir. Park Chan-Wook (2009)

ROMAN POLANSKI (born 1933)

Career

Born in Paris to Polish Jewish parents, young Roman's family moved back to Warsaw in 1936. These dark days in European history (his mother was one of those exterminated in the camps), were evoked in 2002 in *The Pianist*. He made his first feature film in 1962, *Knife in the Water*, an oppressive chamber piece in which two men tear each other apart for a woman's favors. Carrying off the Critics Prize at the Venice Mostra, the movie launched the young filmmaker's career. After *Repulsion* (1965), *The Fearless Vampire Killers* (1967), a jaw-dropping parody of the Dracula myth, propelled him onto the international scene, and soon Paramount offered him a deal to adapt Ira Levin's bestseller, *Rosemary's Baby*. A summit of the genre, *Rosemary's Baby* inaugurates, with Romero's *Night of the Living Dead*, made the same year, the era of the modern fantastic cinema. Polanski applies Kafka's principle to the letter: the more fantastic you become, the more realistic you have to remain. Two years after the murder of his wife, actress Sharon Tate, by the Manson "family" in August 1969, Polanski returned to the cinema with a blood-streaked version of Shakespeare's *Macbeth*, before tackling another genre, film noir. *Chinatown*, a dark and ironic piece, perfectly translates the post-Watergate suspicion that racked America at the time. After *The Tenant*, Polanski, in an adaptation of Thomas Hardy's work, cast Nastassja Kinski in the title role of *Tess*. His career ran out of steam in the 1980s, with *Pirates* (1986), an adventure film pastiche, *Frantic* (1988), a thriller set in Paris, *Bitter Moon* (1992), and *Death and the Maiden* all showing signs of weakness. *The Pianist*, shot in 2002, signaled his return to form.

Style

Two men emerge from the sea dragging a mirror-fronted wardrobe. They try to take the tram, to get a room in a hotel, a table in a restaurant, but their burden arouses irritation, resentment, and, soon enough, anger among all those they encounter. The first known film by Polanski, *Two Men and a Wardrobe* (a student short made at the school in Lodz in

1958) already contains the bases of his future oeuvre: a taste for the absurd, at the intersection between Kafka, Beckett, and Ionesco; a queasy, ironic angle; and, finally, an obsession with confinement—be it physical or mental—as a recurrent symbol of our ontological solitude in this world. Polanski's cinema is always balanced on a tightrope, forcing audiences to choose which way they want to walk: horror, the grotesque, the bizarre, and the ridiculous are all churned up unceasingly, fusing into an unstable, paranoia-inducing universe. In *Rosemary's Baby*, a great film for theorizing, Mia Farrow's growing anguish clashes with her almost caricature humdrum existence, where the most banal situations (Castevet's chocolate mousse) exacerbate the impression of uncanny strangeness. With *Repulsion* (and, ten years later, *The Tenant*), Polanski lays down the rules of cerebral horror, showing Catherine Deneuve, a nondescript manicurist gradually sinking into madness, as the prototype of the modern personality—alienated, unpredictable. In a Polanski movie, the world seems to be going along smoothly enough, but then the tiniest incongruous or unexplained detail sows doubts in the minds of characters and audience alike. The filmmaker likes to recall a saying by a Greek philosopher: "One must keep it dark," seeing this pronouncement as the linchpin of a successful drama: not too clear, not too explicit, but, in the end, enigmatic.

Film THE GHOST WRITER (2010)

Discreet in its classicism, *The Ghost Writer* proves Polanski's continuing ability to extract from the most anodyne situations material for relentless suspense (a GPS leading to an unknown destination, a motel out in the sticks as secure-making as the inn in *The Fearless Vampire Killers*, a game of pass-the-parcel with a piece of exploding paper). The film advances, muted and through the fog of a narrative line that tracks an innocent (Ewan McGregor, with exactly the right dosage of the insipid and the faux naive) employed to write up the memoirs of a British ex-prime minister, Adam Lang, following the mysterious disappearance of his predecessor. Cooped up in an oceanfront bunker, a depressive version of a Frank Lloyd Wright villa, through which two dangerous-looking femmes fatales pace up and down, Lang reminds one of James Mason in *North by Northwest* (that matrix of paranoid Hollywood); the British McGregor would be its Cary Grant figure, shorn of his arrogance and panache, and with less in the way of ropey family drama. The film is located squarely in Polanski territory: a gardener bends over to put leaves in a

The Ghost Writer,
dir. Roman
Polanski (2010)

wheelbarrow but they keep on flying away; the untold threats that disturb the balance of each take; the absurd and vehemently pessimist denouement. *The Ghost Writer* is ostensibly set somewhere out on Cape Cod, but visually the film takes pains to transform this cul-de-sac into an indefinable, nerve-shredding space. Here, geographical confusion (the British coast could be that of the American Northeast) paves the way for political collusion between Downing Street and the CIA that the script patiently brings up to date. After all, Polanski was bound one day to want to get his own back on the United States, which has treated him as a pariah since 1977.

QUENTIN TARANTINO (born 1963)

Career

His story reads like a fairy tale: in 1992, while working in a video store, he meets producer Laurence Bender, who agrees to finance the tightly wrought little crime story Tarantino has just penned. Harvey Keitel reads the script and agrees to act in it for nothing. *Reservoir Dogs* obtains immense critical success and lays the foundations of the Tarantino style: an aesthetic approach to violence, a postmodern flood of cinematographic references (the title is inspired by the kennel in John Carpenter's *The Thing*, the names of the characters are lifted from *The Taking of Pelham One Two Three* by Joseph Sargent, the story derives vaguely from *City on Fire* by Hong Kong filmmaker Ringo Lam), a penchant for pop culture and the exploitation movies of the 1970s, a fragmented narrative line, and the ability to make forgotten actors (Travolta in *Pulp Fiction*, Pam Grier in *Jackie Brown*) appear bang up to date. *Pulp Fiction*, shot in 1994, rams the point home, imposing an aesthetic that will become a must-have in the Hollywood cinema of the time, and gathering an artistic constellation around Tarantino—beginning with director Roger Avary (with whom he had written the bare bones of the scenarios of *True Romance* and *Natural Born Killers*), Robert Rodriguez (*Machete*, *Desperados*), and Eli Roth, whose *Hostel 1 & 2* Tarantino produced. After *Jackie Brown*, a homage to "blaxploitation" film, in 2001 he made a diptych (*Kill Bill Vol. 1 & 2*), a cross between revenge saga and spaghetti western. In *Death Proof* (2007), Tarantino moved his camera out to Texas, to the darkest depths of sleepy-town America to film the misdemeanors and then the punishment of "Stunt Mike," a scar-faced loco played by Kurt Russell, reprising an aging and psychopathic "Snake" Plissken, whose hobby consists in smashing up nice-looking, unsuspecting girls with the aid of a souped-up pitch-black sports car. In 2009, noting that yesterday's cutting edge, however virtuoso it might have been (*Pulp Fiction*, *Kill Bill*), can easily be as stale as rehashed pop, Tarantino tried to break free from the in-your-face style that made his name with *Inglourious Basterds*, a radical response to what was a valid intuition.

Style

At first blush, one might reproach Tarantino for maintaining with the cinema in general, and with the 1970s in particular, a merely nostalgic, fetishistic relationship, for being an incurable geek, capable, like the heroines of *Death Proof*, of blagging *ad libitum* on *Dirty Mary, Crazy Larry* (a road movie by John Hough with Peter Fonda and Susan George), or on *Vanishing Point*, but without making any distinction between them. In other words, for taking delight in wryly harking back to a past that has become cult—a secondhand director. But, take *Death Proof*, for instance: this is less a backward-looking film (though the action is set in the 1970s) than a movie whose deliberate subject *is* anachronism. *Death Proof* is a contemporary piece, where the action takes place today, but where falsely anachronistic effects erupt into the story as if they were the most natural thing in the world. The characters, like Tarantino himself, live in the 1970s, not as the mental refuge of some bizarre sect, but as a perpetual and always accessible mode of the present. In the world Tarantino describes, the 1970s, the icons, movies, and fashions constitute in themselves an inexhaustible source of excitement and inspiration—the last romantic moment in the history of America, constantly reactivated in order to relive its magic. And the present in all this? The answer is supplied by the above-mentioned sequence (undoubtedly the most significant in the movie), when the race between Mike and a horde of stunt-girl furies leaves the rocky paths of the desert and surges out onto a freeway. A return to the present, and an explosive encounter between two ages. Inertia versus energy. There are no Dodges or Ford Mustangs, but uniform lines of indistinguishable sedans and SUVs. So now one can understand why Tarantino takes the side of his characters, however outlandish they may be, since they are the only ones who can breathe a little life, a little chaos into the lethargy of Hollywood, the only ones capable of getting it moving. If a problem does remain, inscribed as it were in the genetic code of this exceptionally gifted storyteller, it is that his impressive control of narrative and tempo, the incredible quality of the script given to the actors, and the genuine pleasure derived from hacking one's way through the luxuriant jungle of quotations seem unlikely to get the movie to linger long in the mind. However alluring it may be, this world lacks a second level, a breadth, or quite simply a vision; an absence that probably explains why his films tend to age rather badly (*Pulp Fiction*, especially).

Kill Bill 2,
dir. Quentin
Tarantino (2003)

Film INGLOURIOUS BASTERDS (2009)

From the opening sequence of *Inglourious Basterds*, Tarantino snuffs out all prospect of the kind of wisecracking hell-for-leather B movie we had come to expect from him (the movie's title is taken from a fun rehash of *The Dirty Dozen* made by Italian Enzo Castellari in 1977, but the loan stops there)—an expectation shamelessly sold to audiences, it must be said, by some intentionally misleading teasers and trailers. Somewhere out in the French countryside, a Nazi officer pays a visit to a farmer suspected of hiding a Jewish family. The eminently classic style, all straight shot and reverse angle and understated panoramas around the two men, sets the tone for the movie. A *Kammerspiel* filmed by Leone in a sequence that functions besides as a variation on the scene that opens *For a Few Dollars More*, *Inglourious* proves once again that Tarantino is the only contemporary filmmaker capable of hypnotizing audiences with dialog written by the book, of racking up the tension to boiling point just by skewing a conversation. Beginning early on in the Occupation, the movie shows Shoshana Dreyfus escaping the massacre of her family by a Nazi colonel nicknamed the "Jew hunter," reemerging a few years later as the owner of a movie theater. Elsewhere in Europe, a band of men once condemned to death, Jews and Americans, carry out punitive raids against the Nazis and soon join up with a German actress and secret agent. Progressively, the little band all converge on Shoshana's cinema for a revenge set piece (this is Tarantino, after all) that blends tragedy, farce, horror, and *Carrie*.

Hewn from five large blocks that take place "in camera" (a farm, a tavern, a cinema, the Fuhrer's office), in Tarantino's sixth film the action set pieces are pared down to nothing, World War II reduced to a cardboard-cutout backdrop for an operetta (or a fairy tale: the words "Once upon a time in Nazi-occupied France" are inscribed at the beginning of film), and it zeroes in almost exclusively on a series of wordy but extraordinary face-to-face encounters. Better than ever before, Tarantino here displays both aspects of his unshakable belief in the capacities of moviemaking: on one side, by refining his style down to an absolute classicism (the very essence of the fascination movies hold?—one screen, two individuals who move, who speak, that's enough); and, on the other, by endowing the cinema with the fabulous and childlike ability to inflect the course of history—or rather, to take its revenge on it. In Tarantino's dream world, it's the Jews who carve swastikas into Nazi faces, and it is cinema (the movie, the theater, the film stock itself) that rids the earth of Hitler and Goebbels.

LARS VON TRIER (born 1956)

Career

Before *Breaking the Waves* (1997), the work of Lars von Trier enjoyed limited exposure. *The Element of Crime*, his first feature (1984), describes in sepia tones the adventures of a private detective in post-nuclear Europe as he hunts down a killer specializing in little girls. A great and experimental film noir, gloriously unhealthy and dank (the original colors were hand-retouched on the film), *The Element of Crime* was an immense success in his native land and earned him a commission from the main Danish TV channel for a series. This became *The Kingdom*, a cathode-ray nightmare set entirely in a hospital peopled by phantom patients, insane doctors, and bizarre visitors. After *Europa* (1991) came the internationally hailed *Breaking the Waves* (1997), a seething melodrama shot using a shoulder-mounted camera, violent and infused with religion. Punctuated by long, statically filmed musical numbers, *Dancer in the Dark* tells of the desperate and doomed love affair between Bess, a barely educated young woman, and a lowly workman, victim of an accident in which he loses both legs. Together with some other Danish filmmakers (including Thomas Vinterberg), Lars von Trier then collaborated on Dogme 95, a film charter that reiterates a number of the principles of Italian neorealism and the French New Wave (no special effects, location shoots, sync sound). *The Idiots*, which came out in 1998, constitutes the first Dogme work. The film shows young people, fascinated by silliness, who decide to behave like "idiots," eliciting around them a series of embarrassing situations. The year 2024 is, finally, supposed to see the conclusion of *Dimension*, the cinematographic edifice he has been constructing since the late 1990s.

Style

Lars von Trier's corpus is characterized by a unified attitude, by a desire to explore uncharted territories, rather than a style. "You want to reinvent the cinema? I'd like to give it a try," he remarked one day in what is the declaration of principle of an exceptionally gifted and also provocative director. A smorgasbord, then, unified by an indefatigable drive to experiment: with deliberately ironic exaggeration and overkill (the lyrical slow-motion shots and the sophistication of black and white have made the opening sequence in *Antichrist* the critical prototype; a horse exhumed from the waters in *The Element of Crime*; the mystic tableaux that interrupt *Breaking the Waves*); with the violent resurrection of long-dead genres (the musical in *Dancer in the Dark*, even the TV series, revitalized in *The Kingdom*) or, contrariwise, a tongue-in-cheek asceticism (Dogme, a flying kick into the precepts of film industry standardization, with the minimalist set for *Dogville* reduced to little more than lines drawn on the ground).

Film THE BOSS OF IT ALL (2006)

At the very start, we are warned by Lars von Trier in person. Here's an unpretentious little film, he tells us, with no particular artistic ambitions, an inoffensive comedy; though it inaugurates a new directorial process ("Automavision," where each shot is randomly generated and computer controlled). A disturbing notion that both cocks a snook at the establishment and challenges the status of the all-powerful auteur filmmaker. Then Lars von Trier steps out of shot and delegates powers to Ravn, who runs a small IT firm with a wholly imaginary proprietor. The latter enjoys all the blandishments of power, while the former bears the burden of responsibility. But when an Icelandic purchaser offers to buy out the business, Ravn's pretence risks exposure and he has to give physical form to the invisible owner. So, to perform the part of the CEO while the contract is being signed, he turns to Kristoffer, an unknown actor of inevitably misunderstood genius, soon known among "his" employees as the "boss of it all." But, with no precise instructions as exactly how to play his role, hindered rather than helped by his laconic "director," the hapless thespian is forced to ad lib and deal with a swarm of eccentric and neurotic employees who each has a bone to pick with the newfound "boss." But it is not the farce of mistaken identity that Lars von Trier peddles. Instead he dissects the mechanisms of decision-making (who takes it? why? and what for?) in a small buisness. Beneath the sitcom veneer, *The Boss* presents a subtle and sardonic investigation of the

Antichrist, dir. Lars von Trier (2008)

question of power in the capitalist system by focusing, not on some vast anonymous and inevitably dehumanizing conglomerate (the classic trap), but on what is an almost family structure. Lars Von Trier's purpose in the movie is not to unmask some diabolical trick—indeed, very quickly the film stymies the binary vision of a world that sets truth against falsehood, and competence against ignorance, showing them instead as working hand in glove, interwoven with one another. Kristoffer's imposture does not falter when it comes into contact with the reality of the firm (its hierarchy, codes, jargon); on the contrary, it reveals how it is the business that is built on sand and how falsehood and flimflam are intrinsic to the underlying system. During one meeting, Kristoffer is supposed to explain to his "employees" the ins and outs of his marketing strategy, and, above all, his global vision for the firm. Masks slip, but not the expected ones. Kristoffer replies to the professionals' questions with questions of his own, destabilizing them and showing how they are unable to articulate

the essential plan behind all the impenetrable technobabble. At this point the movie flips inside out, and one realizes that in this milieu an actor does not constitute an anomaly but its supreme manifestation. Inoffensive comedy? More a caustic if undemonstrative lampoon.

TSUI HARK (born 1951)

Career

He is perhaps the greatest inventor of forms in all contemporary cinema, a magical filmmaker who has created a body of work as eclectic as it is dazzling, and certainly the most significant figure to have emerged on the Hong Kong movie scene since the mid-1980s. Originally from Vietnam, Tsui Hark studied film in the United States in the 1970s before settling in Hong Kong. In 1979, he brought out his first movie, *The Butterfly Murders*, a cross between sword-wielding epic and Hitchcock's *The Birds*, followed by *Don't Play with Fire* (1980), an exposé of the vagaries of bourgeois youth as it slides into terrorism.

In *Zu Warriors*, Tsui modernizes the *wuixa-pian* (Chinese martial arts genre), to which he was to return regularly in the series *Once Upon a Time in China* (1991–95). Director, actor, and a prolific producer (his firm, Workshop, produced the majority of major features in Hong Kong in the 1980s and 1990s), Tsui Hark alternates period pieces (the incredible *Blade*, in 1995) with contemporary movies (*A Better Tomorrow 3*), thus encompassing origin and future in a single sweep, coupling heritage conservation (Chinese ancestral culture) with formal inventiveness. In 1997 Tsui Hark followed in the wake of John Woo, Ringo Lam, and Kirk Wong and moved to Hollywood. It was a free choice, but he also felt worried that the handover of Hong Kong to China might prove catastrophic for artists from the former British colony. But the transplant was not a success (*Double Team, Knock Off*): too radical, too innovative, and too Chinese. Master Tsui packed his bags and returned to his native land with the dazzling *Time and Tide*, a film which, once again, fixed for a further decade the codes of the action movie.

Style

In 2000, it was written, everything had to begin anew from zero, as if, for once, chronological history coincided with the history of form. "It all has to start again. He wasn't the only one to begin everything again. Everything has to begin again with him." In the genesis that opens *Time and Tide*, Tsui Hark redefines the aesthetics of the thriller, peppering it with epic gunfights and breathtakingly inventive forms. He reconfigures the genre, twice: by pushing its basic laws to the extreme (the freeze-frame as radical rewrite and/or dynamic limit of speed) and, even more, by transmuting action into a quasi-climatic phenomenon, liable to affect objects no less than individuals, space no less than human interactions. No encounters, just collisions; no more face-offs, but a vertiginous whirl of contrary forces; no gravity, but a weightless world. To watch a film by Tsui Hark is to see what mainstream cinema lacks, with its industrial logic, its repetitive tropes (why change a winning team?), its dearth of scope, space, and speed. Here, a style is not a cozy investment. Here, there are no lazily rehashed trademarks, no flogging dead horses. Tsui Hark, this is for sure, will never have enough time. His creative bulimia, his inexhaustible energy, his desire to serve the audience more than it can eat forms an integral part of movies that each seem to contain at least one other trying to get out.

Such is his law: a thousand storyboards with grandiose scenes are always better than just one perfectly honed sequence. How many drudges could make (and do make) entire films from just one of his ideas?

Film SEVEN SWORDS (2005)

It is 1660 and the Manchu annex China in order to set up the Qing dynasty. Barely in place, they issue a new decree prohibiting the study and practice of martial arts. A military force of nature, "Fire Wind" sees in the application of this new law a means of getting rich quick, and soon has the regions that are disobeying the law running with blood. Until the day when he chokes on a bone in the shape of a little mountain hamlet, Martial Village, which, with mystical assistance from Master Shadow Glow and seven exceptionally gifted combatants, will resist the invader tooth and nail. *Seven Swords* is a masterly film, at once eye-catching (the opening sequence, all red and gray) and elegant (the violent combats are treated with immense delicacy), which for its author hails a dual return—to the origins both of his art (Akira Kurosawa and his *Seven Samurai*), and of his culture (*wuxia* literature), as if, in an age of increasingly globalized, standardized forms and stories,

Time and Tide,
dir. Tsui Hark
(2000)

it was imperative to reiterate some Chinese fundamentals to the younger generations of Hong Kong. Still, leaving aside the trappings of this costumed fresco, *Seven Swords* holds its own as a topical movie too, an epic treatise on resistance in which it is understood that the invader is China, and the oppressed are the inhabitants of Hong Kong, and that imperialism thrives by obliterating the culture of the people it would dominate (here, the martial arts). The place occupied by *Seven Swords* in Tsui Hark's career is similar to that of *Million Dollar Baby* in Eastwood's: that of a masterly filmmaker, a paradoxical sentinel, obsessed equally by experimentation and by preserving his heritage.

PAUL VERHOEVEN (born 1938)

Career

One of the great satirists of contemporary film, unafraid to cross swords and to raise hackles: Sharon Stone scandalously uncrossing her legs in *Basic Instinct* (1991); atrocities committed by a band of pillaging mercenaries in the Middle Ages (*Flesh & Blood* [1985], his first American movie); buckets of gore in *Starship Troopers*, an antimilitarist diatribe which less perceptive critics reproached for its fascistic aesthetic. While Paul Verhoeven's Hollywood career is well documented, the Dutch part of his catalog is less so. And yet, well before he transferred to Hollywood, the enfant terrible of Dutch cinema (once dubbed the "violent Dutchman") had already sharpened his weapons in five explosive films. His first film in 1972, *Business Is Business*, followed his studies in science and a period of a military service during which he made documentaries; it was his next film, *Turkish Delight* (1973), however, that set the tone, winning the Oscar for Best Foreign Picture. Rutger Hauer, the director's pet actor, stars as a boorish painter who falls for a young middle-class woman whose family is none too pleased. A romantic and trashy number (the hero makes himself a moustache from his partner's pubic hair), uncompromising and outrageous, *Turkish Delight* placed Verhoeven squarely in the provocateurs' camp. The following chapters did nothing to unseat his taste for edgy subjects and no-holds-barred directing: What about Dutch resistance during World War II (the highly controversial *Soldier of Orange*)? What about Catholicism's hold over present-day society (*The Fourth Man*)? And the disorientated, marginal youth in *Spetters* ("a committee was set up to prohibit the film, condemned as repugnant. If I left my country, it was chiefly because the government considered me indecent and decadent—it's probably true—and no longer wanted to provide me with subsidies to make movies.") Verhoeven moved to the United States, making seven films, including *Hollow Man* (2000), a sulfurous rewrite of *The Invisible Man* hard on the heels of the Monica Lewinsky affair, before returning to Holland to shoot *Black Book*.

Style

No sooner had he touched down in Hollywood than Paul Verhoeven began to use genre cinema (thriller, science fiction, the fantastic) as a Trojan horse to smuggle in subversive, disturbing, deliberately ambiguous films that delineate the downside of an America still in the thrall of prurience (*Basic Instinct*, *Hollow Man*), patriotism (*Starship Troopers*, and its final sequence based on the Alamo with giant insects taking the place of the Indians), and an obsession with security (all guns blazing in Detroit with *RoboCop*). In *Showgirls*, he analyzes the vulgarity of the American dream, with Las Vegas as a kitsch precipitate of a nation that, deep down, only venerates sex and money. *RoboCop*, Verhoeven's adaptation of a novel by science-fiction author Philip K. Dick, unfolds as a subtle metaphor of the fate of workers for whom rebellion remains possible, but only in a virtual world. Iconoclastic, never afraid to use kitsch and ghastly bad taste to accentuate the caricature, Verhoeven's style is rooted in a context, 1980s America, which, aided and abetted by Ronald Reagan, *Rambo* (chapter two), and Wall Street yuppies, repainted its battered myth in the gaudiest colors it could get its hands on. Sorely mistreated during the previous decade, the foundation values of the nation—heroism, individualism, the American way of life, the films of Walt Disney—earned a second wind with the retro comeback of a triumphant and all-conquering US of A, which the Hollywood movies of Verhoeven set out to debunk.

Film BLACK BOOK (2006)

The Hague during the German occupation. After Nazi soldiers massacre her family, Rachel Stein, a young Jewish woman, joins the Dutch Resistance, and, under the name Ellis de Vries, agrees to seduce a Nazi officer, becoming his mistress. With *Black Book*, Paul Verhoeven returns to mine the vein of *Soldier of Orange* (a historical saga set in World War II) and, in *Flesh & Blood*, to open the "black book" of his country's history. By keeping to the naive point of view of this Lolita-like Mata Hari (Carice Van Houten), Verhoeven, and the audience with him, throw off their preconceptions and let the story, and history, unfold. It is only after her family is slaughtered that the heroine becomes aware of the true situation, a state of affairs first made problematic by the growing humanity of the Nazi officer, and then shattered following the unthinkable (but incontrovertible) discovery that a Jewish notable has acted hand in glove with the Gestapo. When the hour of Liberation sounds, abjection is exacted by other hands: card-carrying

Starship
Troopers,
dir. Paul
Verhoeven
(1997)

villains are celebrated as Resistance heroes, courageous combatants are shot down like dogs, others turn their hand to torture for the "good cause," and Ellis, accused of having had dealings with the Kraut, is humiliated, has her head shaved, and is drenched in excrement.

Paul Verhoeven has lost none of his healthy horror of clear-cut distinctions and entrenched positions. The majority of his characters run through a wide gamut of emotions and positions with respect to history, their sinuous path resembling a broken, rather than a continuous, line. However, if there is a line unflinchingly drawn in the movie, it is less the overworked divide between the villains (the Nazis and their collaborators) and the goodies (the Resistance and the victims), between total Evil and absolute Good (two concepts quite alien to the cinema of Verhoeven), than that between opportunism and survival. In consequence, the hermetically sealed borders, the usual distinct images (and taboos?) about Nazism and the extermination of the Jews are treated as permeable. Without ever falling into what would be an absolutely unacceptable symmetry between the two camps, we are informed, in a number of chilling scenes, how history is written in shades of gray rather than in a unified monochrome.

ROB ZOMBIE (born 1965) and ELI ROTH (born 1972)

Career

These two are leading figures in the revival of the contemporary horror movie, a genre whose power of formal invention and critical impact is a matter of record. Founder member of the band White Zombie, and a horror film screenwriter, Rob Zombie moved on to direction in 2003 (*House of 1000 Corpses*, a reworking of Tobe Hooper's *The Texas Chain Saw Massacre*), going on to make *The Devil's Rejects* in 2005, a hyperviolent epic deeply marked by the 1970s (Lynyrd Skynyrd for the soundtrack and a final sequence inspired by those of *Bonnie and Clyde* and *The Wild Bunch*), about a family of marginal psychopaths pursued by an obsessive sheriff. Zombie then shot remakes of *Halloween 1* and *2*.

In 2005, *Hostel*, Eli Roth's second film (as producer and actor) marks a turning point in the history of the genre, showing the nightmare of three young American tourists, who, in a small town in Eastern Europe, fall into the clutches of torturers paid to provide for the sadistic viewing pleasure of wealthy businessmen.

Style

In spite of their respective idiosyncrasies (outlandish violence, immoral and vulgar characters for Zombie, realistic ultraviolence and cynicism for Roth), the two moviemakers are today seen as leaders of cinema hugely inspired by the 1970s that opts for an unflinching horror mode quite at odds with the popcorn irony of the 1980s and 1990s. The diptych *Hostel 1* and *2* also constitutes—and this is no small accomplishment—one of the most intelligent and subversive analyses of the pathology underlying the logic of capitalism and, beneath some superficial glibness (the horror market reconfigured by its creator as "import/export"), reveals distant echoes of Nazism in a popular and more successful version of Nicolas Klotz's *Heartbeat Detector*. Smoke stacks, cremation, torture, barbed wire, victims in train trucks: at every turn both films reactivate the imagery of the camps, reinserting it, in the form of a suppressed drive, within the globalized economy, complete with its sales representatives, its contracts, its stock market, its merchandise, and its rejects (the gangs of poor children who survive by racketing tourists, but whose lives are seen as worthless). On the scale of hatred, an American, because of his arrogance and the policies of his administration, is worth more than a European, and the least manufacturing defect (one of the young women is accidentally disfigured) immediately devalues the product. How can the horror of the world again be made palpable for contemporary eyes saturated with violent fictions? Eli Roth manages it—if, that is, one admits that the mere idea of the unbearable, its rejection from the image, is no longer enough to convey the abjection of the world, and that to including hyper-, often sick-making gore is necessary to finally put to bed the enduring myth that certain types of image are incompatible (the Holocaust and the genre movie).

Film HALLOWEEN (ROB ZOMBIE, 2007)

A remake of the eponymous film made by John Carpenter in 1978, *Halloween* shows Michael Myers's family in pieces, back when he was a child, with his slob of a father, a hapless mother forced to perform striptease to make ends meet, and three offspring left to their own devices. Insults, noise, chaos—and then the young Michael Myers, angel-faced and fair-haired, patiently gutting rodents in the bathroom washbasin. Dramatically absent in Carpenter's movie, the family here becomes a seedbed of unremitting violence, the matrix of the exponential horror that crystallizes in the mind of Michael, only elucidated by the child psychiatrist who wins his trust. The role of Dr. Loomis is played by Malcolm McDowell, so it is as if the Alex of *Clockwork Orange* has crossed back over the frontier of madness to finally face his child double. Rob Zombie immediately finds the correct tone in which to relate to the original. Present like a persistent ghost (in discreet and always intelligent quotations: the musical leitmotif no longer announces the presence of the monster, but is there to accompany the untold pain suffered by a kid rejected by all), it remains in the distance, since—though starting from similar material—*Halloween* (2007) explores a different potential path from its model. The film proceeds in two stages: anamorphosis, followed by compression. Anamorphosis: the first part is stretched out and explored, unpicking what *Halloween* (1978) dispatched in ten minutes. The horror of the family, the origin of the catastrophe, the birth of a pathology that the parents never see coming, Zombie provides a hysterical twist to Carpenter's chillily theoretical masterpiece, transfused with the melancholy imprinted on

Halloween,
dir. Rob Zombie
(2007)

the body of a wild child (the magnificent sequence in a sana-
torium, set against Albinoni's *Adagio,* where Michael patiently
constructs his wall of silence). Then compression: once an
adult, Michael escapes from the asylum and returns to
Haddonfield for a speeded-up retread of the original film.
Carpenter had quickly liquidated the humanity of the character to make him into the abstract incarnation of a pure state
of evil, a kind of absolute Other, whose mask, white and
frozen, spoke of radical autism. Zombie, deploying a rough
and ready mannerism, forsakes the fear sequences that
Halloween 1978 treated with such brio, and concentrates
on the violence inside the character, a victim among the victims. This Michael Myers kills those who do not understand
him, in rage, certainly, but with no sadism (a thousand miles

from the traditional slasher movie and its armory of sharp
instruments). For John Carpenter, the issue was to fight the
Other, and his *Halloween* is an initiatory horror movie. For Rob
Zombie, in adopting Michael's point of view and in breaking
the killer/victim opposition, the problem is different: How can
a society fail to understand the Other to the point of making
him into a monster?

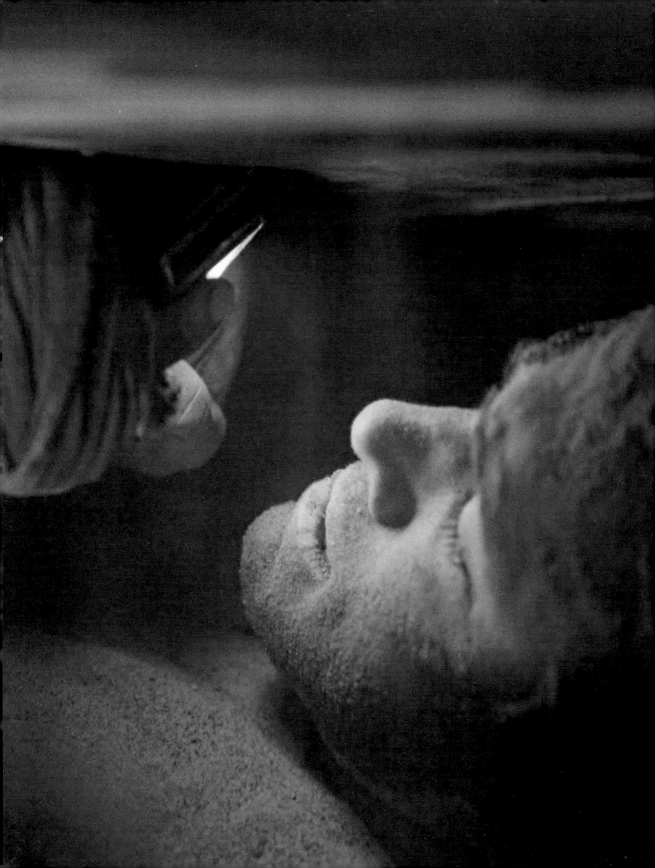

Buried,
dir. Rodrigo Cortès
(2010)

APPENDIXES

FINAL CREDITS

Short of sneaking out early, there's no escape. The final credits, with their long litany of names—of the director, the actors, and sundry extras and technicians—accompanies every film, whatever its country of origin, budget, or genre. It may not be hard to imagine the function of the director (or filmmaker), the composer, and the costume designer, not to mention the actors, but in other cases, viewers will often find themselves asking: *So, what exactly do they do?* Here are some explanations.

Screenwriter (scriptwriter)

The person who arranges a storyline and dialogue that he hasn't necessarily created (as, for example, with an adaptation for the screen of a novel or play), rewriting it for a movie in the coded language of a film script (screenplay), complete with scene divisions, locations, etc. How can the length of a movie be gauged from its script? On average, one written page is equivalent to one minute of film, though this is only a rule of thumb (for instance, the initial script for Michael Cimino's *Heaven's Gate* ran to ninety pages, but the film lasts nearly three hours).

Editor

The person, who, under supervision from the director, cuts, organizes, and reassembles the "rushes" (the many meters of film used during the shoot) into sequences for a movie. Editing represents a crucial stage in the filmmaking process (it is arranging its takes that gives a scene meaning), to the point that many directors are of the opinion that a movie is really made in the editing suite.

Storyboard

A kind of cartoon strip drawn before a movie shoot. A graphical document that

certain directors are especially fond of (Hitchcock, for example), it features precise technical information (angles, edit cuts and links, camera movements), allowing the filmmaking team to visualize the appearance of each take at the shoot.

Producer

First and foremost, this is the individual (or one of them) who finances, or obtains financial backing for, a movie. He or she may also contribute artistically to the movie by choosing the actors and the technicians or by mediating in the (sometimes fraught) relationship between a film director and his crew.

Executive producer

If the producer supervises expenditure within an allotted budget, the executive producer oversees the legal and financial aspects of a movie, together with its overall management. In collaboration with the filmmaker, it is he who establishes a budget for each sector (lighting, costumes, special effects, postproduction) and is responsible for the production of the film with respect to backers and coinvestors (TV companies, local and foreign production companies).

Casting director

The person responsible for finding actors for a movie. Casting directors work in collaboration with the director and/or the producer for the stars and leading roles, but alone for the supporting roles and extras, before leaving the final decision up to the filmmaker.

Director of photography

One of the key individuals in the making of any movie, the DP prepares the camera crew for each take. He may also decide on the type of camera, on the lenses and filters, and on the exact movements required (dolly, crane), as well as on the lighting (selection and siting of the light sources). Sometimes he may actually film the scene, manning and guiding the camera himself, in the guise of chief cameraman or camera operator.

Production designer (artistic designer)

This "super set designer" is responsible for the global visual impact of the movie (lighting, set, costumes, hairstyles, accessories), whose coherence she or he has to ensure.

Clapboard

A small, hinged device ("clapperboard," "sync slate"), inscribed with the name of the filmmaker and the director of photography, as well as with the number of the take, shot, and scene, etc., which is audibly "clapped" whenever the camera turns. It also allows the image and sound, which on shoot are recorded on two different media, to be synchronized at edit.

FROM TOP TO BOTTOM: *Crash*, dir. David Cronenberg (1996), *Dirty Harry*, dir. Don Siegel (1971), *Heat*, dir. Michael Mann (1995), *Point Break*, dir. Kathryn Bigelow (1991), and *The Birds*, dir. Alfred Hitchcock (1963)

INDEX OF PROPER NAMES

INDEX

254

Photographic credits

©1934–1959 Universal Pictures International, DVD Carlotta Films: p. 51; ©1959 Turner Entertainment Co. DVD, Warner Home Video: p. 132 above; ©1966, Turner Entertainment Co. DVD, Warner Home Video: p. 125; ©1969 Mercury films, Pan Latina Films, Peliculas Ibarray cia DVD ©2002 One plus one video: p. 120; ©1976 Metro-Goldwyn-Mayer Pictures Inc. All rights reserved DVD: p. 100; ©1991 Tristar Pictures Inc, all rights reserved, DVD ©1998 Columbia Tristar Home Video. All rights reserved: p. 107; ©1992 Morgan Creek International, Inc. 8 Twentieth Century Fox Film: p. 19 below; ©1992 Studio Canal images. All rights reserved, DVD©2006 Studio Canal Vidéo: p. 89; ©1996 Warner Bros, DVD Warner Home Video: p. 49 below; ©2000 Block 2 Pictures Inc. © Video 2001 Paradis Distribution. All rights reserved: p. 53; 2003 HBO ©2004 MK2S.A. © Canal+ May2003 ©BBC Northern Ireland: p. 93; 2006 Buena Vista Home Entertainment (France), ©2006Disney/Pixar, Lucas film Ltd. 8 TM. All rights reserved: p. 83 below; ©Allan Young Pictures SRL 2001. All rights reserved: p. 59 below; ©American Zoetrope/Eternity Pictures/Muse Productions/Virgin Suicides LLC: p. 21 above; Angel Studios/Bazmark Films/Twentieth Century Fox Film Corporation: p. 79 above; Aardman Animations/DreamWorks Animation: p. 83 above; Argos Films/Oshima Productions/Shibata Organisation: p. 126; ARP Sélection/Canal+/Centre National de la Cinématographie (CNC)/Centre de Cinéma et de l'Audiovisuel de la Communauté Française de Belgique/La Laterne Nationale/La Regie Wallone/Les Films du Fleuve/October Films/Radio Télévision Belge Francophone (RTBF): p. 109; ©Australian Film Commission, The McElroy 8 McElroy/Picnic Productions Pty. Ltd/Z: p. 21 above; ©Australian Film Commission, The CiBy 2000/Jan Chapman Productions/New South Wales Films 8 Television Office: p. 51 right; ©Austrian Film Institute/Wega Film/Wiener/Filmfinanzierungsfonds/Österreichischer Rundfunk: p. 64 above; ©A8M Films/Channel Productions/Universal Pictures: p. 83 above; ©AVCO Embassy Pictures/EDI/Debra Hill Productions: p.155 above right; ©Berit Films/RKO Radio Pictures: p. 111; CAT'S Collection: p. 30, p. 31 above, p. 74, p. 75 below, pp. 85, 98, 142 [Aguirre],182, 186, 190, 192, 193, 196, 198, 204, 207, 222, 230, 234, 242, p. 157 above right, p. 157 below, p. 162, p. 166 above, p. 169 above, 174; CAT'S Collection ©Ad Vitam Distribution: p. 99; CAT'S Collection ©Allied Artists Pictures: p. 142 [Blow-Up]; CAT'S Collection ©AMLF/United Artists: p. 244; CAT'S Collection ©Bandai Visual Company/Bac Films: p. 223; CAT'S Collection ©Buena Vista Pictures: p. 45 above; CAT'S Collection ©Buena Vista Pictures /Bac Films: p. 224; CAT'S Collection © CJ Entertainment/ CTV International: p. 112; CAT'S Collection ©CJ Entertainment/Le Pacte: p. 235; CAT'S Collection ©CJ Entertainment/Wild Side Films: p. 34; CAT'S Collection ©Columbia Broadcasting System(CBS): p. 159 above right, 159 below right; CAT'S Collection ©Columbia Films: p. 153 middle; CAT'S Collection ©Columbia Pictures: p. 87 below, pp. 214, 228; CAT'S Collection ©Compton Films: p. 26; CAT'S Collection ©Dimension Films, Andrew Cooper: p. 238; CAT'S Collection ©Dimension Films/ MGM: p. 247; CAT'S Collection ©Film MGM: p. 147 above; CAT'S Collection ©Film Warner Bros. Pictures: p. 48, p. 73 below; CAT'S Collection ©Focus Features: p. 202; CAT'S Collection ©Fortissimo Films/Pan Européenne Distribution: p. 43 above; CAT'S Collection ©GEF/CCFC: p. 32 right, p. 33; CAT'S Collection -GFD: p. 149 below; CAT'S Collection ©Gramercy Pictures: p. 200; CAT'S Collection ©Lions Gate Films: p. 216, 246; CAT'S Collection ©Mars Distribution: pp. 232, 233; CAT'S Collection ©MGM: p. 29, p. 179 above; CAT'S Collection ©Minerva Film/ Francinex: p. 24; CAT'S Collection ©Miramax Films: p. 188; CAT'S Collection ©Miramax Films/TFM Distribution: p. 239; CAT'S Collection ©Paramount Pictures: p. 68 left, 114, 179 below left, 210; CAT'S Collection ©Pathé: pp. 220, 221; CAT'S Collection ©Pixar Animation Studios/Walt Disney Pictures: pp. 3, 47; CAT'S Collection ©Sacher Distribuzione/Bac Films: p. 231; CAT'S Collection © Seda Spettacoli: p. 102; CAT'S Collection ©Show East/Bac Films/Wild Side Films: p. 1; CAT'S Collection ©Sony Pictures Entertainment/Columbia Pictures: p. 189; CAT'S Collection ©S.N.Prodis: p. 142 [The Samurai]; CAT'S Collection ©Swift Productions/ Centerstage Productions/Equation Distribution: p. 23 below; CAT'S Collection ©Tadrart Films, photo Roger Arpajou: p. 206; CAT'S Collection ©Twentieth Century Fox: p. 226; CAT'S Collection ©Twentieth Century Fox Film: p. 77 above; CAT'S Collection ©Twentieth Century Fox Film Corporation: pp. 6, 12, 46, 56, p. 57 above, p. 75 above, p. 79 middle, p. 159 below left, p. 194; CAT'S Collection ©United Artists: p. 97, p. 169 below, p. 183 middle; CAT'S Collection ©Universal Pictures: p. 23 above, p. 118, p. 119 left, p. 139 below, p. 208; CAT'S Collection ©Universal Pictures/Paramount Pictures: p. 183 above; CAT'S Collection ©Universal Pictures/UIP: p. 2, 8, 229; CAT'S Collection ©Voltage Pictures/Grosvenor Park Media: p. 195; CAT'S Collection ©Warner Bros.: p. 19 middle, pp. 209, 183 below; CAT'S Collection ©Warner Bros. Pictures: pp. 4, 5, p. 43 below, pp. 66, 69, p. 73 above, pp. 94, 96,128, 142 [The Searchers], p. 179 middle, p. 179 below right, p. 205, p. 176 above, p. 176 below; CAT'S Collection ©Warner Bros, Renn Productions: p. 88; CAT'S Collection ©Warner Bros. Seven Arts: p. 59 above right; CAT'S Collection ©Warner Soge films S.A/Pathé: p. 52 above; CAT'S Collection ©Werner Herzog Filmproduktion/Gaumont: p. 103; CAT'S Collection ©Xstream Pictures/Memento Films: p. 218; CAT'S Collection ©Xstream Pictures/AdVitam Distribution: p.219; CAT'S Collection ©Zentropa Entertainment: pp. 7, 241; CAT'S Collection ©Zentropa Entertainments/Trust Film Svenska/Filmi Väst/Liberator Productions: p. 240; ©CBK/Filmové Studio Barrandov/Sebor: p. 27 above; ©Ciné-Alliance: p. 108; p. 153 below left: Cinema Center Films/Stockbridge-Hiller Productions; ©Columbia Pictures Corporation/Jersey Films: p.71 below; Copercines, Cooperativa Cinematográfica/Devon Film: p.163; ©Craven Maddalena Films/Dimension Films/ Konrad Pictures/ Maven Entertainment/ Miramax Films: p.139 above; ©Dimension Films/Nightfall Productions/Spectacle Entertainment Group/Trancas International Films/The Weinstein Company: p. 60; Dimension Films/Troublemaker Studios/Rodriguez International Pictures/The Weinstein Company: p. 105 below; Rights reserved: pp. 25, 36, 40, 42, 101 above, p. 101 below, pp. 104, 116, 117 right, 119 right, 122, 130, 131, 132 below, 133 right, 134 left, 134 right, 136, 138 above, p. 142, 171 below, p. 161 left; DR/Author archives: p. 16 above, p. 17 below, p. 21 middle, p. 27 below, p. 31 below, p. 39, 41, 44, p. 49 middle, p. 55, p. 57 below, pp. 58, 59 above left, p. 61 above, p. 61 below, p. 62–63, 70, 72, p. 77 below, p. 81 right, p. 86, p. 87 above, pp. 113, 117 left, 121, 124, p. 133 left, 135, p. 151 above right, p. 151 below right, p. 153 above, p. 153 below right, p. 155 below right, p. 157 above left, 159 above left, p. 165, p. 166 below, p. 173 below right, p. 181 above, p. 181 below, pp. 185, 191, 197, 199, 201, 203, 211, 212, p. 213 above, p. 213 below, pp. 215, 225, 227, 236, 237, 243, 245, p. 250 above left, p. 250 above right, p. 250 above middle, p. 250 below middle, p. 260 below; ©Dream Works SKG/Pathé/Aardman Animations: p. 82; ©DVD Warner Home Video: p. 15; ©Embassy International Pictures: p. 71 above; ©EMI Films/Universal Pictures: p. 161 right; ©Euro International Film(EIA)/Les Films Corona/Selenia Cinematografica: p. 172; ©Everyman Films/Incorporated Television Company (ITC): p. 171 g; ©Fads in Cinema Associates/Palomar Pictures (I): p. 151 left; ©Film©1949 RKO, DVD ©editions Montparnasse: p. 19 above; ©Focus Features/Pathé Distribution/Medusa Film/Tohokushinsha Film/American Zoetrope: p. 45 below; ©Fox Searchlight Pictures/Protozoa Pictures/Phoenix Pictures: p. 149 middle; ©Gaumont: p. 16 above; ©Haxan Films: p. 37; ©Indian Paintbrush/This Is That Productions/Your Face Goes Here Entertainment: p. 91 below; ©Légende Films/Gaumont/Légende des Siècles/TF1 Films Production/France 3 Cinéma/SMTS/KS2 Cinéma/Alva Films/EOS Entertainment/Eurofilm Stúdió: p. 65 below;©Lucas Film/Twentieth Century Fox Film Corporation: p. 137; Lions Gate Films/ Discovery Docs/Real Big Production :p. 217; ©Lionsgate/ The Weinstein Company/ Millennium Films/Nulmage Films/Equity, Pictures Madeleine Films/Parc Film: p. 79 below left; ©MCMXCIV Warner Bros Productions, Ltd., Monarchy Enterprises B.V., Regency, Entertainment (USA) Inc., All rights reserved DVD Metropolitan Film 8 Video: p. 105 above; ©Medienfonds GmbH 8 Co. KGIV: p. 77 middle; ©Metro-Goldwyn-Mayer (MGM)/Loew's (as Loew's Incorporated): p. 123; ©Minerva Film/Francinex: p. 110; ©Nikkatsu: p. 173 left; ©Outlaw Productions (I)/ Virgin: p. 138 below; ©Pandora Filmproduktion/ Arbeitsgemeinschaftderöffentlich-rechtlichen Rundfunkanstaltender Bundesrepublik Deutschland/Degeto Film/Plywood Productions/ Bac Films/Canal+/JVC Entertainment Networks: p. 173 above right; ©Paramount Pictures/Skydance Productions/Scott Rudin Productions /Mike Zoss Productions: p. 68 right;©Paramount Pictures/Patron Inc.: p. 140; ©Paramount Pictures/Scott Rudin Productions: p. 171 above;©Partisan Productions: p. 145 right; Pathé Entertainment/Percy Main/Star Partners III Ltd/Metro-Goldwyn-Mayer (MGM): p. 181 middle; ©Seda Spettacoli: p. 149 above; ©SLM Production Group/New Century Productions/United Artists: p. 177 left; ©Studio Canal +/Les films Alain Sarde/ Universal/Archives Flammarion: p. 32 left; © Summit Entertainment/Temple Hill Entertainment/ Maverick Films/Imprint Entertainment/Goldcrest Pictures/Twilight Productions: p. 84; © Tessalit Productions/Kiss Films/France2 Cinéma/France3 Cinéma/Studio Canal/Taza Productions/Tossili Films: p. 65 above; ©The CKK Corporation/Overseas Film Group: p. 175 above; ©The Directors Company/The Coppola Company/American Zoetrope/Paramount Pictures: p.167; ©The State Hermitage Museum: p. 127; ©Tim Burton Productions/ Warner Bros. Pictures: p. 49 above; Titanus (Rome)/Société Nouvelle Pathé Cinéma/ Société générale de Cinématographie (S.G.C.) (Paris): p. 145 left; ©Twentieth Century Fox Corporation: p. 141; ©Twentieth Century Fox Film Corporation/Conundrum Entertainment: p. 147 below; ©Twentieth Century Fox Film Corporation/ Paramount Pictures/Lightstorm Entertainment: p. 52 below; Universal Pictures: p. 155 below; ©Universal Pictures/Apatow Productions: p. 91 above; ©Universal Pictures/Atmosphere Entertainment MM/Exception Wild Bunch/Romero-Grunwald Productions: p. 175 below; Universal Pictures/Motion Picture THETA Produktionsgesellschaft/Kennedy/Marshall Company, The Ludlum Entertainment: p. 177 right; Versus Entertainment/The Safran Company/Dark Trick Films/Studio: p. 248; ©Walt Disney Pictures/Pixar Animation Studios: p. 81 left; ©Warner Bros. Pictures/Amblin Entertainment/Malpaso Productions: p. 50; ©X Filme Creative Pool /Wega Film/Les Films du Losange/Lucky Red: p. 64 below; ©Zentropa Entertainments/ Trust Film Svenska/ Filmi VŠst/ Liberator Productions: p. 79 below right, 80

255

SELECTED BIBLIOGRAPHY

Amiel, Vincent, and Pascal Couté. *Formes et obsessions du cinéma américain contemporain (1980–2002)*. Paris: Klincksieck, 2004.

Bazin, André. *What Is Cinema?* Berkeley: University of California Press, 2004. (2 vols.).

Biskind, Peter. *Easy Riders, Raging Bulls: How the Sex-Drugs-And-Rock 'n' Roll Generation Saved Hollywood*. London: Bloomsbury, 1999.

Biskind, Peter. *Seeing Is Believing: How Hollywood Taught Us to Stop Worrying and Love the Fifties*. London: Bloomsbury, 2001.

Bondanella, Peter. *Italian Cinema: From Neorealism to the Present.* London: Continuum International Publishing Group Ltd., 2001.

Brenez, Nicole. *De la figure en général et du corps en particulier. L'Invention figurative au cinéma*. Brussels: De Boeck University, 1998.

Chion, Michel. *Audio-Vision: Sound on Screen*. New York: Columbia University Press, 1994.

Coursodon, Bernard, and Bertrand Tavernier. *50 ans de cinéma américain*. Paris: Omnibus, 1995.

Daney, Serge. *La Rampe*. Paris: Éditions de l'Étoile/Cahiers du cinéma, 1996.

De Baecque, Antoine. *Camera Historica: The Century in Cinema*. New York: Columbia University Press, 2011.

Deleuze, Gilles. *Cinema 1. The Movement-Image*. London: Continuum International Publishing Group Ltd., 2005.

Deleuze, Gilles. *Cinema 2. The Time-Image*. London: Continuum International Publishing Group Ltd., 2005.

Elsaesser, Thomas, ed. *The Last Great American Picture Show. New Hollywood Cinema in the 1970s*. Amsterdam: Amsterdam University Press, 2004.

Epstein, Jean. *Critical Essays and New Translations (Film Theory in Media History)*. Edited by S. Keller and J. N. Paul. Amsterdam: Amsterdam University Press, 2011.

Farber, Manny. *Farber on Film: The Complete Film Writings of Manny Farber*. Edited by R. Polito. Amsterdam: Amsterdam University Press, 2011.

Leutrat, Jean-Louis. *Vie des fantômes*. Paris: Éditions de l'Étoile/Cahiers du cinéma, 1995.

Rieupeyrout, Jean-Louis. *La grande aventure du western 1894–1964*. Paris: Éditions du Cerf, Ramsay Poche Cinéma, 1987.

Tesson, Charles, ed. *L'Asie à Hollywood*. Paris: Éditions de l'Étoile/Festival de Locarno, 2001.

Tesson, Charles. *Photogénie de la série B*. Paris: Éditions des Cahiers du cinéma, 1997.

Thoret, Jean-Baptiste. *Le Cinéma américain des années 70*. Paris: Éditions de l'Étoile/Cahiers du cinéma, 2006.

Truffaut, François. *Hitchcock: A Definitive Study of Alfred Hitchcock*. New York: Simon & Schuster, 1986.

Wood, Robin. *Hollywood from Vietnam to Reagan*. New York: Columbia University Press, 2003.

ACKNOWLEDGMENTS

I would like to thank Élisabeth Couturier for her enthusiasm and confidence. And Julie Rouart, for her energetic commitment, as well as Camille Giordano, the infallible guardian of this book. A thank-you to all three good fairies for their unbelievable patience. And thanks to Martine de Lebret of Cat's Collection for her watchful eye and for always being on hand when needed.

Translated from the French by David Radzinowicz
Copyediting: Penelope Isaac
Design: François Huertas
Typesetting: Claude-Olivier Four
Proofreading: Chrisoula Petridis
Editorial Assistance: Joshua Wilson
Color Separation: Reproscan
Printed in Portugal by Portughesa

Originally published in French
as *Cinéma contemporain: mode d'emploi*
© Flammarion, S.A., Paris, 2011

English-language edition
© Flammarion, S.A., Paris, 2012